This book is dedicated to -

The sacred memory of the Martyrs of 1971 war;

To my parents Mrs. Kamla Tandon & Dr. A.C. Tandon who encouraged their bookworm kid, ensuring his access to a wide genre of books and inculcated sterling humanitarian values in their children Anshuman & Dr.Anju Bhagirath.

To my extended family - Abha & Ashok Tara for their love and warmth;

To my dear wife Saruchi & daughter Arushi for being my pillars of strength;

To my Mamaji Late Wing Commander C.S.Kataria, veteran of 1965 & 1971 wars, who laid down his life in 1989, while operating his last flight.

TIGERS DON'T BLINK

True Story of a brave unarmed Indian Army Major (Ashok Tara) who single-handedly in a daring hostage rescue operation saved Sheikh Hasina's family from the trigger-happy Pakistan Army during the Bangladesh Liberation War (1971)

Life & Times of

Col (Retd.) Ashok Tara, *Vir Chakra*

ANSHUMAN TANDON

PRABHAT
PRAKASHAN

Published by
PRABHAT PRAKASHAN PVT. LTD.
4/19 Asaf Ali Road,
New Delhi-110 002 (INDIA)
e-mail: prabhatbooks@gmail.com

ISBN 978-93-5521-831-5
TIGERS DON'T BLINK: LIFE & TIMES OF COL. (RETD.) ASHOK TARA, VIR CHAKRA
by Anshuman Tandon

Edition
First, 2024

Price
₹ 500 (Rupees Five Hundred Only)

Printed at
Japan Art, Delhi

Col. Ashok Kumar Tara, VrC
Indan Army Veteran (Retd.)

Dear Anshuman,

Having an idea and turning it into a book is harder than it may sound. It certainly is a significant undertaking and requires a great deal of research and attention to detail - am sure the experience is internally challenging and rewarding.

I would like to take this opportunity to express my gratitude for highlighting my experiences and contributions in a way that is both informative and captivating.

Your ability to capture the essence and vividly depict my legacy through your unique perspective is truly remarkable.

The book offers a captivating and insightful account of how strong values and principles, which form the cornerstone of my being, enabled me to surmount personal and professional challenges with much resilience and determination.

Thank you once again for making my legacy an eternal part of both our country's and military's history.

It is an honor to be associated with this enduring heritage, and I take great pride in it
– **Jai Hind**

Sincerely,
Colonel Ashok Kumar Tara (VrC)
Indian Army Veteran (Retd.)

30 Apr 2023

Author's Note

"A breezy tale that transports you to the 60s & 70s. A gripping extraordinary story of an ordinary boy from the by-lanes of west Delhi."

Retd. Col. Ashok Tara (Vr.C.) a decorated war hero, is respected in both India and Bangladesh. He has seen action in both 1965 and 1971 Bangladesh War of Liberation. Tara's story in the backdrop of 1965 & 1971 wars is full of adventures and surprising turns and twists. Ashok Tara, a thorough gentleman and an officer is a man of many parts - war veteran, dedicated family man, a dependable friend, keen sportsman, next door amiable neighbour and a social worker. It is the story of a humble and a jovial army man who in the face of certain death transforms into a 'Tiger, Who Doesn't Blink'.

Col. Tara's life coincides with the building of modern India, evolution of Delhi as a large megapolis, changing cultural and family dynamics and many other important historical events. I was amazed to discover that Col. Tara was first amongst the Indian Army officers, to enter Bangladesh and apparently the last one to leave. His unit was also amongst the first ones to reach Dacca.

I have thoroughly enjoyed writing this book and want to thank the entire Tara family. I wish to thank my parents Dr. A. C. Tandon & Mrs. Kamla Tandon for the values they have inculcated. My wife Prof. Saruchi Tandon and my daughter Arushi, from whom I stole many moments to write this book. My sister & brother-in-law Dr. Anju & Dr. Rajnish Bhagirath. I wholeheartedly thank Vijay, Sukriti Arora, Ramneek Singh, Zia, Dola, Yogesh Saluja, Puru Manchanda & Akshat Chopra for their invaluable help I wish to thank Prof. Subash Chandra Sabharwal and Mr. Veena Sabharwal for their support. Last but not the least, I thank all my colleagues and friends who listen intently to the stories collected by this raconteur.

Introduction

Winters, 2013

It was late evening, winters of 2013, I was at the Press Club of India with friends having a light banter. Saruchi, my wife called to come home immediately to plan next day's visit to my daughter Arushi's school. I excused myself from the iconic bar corner where my friends Vijay Kumar, Ravi Bhardwaj, Jasween Jassi, JS Malhotra, GS Kaura and Yogesh Kumar were engaged in an animated discussion. As I drove past the All India Radio and the Parliament house, I tuned on to radio. RJ was talking about a special guest she had for the evening – A hero of the Bangladesh war who was honoured by Govt. of Bangladesh. I had tuned late and missed the name of the hero. A retired army officer with baritone voice described the famous battle of Gangasagar during the Bangladesh Liberation War in which he had been awarded the Vir Chakra. Driving past the Willingdon hospital, I reached the thick forested ridge where fog thickened and there was condensation on my wind screen. I halted my car next to the forest and decided to listen to the amazing story. He recounted, as to how he alone as a young unarmed Indian army major faced an armed to teeth Pakistani Army unit, to rescue the family of Bangabandhu Sheikh Mujibur Rahman's family. I had goose bumps listening to his bravery in the face of certain death. He described his meeting with

Bangabandhu on his return to Bangladesh. The fog eased up a bit as the programme ended. The name of the road on the ridge where I had stopped to listen to Col.Ashok Tara is now known as 'Bangbandhu Sheikh Mujibur Rahman' road.

I came back home and recounted the story of valour to my father Dr. A.C. Tandon who had been part of the St. John's ambulance and Senior Under officer with NCC in Punjab during his school and college days. My mother Mrs. Kamla Tandon became emotional as she was reminded of her brother Wing Commander C.S. Kataria who had served during 1965 and 1971 wars. Mamaji unfortunately lost his life when his helicopter crashed in Nagaland in 1988. I had grown up listening to war time stories from war heroes at various Air Force stations.

March 2017

I first visited Dhaka in 2017 as part of Indian Engineering exhibition troupe. At the Shal Jalal Airport, we were received by Mr. Kaleem Akhtar, Powergrid Corporation of India's resident engineer posted in Dhaka. An extremely pleasant personality hailing from Saharanpur, he was popular with the local Power Sector fraternity. Many people visited our stall; I was impressed by the enthusiasm of the young engineers who quizzed us about new technologies. It was a country on the move. The warmth of the people touched me. I met an elderly Bangladeshi gentleman who recalled the days of the Liberation war. I was touched when he said in a voice choked with emotion, "There is no parallel in the history of mankind, like struggle of the people of Bangladesh. We fought for our language."

In the evening, once the engineering exhibition closed, we saw a huge crowd walking towards the Expo centre auditorium. The Fashion Design Council of Bangladesh had organised a show showcasing its prowess. Bangladesh is a world leader in export of garments & textiles. I, Kaleem Akhter and Pragya Sharma were standing outside the auditorium trying to figure out whether we could get in uninvited, when one of the young organisers came to me and enquired – "Where are you from?" I said, "India". "Please be our guest", he said. We were guided to VIP seats. Maheen Khan a well-known pioneer in the design industry of Bangladesh presided over the events. The presentation of

Khadi in the sub-continent was amazing. A special refence was made to the freedom struggle and Mahatma Gandhi. Young girls and boys showcased designs to soul stirring Bangla music. In my spare time, I visited the Dhakeshwari mandir & Gurudwara in the University area. Guru Teg Bahadur had visited Dhaka and his holy slippers are kept there. I asked my driver to stop at the 'Aparajeyo Bangla' monument designed by Syed Abdullah Khalid and stood there for a few moments in the memory of people who had lost their lives in the freedom struggle. It is an awe inspiring sculpture which captures the essence of the heroic struggle waged by ordinary men and women of Bangladesh against extreme brutality. With my deep interest in the art, culture and literature of the sub-continent, it was impossible for me not to visit the memorial of the great poet of the Sub-continent Kazi Nazrul Islam, who is revered in both the countries. I asked my driver, if he could take me to the memorial of Kazi Nazrul Islam. The mausoleum was closed. I requested the gate keeper to let me in. Once he came to know that I was from India and would not be able to come again later, he allowed. He was surprised but very pleased that a non Bengali would want to visit. I spent a few minutes at the grave of the great philosopher poet. My next stop was Bangabandhu Memorial Museum, Dhanmondi, where I paid my respects to the great leader of the sub-continent Sheikh Mujib-ur-Rahman. I wound up visit with a trip to Bashundhara city. As I entered the iconic store Aarong, I was greeted by the young energetic team manning the store. They could guess I was a Punjabi. With my jovial self, I became an instant hit amongst the young crowd. They were very courteous. They kept the store open for us even as the entire mall closed. Unfortunately, I have forgotten their names. But I salute the spirit of these young boys and girls which is rapidly transforming their great nation. It was a great trip professionally & personally, as I took the flight back home.

As the flight from Dhaka landed at Delhi Airport, everyone scrambled to pick up their cabin bags and made a dash for the exit door. The flight had been delayed at Dacca. I stayed put as I generally like to get after the impatient rush is over. Also, I had a number of hand bags post shopping from Bashundhara city market, Dhaka for my wife, Saruchi and daughter, Arushi. Arushi was supposed to come back from her college in New Jersey, USA, in a couple of days. Passengers brushed past in hurry, as the flight had been delayed at

Dhaka. I saw a very dignified elder lady struggling with her baggage. My parents' value system passed on to me has ensured that I can never look the other way in case anybody needs help. Seeing her predicament, I offered to help her and carried some of her bags apart from my own. As I put down her bags in the trolley at Delhi airport terminal, she thanked me and gave me her card. 'I am Tuhfa Zaman Ali' wife of the Bangladesh High Commissioner to India, Syed Muazzem Ali.

She enquired about me and my family and the purpose of visit to Bangladesh. She invited me and my wife to have lunch at their residence. In turn I invited them for a typical Punjabi treat of Makki di Roti with Sarson da Saag, adding that my wife Saruchi is a great cook. I gave her my visiting card too. I had forgotten the episode till I received a mail about 8 months later from the Bangladesh High Commission inviting me to the victory day celebrations at India International Centre. Famous singer Mitali enthralled the audience with soulful Bengali numbers. She is a Bengali married to famous singer Bhupinder who is a Punjabi. She sings beautiful Punjabi numbers too. At the end of the cultural program, veteran army officers were felicitated. The audience clapped as Colonel (Retd.) Ashok Tara was felicitated by the then High Commissioner Syed Muazzem Ali. I was instantly reminded of the radio programme that I had listened to a couple of years ago. A very handsome man; he looked every inch a commando, who can give enemy a bloodied nose. Mr. & Mrs. Ali were very courteous to us, we thanked them for inviting us. It is here that I and Saruchi met Abha and Ashok Tara for the first time. It seemed we had known each other since ages. Col. Tara was his jovial self cracking jokes with me in Punjabi. My wife Saruchi was pleasantly surprised to find out that he was from the first batch of the ARSD college where she is teaching now. Col. Tara calls her Guruji.

They invited us to their house, the very next weekend. I was active in theatre and was collecting stories of the Punjabi diaspora especially who were affected by partition. I wanted to do a play on his life in Punjabi. My wife suggested why not write a book on his life and Mrs. Abha Tara seconded the idea. It was at this time that I decided to write a book on him and tell his amazing story to the world. The book took shape chapter by chapter over many months, during which we visited their place umpteen times and they visited our house. It was as if we have known each other for ages. They became an integral part of our lives. It was during the first lockdown that I could get time to work seriously and sift through the notes. The book was stalled as I was admitted to hospital due to covid and had a brush with death. The book was almost complete when the second wave came. It was much more deadly than the first one. I volunteered to help covid victims over next two months. The book was delayed for one reason or the other, but Col. Tara and my mother kept on encouraging me. During the course of the book, I discovered many unknown facts about the war which have been brought about in the book. This book has been narrated as a biography but in an autobiographic style.

❑

Contents

CHAPTER 1

A Granddaughter's Hero and Hostage Crises

2016—Haileybury College, Keysborough, Melbourne

It was a sunny, cheerful morning in Melbourne. The primary school was abuzz with energy. In the fourth-grade classroom, the children greeted their English teacher. She said that she had a new task for them. "I know all of you have your heroes. I want you to share them with us. I want all of you to write about who you admire the most and more importantly, why. We shall discuss the best essays tomorrow."

For the next hour, the class was busy writing about the people they revered — an impressive pantheon from mythical characters to real people — Spiderman, Batman, politicians, film stars, sportsmen and the likes.

Next day, the class greeted the teacher with more enthusiasm, eager to know who did the best. "Dear children, I am impressed with your essays and the heroes you talked about in them," she said. "You were all very good. But I would like to share one essay which had the most extraordinary story, not about a superhero but a decorated war veteran. Rhea Tara, please come forward and share what you wrote with your friends."

Rhea remarked, "My hero is my grandfather, Colonel Ashok Tara. He has participated in two wars and is a gallantry award winner. He has saved many lives, unmindful of his own and he is very brave. His father, my great-grandfather, was also an army man, who had seen action in World War II while serving in the British Indian Army."

The teacher further added, "It is a matter of great pride for us that her grandfather takes part in the annual ANZAC (Australia and New Zealand Army Corps) veterans' parade in honour of the martyrs of World War I in the Battle of Gallipoli. As you all know, it is held on 25th April every year and is a national day for us in Australia. We are all honoured and proud to have her in our midst. Her grandfather is a role model for her, and I think he would be for all of us, now. Can we all clap for her?"

The teacher, as well as the entire class, applauded in unison. My ecstatic granddaughter came back home elated and narrated the story to her parents.

My children had migrated to Australia in the late 2000s. Each year, Abha, my wife, and I, visit my daughter Anshu, my son Ashish, his wife Sanyogita, and their daughter Rhea. It is a summer ritual for us to travel to Australia to be with them for about six months. We look forward to this annual vacation and so do our children. One of the favourite pastimes of grandparents is to tell stories of their heydays and family anecdotes to their grandchildren. This informal oral history project has been time-tested across the world and both parties look forward to it.

Tuesday, November 5, 2019—Elmwood Boulevard, Melbourne

You can take an Indian out of India, but not India out of him. I stay in touch with the happenings in the country whenever I am abroad. For three days, the Indian news channels were agog with an ugly clash that had broken out between the lawyers and the policemen at Tis Hazare courts in Delhi over a petty parking issue between a lawyer and a constable. It took just minutes for the matter to spiral out of control. A heavily outnumbered police contingent, when surrounded by angry lawyers, had opened fire and a lawyer got hurt. Outraged, the group retaliated and cornered policemen in a small building. They held them hostage until more policemen arrived to rescue their fellowmen.

Lawyers and cops are two sides of the same coin as upholders of the law. Like the army and paramilitary forces, both entities have their respective uniforms, but the police are an armed force. It was distressing to see the unwarranted clash. Unlike the earlier days, social media and other communication channels are quick to take the news to the decision makers on a real-time basis; thereby enabling a swift administrative response, but somehow, the entire machinery was caught unaware in this case. It was merciful and miraculous, to an extent, that nobody died despite the scale of anger. There were versions and counterclaims from both sides and media flashed some disturbing images. My WhatsApp was buzzing with many videos of the clash.

In a way, social media is both a boon and a bane. Perhaps, the families of lower ranking constabularies could take it no longer and hundreds of them observed a fast in front of the police headquarters. A peaceful demonstration, but something not seen for decades. They dispersed after 11 hours of a sit-in and assurances from senior police officers. Their demand was to restore the dignity and the rights of police personnel and their families. There were sane voices from all sides, including the judiciary, over the next two days. Police is an armed force and there have been instances around the world when things have gotten out of hand under extreme provocation and sometimes over trivial issues. The lawyers, too, went on a strike to vent their angst. The Indian judiciary, which prides itself in being the most independent and professional one in the world, refused to take sides and summed up the case with the old Indian saying that one hand doesn't clap alone. The storm had passed and the resilient social fabric of democratic India was restored. I heaved a sigh of relief. I knew that public memory was short and they would forget the episode soon. It would remain only as a part of newspaper archives.

I had been glued to the television for almost three days. I had not slept properly, watching the drama unfold on TV, WhatsApp, and YouTube. My wife chided me to sleep.

It was midnight in Melbourne, as I lay on my bed in a slumberous state, my mind wandered off to 1973. I saw myself, a much younger Ashok, dashing at a speed, typically reminiscent of my college sporting days as a forward. I could hear bullets whizzing by. A near-forgotten episode of my life came back to me vividly. It was the 1973 UP Police revolt.

August 1972—Mizoram to Kanpur

My unit, 14 Guards, was back in Mizoram from the recently concluded Bangladesh Liberation War. Its heady hangover was not quite over. The evenings in the mess were still agog with high spirits, a victor's swagger, and tales of bravery and valour. Lieutenant Colonel V N Channa, our commanding officer, informed that at the completion of the Mizoram tenure, 14 Guards was to move to Kanpur, Uttar Pradesh, by the end of August 1972. The unit conducted its training in the hills of Almorah, UP.

Mizoram and Kanpur are about 2,000 kms apart. From the scenic hills of the North-East, we were to move into the heart of the vast Indo-Gangetic plain. The 14 Guards had seen a lot of action in the hills and it was a different feeling to come to the plains. We were sure that adventures were past us. Life was idyllic in Kanpur. Its cantonment and the city were good places to be in. Kanpur, spelled as Cawnpore during the British times, is a large city in the state of Uttar Pradesh. Also called the 'Manchester of India', it is a major commercial centre located on the western banks of the mighty River Ganga.

It was also an important British garrison town. The Kanpur cantonment was established in the year 1811 and is situated on the right banks of the Ganga, bound by the city on the remaining three sides. It is the largest cantonment in India, both by area and population. On the river edge of the cantonment, is the Satti Chaura Ghat also referred to as the 'Massacre Ghat'. Satti Chaura Ghat has a temple that predates colonial times. The ghat, which is a broad flight of steps leading down to the river, was witness to one of the grimmest chapters in the Sepoy Mutiny of 1857, or the First War of Independence. It is said that during the rebellion, the rebel sepoys held some 900 British officers and civilians, including women and children, hostage. The hostages were given safe passage to move to Allahabad, now Prayagraj. The massacre started while they were climbing the boats and rafts floating in the Ganga. There is confusion regarding how the massacre started, but there is no question that the hostages were being allowed to leave when the firing suddenly started. Nobody knows who fired first, but things went out of control in minutes. Almost all the British men were killed.

Some two hundred British women and kids who survived the massacre were later killed in the Bibighar massacre. Almost everyone agrees that the rebel sepoys refused to shoot the unarmed ladies and kids in Bibighar. The dirty job was said to have been done by some local butchers under the command of a courtesan named Hosseni Begum. There are gut-wrenching accounts of that carnage. Only four men and two women survived from the entire lot. The British retribution was equally brutal. Bibighar translates roughly to 'The House of the Ladies'. It was a small, villa-like residence in the cantonment magistrate's compound. They later built a memorial at the site of the well in which the bodies of the British women and children had been dumped.

Marble statue over the Memorial Well.

Every soldier knows that he can get into a tricky situation at any time. One such event was during the stand-off between India and Pakistan in February 2019. Wing Commander Abhinandan Varthaman of the Indian Air Force was taken hostage by the Pakistan Army when his fighter aircraft crashed into Pakistan-occupied Kashmir (PoK) after an aerial dogfight. Thanks to social media, his capture and initial interrogation unfolded on real-time basis to the world. Despite being battered and bruised, the calm demeanour with which he faced his captors was in the highest standards of the armed forces. Anybody else would have wetted his pants. Wing Commander Abhinandan returned home and lived to tell his tale. He was awarded the Vir Chakra.

As a soldier, one has to learn from all wars, battles, skirmishes, and tense or volatile moments from the past. Lessons learned from every such incident will have a bearing on future conflicts and strategies. One has to dispassionately analyse these incidents. A hostage crisis is a tricky situation and things can get out of hand quickly. So are rebellions. As an army man who has seen many a battle and knows that war can be a dirty game, I have yet to come across a soldier who, upon retirement, does not root for peace and safety for all.

I have recounted three stories of rebellions and hostages, almost 160 years apart. These are a prelude to my next true story that takes me to the center stage of a similar situation.

1973—UP Police revolt, an army officer is taken hostage

Uttar Pradesh Provincial Armed Constabulary (UP-PAC) or Pradeshik Armed Constabulary (PAC) is the armed police of UP. They are stationed at key locations across the state and activated only upon orders from the deputy inspector general and other high-level authorities. They are usually assigned to VIP duties or to maintain law and order during festivities, elections, natural disasters, communal riots, etc. Even though they are equipped with semi-automatic rifles, they usually carry lathis—batons made of bamboo—while controlling the mob during an unrest.

On May 23, 1973, all examinations of Lucknow University were called off as some incidents of rioting and arson were reported. A revolt had been started by the PAC unit deployed on the campus of Lucknow University, and even students had joined them.

The 1973 PAC revolt was a mutiny by three battalions of the armed force located at Bareilly, Meerut and Agra. Lucknow, however, became its ground zero. The PAC had the following complaints:

a. Strong discontentment regarding meagre wages.

b. Menial jobs were given to them such as washing clothes or utensils at a senior's place.

c. No residential quarters, mess facilities, vehicles, or leaved despite long hours of work.

d. They were not allowed to make an association or union.

As the revolt progressed, there were rumours that a PAC unit intended to loot the armoury. The Indian Army was called in to quell the paramilitary forces in the state as the rebellious wave had also reached the PAC unit in Kanpur. They had taken families of senior police officers as hostages.

On May 24, 1973, I was ordered to move with Alpha Coy to Kanpur PAC lines to suppress the revolt and to save the lives of officers and their families held in custody. My wife, Abha, was in the officer's quarters in the cantonment with my two-year-old daughter. Like most uniformed personnel wives, she had no inkling as to what I was up to or where I was. All she knew was that I was going on some important mission.

I reached the PAC unit in Kanpur with a small reconnaissance (recce) group in a civil dress to hide my identity. The rebel policemen got wind of our plan. Once our recce group reached the outgate of the unit, they stopped and surrounded us. I was in the front, and got separated from my group. While the rest of the party could come back to the base, I was taken hostage. In a state of panic some of the policemen abused me and rained lathi blows on my back. The rebel policemen kept me under house arrest in their guest house. A family of a senior police official with a child was also hostage in the same guest house.

I had been in many a tricky situation before, both during wartime and my stint in the North-East. This was not the first time that I had to rescue a family who was being held hostage, except this time, I was a hostage too.

My unit was aware about my situation and I knew they would now be on high alert to rescue their officer. But a hostage, too, has to be extremely alert. Nothing can be taken for granted. A hostage can be both a bargaining chip as well as a dirty baggage for his captors. He can be an easy target for revenge if the external forces inflict damage on the rebels. Or he may just be unlucky and get caught in the crossfire.

I did not disclose my identity as an officer to them. However, they came to know that I am an officer. I gave them a story about how my commanding officer had sent me there with no proper briefing or instructions. I listened sympathetically to my captors and encouraged them to air their grievances. I sympathised with their cause and identified as one of them. I assured the captors that I was on their side.

They took me to an officer's house where I saw the captured family. His young wife and their five-year-old child were terrified. I realised that any plan of my escape had to include the hapless family, too. The plan had to have three elements—identifying the escape route, gaining confidence of the captors, and waiting for the opportune moment to escape. It was either escape or wait for rescue operations to get underway. I knew any rescue attempt would have serious repercussions since it was a sensitive issue, internal to the country, with political ramifications.

A sentry guarded the house while others left to take their positions. My jolly and friendly nature has come to my rescue several times. I struck up a sympathetic and friendly conversation with the sentry to gain his confidence. "I am happy to be of use to your cause," I said. Once I had gained his trust, he allowed me to move around the house. This allowed me to map everything I could see. He had no idea that he was dealing with a war veteran, a daredevil sportsman commando who would later become a trainer. As an unarmed hostage, my best weapons were mind games. On the inside, I was on full alert but a sleepy, hapless hostage by all outward appearances. I had, by now, memorised the entire map of the house and had calmly surveyed the area from the window. I had the entire escape route ready for myself and the family.

In the evening when the cook arrived, I was able to secure the opening of the backyard door on the pretext of letting in some fresh air. That night, I engaged in a 'sleep duet' with that sentry. He would slowly get into sleep and then suddenly nod and wake up. I would follow suit with my eyes half-shut while watching him. He was struggling with his sleep while I was wide awake. I sensed my opportunity in the wee hours of May 25, when the sentry's rifle was on the floor; his head resting firmly on his chest and gentle snores emanating from his nose. I moved slightly away from the front of the house towards the back door and facilitated the family to escape from there into an open field and signalled them to run. Meanwhile, my unit, 14 Guards had sent more troops.

The troops took position around the PAC camp area. At about 4 a.m., they issued a warning on a loudspeaker to release me and the others. The rebels turned down the offer. The sentry also woke up, grabbed his rifle, and moved towards the front. They were given another warning to release the hostages. This was again treated with contempt by the rebelling policemen. They shouted back and refused to surrender either the hostages or themselves. It was dark, but I could see the silhouettes of army men moving at the other side of the barbed fence and take positions. Suddenly, the army troops fired, creating an upheaval in the rebel ranks. There was a panic-stricken flurry as they had not expected the army troops to fire. The rebel policemen panicked and they, too, retaliated with fire.

I took advantage of the turmoil and before the sentry realised, I dashed towards my troops from another direction to avoid getting into the direct line of fire. I could hear frantic shouts of 'bhag gaya' (he has run away) behind my back. The rebels directed fire at me. I could hear bullets whizz past me, so I made one of the best dashes of my life. The football forward in me took over as I ran the 100 yards at full speed. Seconds seemed like hours as I jumped over the wire fence to join my men, my unit. As I lay prostrate on the grass, I wanted to shout to my men not to kill them as they were not the enemy but our own men.

My escape, even under the shower of bullets and the rescue of the police officer's family had broken their unyielding stance. Unnerved, the rebels knew they could not hold out against the army. They soon surrendered. The revolt was suppressed in totality.

After the unrest gained nation-wide attention, Chief Minister Kamalapati Tripathi resigned on June 12, 1973, and President's rule was imposed. There was no commendation of certificate as the case became a political one. The incident was lost in the mist of time and the inner recesses of my memory till I saw the lawyer–police commotion in Delhi on television, that too while I was vacationing in Australia with my son and his family.

The entire family was amused as Abha recalled with indignation as to how I had not told her before going for the operation that night and told her that I would come late. She recalled having woken up at about 4 in the morning to the sound of firearms and she mistook it for firecrackers. A word had got around the Cantonment regarding my predicament. A wife of another officer, told her that I had been taken as hostage. She anxiously waited for me to return. I remember the relieved look on her face when I came back home limping. I kept quiet about the episode but the lashes on my back and bruises said everything.

In 70s, dacoits were very active in and around the Kanpur area. One night some dacoits had entered the outer fringes of the cantonment from the Ganges side. An on duty guard alerted me. I took my faithful Alsatian dog to chase the dacoits. Two sentries on duty joined me later. Entire family was amused when Abha recalled as to how she had confronted me as to how could I leave her and one year old daughter all alone. "You even took the Doggie who was ferocious enough to confront any stranger." All I could do is smile sheepishly and children laughed at the events and light hearted banter between their parents over events that happened almost 50 years ago.

Later, in 1973, Lieutenant Colonel V. N. Channa, my commanding officer, was posted out and Lieutenant Colonel Satish Chadha took over the command of 14 Guards at Kanpur. Thus yet another eventful year of my life came to an end on a very happy note on December 12, 1973, when I was blessed with my son Ashish in Kanpur.

❑

CHAPTER 2

Roots in Pindi

Sagri Village, Rawalpindi District—Undivided India

Saaneha ye meri zindagi seh gayi,
main yahan aa gaya woh wahan reh gayi!

Kuchh na main kar saka, dekhta reh gaya,
kuchh na wo kar saki, dekhti reh gayi!

Log kehtey hain, taqseem sab ho gaya,
jo nahi bant saki cheez wo reh gayi!

Rastey mein khadi ho gayii sarhadein,
Sarhado'n pe khadi be-bassi reh gayi!

Inn zameeno ne kitna lahoo pi liya,
ye khabar aasmaano talak hai gayi!

Yaad Pindi ki aati hai ab kis liye?
meri mitti thi Jhelum mein wo beh gayi!

De gayi ghar, gali, shehr mera kissey,
kya pataa kis se Bakhshi wo kya keh gayi!

—Anand Bakshi 'Rawalpindi'

I survived the tragedy of separation (from my motherland),
I left unwillingly, and she grieved silently with a glance forlorn,

People say everything was partitioned but memories.
There were new boundaries erected on the way,
Helplessness came standing on that.

Even the heavens shook at the bloodletting for lands,
This news has spread far upto the skies.
Why do I remember my village even now?
It had my body and soul in the mud that Jhelum washed away.

I wonder who got my town, lanes and home,
I know not what the helpless boundaries bequeathed and to whom.

I was born on February 27, 1942, in a family of agriculturists hailing from Sagri Village of Rawalpindi, which is now in Pakistan. I was born in a Military Hospital, Aurangabad Cantonment in Maharashtra, where my father, an army man, was posted. A man's personality is shaped by a number of factors that surround him since his birth; the place where he is born, the family that he is born into, the era and circumstances that he grows up in. Family, friends, area, culture, language, contemporary times—all contribute towards the making of a man. Before I move to the center stage of my life and action, I want to introduce you to certain characters who have shaped my personality.

Rawalpindi Cantonment

53rd Regiment of the British East India Company army took quarters in Rawalpindi city after the Sikh rulers surrendered to General Gilbert in 1849. It had been an important region since the pre-partition era with a rich history. In 1851, James Broun-Ramsay, the First Marquess of Dalhousie, announced a permanent military cantonment in the city. The city's Garrison Church was built shortly after in 1854. The municipality of Rawalpindi was constituted in 1867 and many civil and military buildings were built. The city was also connected to the railways that further connected India to the North-West Frontier in Peshawar. In the 1880s, Rawalpindi's cantonment served as a feeder to other cantonments throughout the region, through the Commissariat Steam Flour Mills, first of such mills in Punjab.

Rawalpindi flourished as a commercial centre. A major portion of Kashmir's trade also passed through it. The cantonment became a major centre of military power of the British Raj after they established an arsenal in 1883. They established a shopping district for the city's elite, an archway in Saddar Bazaar in honour of Brigadier General Massey. Sardar Sujan Singh opened a large market in central Rawalpindi in 1883. In 1901, Rawalpindi was made the winter headquarters of the Northern Command. By 1921, Rawalpindi Cantonment overshadowed the old city with more than half of the city's total population. The erstwhile small town was elevated to a large city in Punjab. Its agreeable climate, and the nearby hill station of Murree, made it a favourite first posting for newly arrived soldiers from England. During World War 1, Rawalpindi district stood first in recruiting for the British war effort. The British Government channelled liberal financial assistance into the area in return. By 1921, it was one of the largest seven cities of Punjab, which, in those days, stretched from Delhi to Peshawar.

Rawalpindi was the headquarters of the Northern Command of the British Indian Army. It was also the largest British cantonment in the region. On August 14, 1947, it was chosen as the headquarters for the Pakistan Army. This was perhaps the beginning of a Punjab-centric evolution of Pakistan. This was despite Karachi being selected as the first capital of the new nation. Pakistan later built its brand-new capital in Islamabad, close to the historic city. The Rawalpindi headquarters or GHQ of the Pakistan Army would now be base for almost permanent, direct or covert hostilities against India, and sadly, also against its own people of ethnicities other than Punjabi.

My family roots

The area that my family belonged to had an important link with the armed forces. My family were primarily agriculturists. My great-grandfather had lands in village Sagri. He had four children, and among them was my grandfather, Tulsi Ram, who was born in 1885. He married my grandmother Lakshmi in 1905 in a grand ceremony. It was a time of relative bliss for Punjab, and of course, for Rawalpindi and its surroundings. The district was prospering, and it had a lot of opportunities both in terms of business and jobs. Most of the jobs were coming from the army and its allied services. Rawalpindi had a tumultuous history, but from the 18th century onwards, it had progressed under the Sikh and British rule. It became an important centre for trade, administration and the military.

The idyllic countryside bliss of my grandmother was to be shattered soon after her marriage. My father was two when my grandfather suddenly passed away. My father was named as the Chattarpati, the title held by the famous medieval Maratha warrior, Chattarpati Shivaji. My father had a sister, Vidya, who was about five years elder to him. Life was tough for a young widow during those days, which were full of superstitions. Until the passing of various acts in the independent India regarding property inheritance for women, the agriculturists followed their own customs regarding inheritance. My grandfather's family, however, gave a fair share to my grandmother and her kids. Anybody who hails from agrarian families of Punjab knows how difficult it was to survive for a widow during those days.

Punjab was notorious for fratricide over agricultural lands. People were reluctant to divide lands even among their brothers and cousins, let alone sisters. The ancient customs prevalent in the area completely excluded the females of a family from any share of the property. A widow with only daughters was entitled to some share in the crop, but her daughters were strictly excluded. It is rumoured that after Independence, several widows in the countryside were killed once the farmers realised they would have to share their lands with cousin sisters.

My father's family gave my *dadi* (paternal grandmother) her share in the crop till partition of the country. Even when they migrated to India and were provided compensation by the Indian Government, they continued giving her what was due. Later, my Bua (paternal aunt) Vidya, who by then, had become a widow herself with three young kids, was given the entire share of the ancestral property by my father. Both my parents were working and had well-paying jobs. They did not want any share in the ancestral property. After partition, my Bua was allotted a flat in Lajpat Nagar. I have since lost touch with her descendants. I was lucky to have been born into a family that was ahead of its times. Our parents taught us to reject the archaic rules and rituals. I especially credit my mother for shaping my personality as well as of my siblings, about whom I will discuss in the coming chapters.

Dadi was a fiercely independent lady with her own mind and indomitable courage. Once a pregnant lady urgently needed a doctor at night. During those days, people avoided crossing jungles at night because of the fear of spirits and ghosts and, of course, other perils. Brave Lakshmi, with a fire torch (*mashaal*) in her hand, accompanied the lady to the midwife by crossing the jungle at night.

The rural folk, irrespective of religion, were riddled with superstitions and orthodoxy, and these could be really unpleasant for a widow. It was sad that widows were not even allowed to attend weddings. *Dadi* despised superstitions all her life and loved to break taboos and stereotypes. This was extraordinarily courageous in days when words like feminism and women's emancipation were unheard of. Her aversion towards such practices was passed onto my father and later his children. I am often amused to see many of them still being followed even by highly educated and well-placed men and women. I revel in breaking the taboos and superstitions even now.

Dadi allowed her only son to join the army, which, at that time, was the British Indian Army. Once when my father was posted across River Chenab on the other bank, somebody told my grandmother that her son was ill. Nothing could stop her, not even a river in spate. She crossed the Chenab with the help of an earthen pitcher and arrived to see and nurse her beloved son. Punjabi folklore and songs are replete with Sohni crossing the river in spate with an earthen pitcher to meet her beloved Mahiwal. But here was a mother who dared to cross it for her son. She died in the year 1960, aged about 70 years. She died a contented soul with all of us by her side. She had been a fighter all her life and had taken myriad problems of life head on. Her determination and ideals live on within us.

My father grew up under her strict and watchful eyes. He did his graduation from Government College, Lahore, and joined the army. Later, in 1942, he actively participated in the Burma campaign, World War II.

I am aware of only two other relatives from my grandfather's side. They were my father's first cousins. One was an employee of the Post and Telegraph Department who died in 1980, aged 82 years. The other one retired as an honorary captain from the Indian Army and died in 1985, aged about 85 years. I am not in touch with their descendants.

Riyasat Jammu & Kashmir

Maharaja Hari Singh ruled the kingdom of Jammu and Kashmir at the time of Independence. My mother's family hailed from there. I was very attached to them. My *Nanaji* (maternal grandfather) had a profound impact on my personality. His name was Darbari Lal, and he was a tehsildar (Revenue Officer) in the princely state, an influential officer in the rural areas. My *Nani* was Roopwati, a doting mother and grandmother. *Nanaji* was in the Maharaja's service and was posted in the Jammu region. Rawalpindi was about 200 kms from there and travel between the two regions was common and frequent, something which is unthinkable today. *Nanaji* was a fearless man of principles. During partition, many people from Rawalpindi and surrounding areas crossed over to India via Jammu because of the proximity, and also because it was impossible to cross over from Pakistan Punjab side via Lahore. This was also facilitated because of a train link between the two cities at that time.

Darbari Lal and Roopwati had four children, sons Kailash and Kapil Dev, and daughters Damyanti and Kulwanti. My older *Mama*, Kailash, held a degree in MA in Economics. It was rare in those days. He started his career as a professor of economics at Hoshiarpur and later joined the Ministry of Finance, Government of India. He went on to become an adviser at UNO in USA. *Nanaji* was a visionary and an advocate of female literacy. Both his daughters were educated. My *Maasi* (maternal aunt) Kulwanti did her BA from Jammu and Kashmir, which was comparatively quite rare in those days. My mother, Damyanti, was the elder one and did her matriculation from Jammu and Kashmir and she later completed her education in Delhi after marriage. My younger *Mama*, Kapil Dev, was a garment exporter.

It was in the year 1923 that *Nanaji* arranged for a match for his daughter Damyanti with Chattarpati of Sagri. They were blessed with three sons and a daughter. I was the third child. Our *Nanaji* had a profound impact on our lives. As children, we spent a lot of time in our *nanka*, the maternal grandparents' house.

Nanaji was an avid and skilled *shikari* (hunter). He would often take us to shikaars (hunts). A memory during one such expedition is clearly etched in my mind. I must have been 12 years old. The party left for the jungle with rifles and ammunition on a routine hunt. I was under *Nanaji's* tutelage. An unsuspecting bird was perched on a tree. As I was about to aim and shoot, *Nanaji* intervened and stopped me. He told me I was in a position of superiority, armed with a rifle, with a clear intent to hunt. It was only ethical we make the bird aware that you intended to hunt it, and that you must give it a chance to escape. I never forgot that lesson. There were times during the war when I had spared the enemy who was willing to surrender. Today, hunting wildlife is a crime and rightly so, as various species are critically endangered. But this was when people used to hone their shooting skills in the wild in the absence of any shooting ranges for aspiring sportspersons.

1947—Partition of India

The Rawalpindi region was awarded to Pakistan during the partition of India. The area's first partition riots erupted on March 6, 1947. Rawalpindi's Hindu and Sikh population, migrated to India en masse. My immediate and extended family, including my grandmother, migrated to India, never again to see the land that had belonged to their forefathers for centuries. With over 1.5 million dead and the migration of over 10 million people, it was nothing short of a holocaust and one of the biggest forced migrations in the world. The *bazaars,* lanes, and *havelis* of Rawalpindi would surely have missed its sons and daughters. But many of them who migrated to India made their birthplace proud. I name a few of them–Sahni brothers, Balraj and Bhisham, Kartar Singh Duggal, Anand Bakshi, etc. Bhisham Sahni wrote a soul-stirring novel on partition, *Tamas*. I have reproduced a poem 'Rawalpindi' at the beginning of this chapter, penned by Anand Bakshi, the famous poet and lyricist. Being a cricket lover, I loved watching 'The Rawalpindi Express' Shoaib Akhtar bowling to his opponents. Today, there is a sense of kinship and love when I meet people from across the border in Punjab. We are, after all, the same people sharing the same language, culture, heritage and history. However, I feel sad when the state of Pakistan carries on with its policies to destablise the entire south Asian region. Poverty is the real enemy of the region and not each other.

After World War II was over, my father took retirement from the army and shifted to Delhi in 1946. Our immediate family was spared the mayhem and immense grief that partition had caused for most of the Punjabis stuck on the wrong side of the border, both in India and Pakistan.

After retirement, he joined the Society for the Prevention of Cruelty to Animals (SPCA), which is a common name for non-profit animal welfare organisations around the world. The oldest such organisation is the Royal Society for the Prevention of Cruelty to Animals, which was founded in England in 1824. We, as a family, strongly believe in animal rights.

Notwithstanding the sad months of partition, in 1947, a new era was about to begin in free India. It was almost a fresh start from the scratch. What matters in the long run is how people of the subcontinent have fared since 1947 when they had the freedom to chalk out and write their own fortunes. How they have fared on crucial socio-economic parameters like education, poverty alleviation, literacy, jobs, happiness index, gender parity and so on. The young readers should evaluate where we went wrong and what we did right and figure out ways to regain our lost glory. They must find out how to make this once prosperous and gifted land and its people shine in the world. When I write this, I mean the people of this entire subcontinent. I wish peace and prosperity to one and all, and may we never see the bloodshed that we have been witness to, across centuries.

❑

CHAPTER 3

Mischief and Marbles

My heart leaps up when I behold
A rainbow in the sky:
So was it when my life began;
So is it now I am a man;
So be it when I shall grow old,
Or let me die!
The Child is father of the Man;
And I could wish my days to be
Bound each to each by natural piety.

—William Wordsworth,
'My Heart Leaps Up' (1802)

Delhi—The sleepy town turned megacity

Those were the post-partition years. Rajendra Nagar, Patel Nagar, and Karol Bagh had emerged as major settlements on the left side of a densely forested ridge. On the right was New Delhi. Paharganj, next to Karol Bagh is where New Delhi Railway Station is located. It was an area sandwiched between Old and New Delhi. The area beyond this region was almost a wilderness till the refugees arrived in huge numbers after the partition. The ridge with *Bhuli Bhatiyari ka Mahal* (a hunting lodge built by Feroz Shah Tughlaq) is still a jungle and the green lung of the capital. With refugees being granted land in Patel Nagar and Rajendra Nagar, much of the jungle was cleared and the entire region started bustling with activity. However, it was nothing like the human beehive it is now.

In 1947, Delhi, by virtue of being the capital, had people from every community – from Peshawar to Chittagong, from Baltistan to Kashmir to Kanyakumari. Apart from this, were the original inhabitants of the city living in Shahjahanabad or Old Delhi. They had been living there for centuries and had their own unique culture. The old city had several magnificent monuments from the Mughal era, like Chandni Chowk, Red Fort, Jama Masjid, etc. The British built a brand-new capital for governing the country, after the shift from Calcutta to New Delhi was announced in the durbar of 1911. The inauguration ceremonies began on 10th February 1931 by Lord Irwin, the then Viceroy. The British-era monuments like India Gate and Connaught Place impart a unique colonial charm to New Delhi, referred to as Lutyens Delhi after the famous architect who designed it. If you are in Delhi, please take a slow ride from the President's House towards India Gate. It is one of the most beautiful and romantic drives in the world.

If the Bengali bhadralok came with the shifting of the capital from Calcutta to Delhi, the first influx of Punjabis came to Delhi in big numbers during the city's construction in the 1920s and 30s. One has to visit the Imperial Hotel to know about the five Punjabi families from West Punjab who were involved in the making of New Delhi. This first batch of Punjabis in Delhi of 1930s (the civil contractors and government servants) had played an important role in establishing Gurdwaras and Arya Samaj mandirs in the upcoming capital of India. The second batch were the civil servants, army men, business owners and railway employees. The third batch comprised of the countless Hindu and Sikh refugees who poured into India during the partition.

The Punjabi refugees changed the complexion of the old city. While in West Punjab, they had played a major role for centuries as business owners. They had trade links with Iran, Afghanistan and Central Asia. They also had the benefit of quality education system in Lahore and other major cities in West Punjab (now Pakistan). The Punjabi refugees dominated Delhi's landscape as business owners, academicians, doctors, bureaucrats, politicians and artists etc. With the passage of time, other communities, too, have migrated to the city in large numbers and enriched its culture and composition.

It is a matter of pride that one can hear almost all languages and dialects of the undivided India in today's Delhi. The city has become a melting pot for countless communities, big and small. From a sleepy bureaucratic town of the Raj, Delhi, with its 25 million strong population, is one of the largest megacities of the world. Legend has it that Delhi was built and destroyed seven times. The Delhi of today is far bigger and grander. If you happen to be a foodie, Delhi is the place to be—every known cuisine in the world can be had here. The Mughlai and Punjabi cuisines are amazing. Old Delhi has its own unique dishes, not to be found anywhere else in the city or the country. Modern-day Delhi has a thriving expat population from Asia, Africa and Europe, who bring in their own flavours. I am sure the British author and historian William Dalrymple, who made this city his home, will be more appropriate to discuss all things about Delhi and India. This is the beauty of India that encompasses in its bosom, probably the biggest diversity on Earth with minimum conflict. As I travel the world, I find no other place as big a melting pot of diverse cultures, religions, and languages as India. I am pained when biased people create anti-India narratives.

In dinoñ garche dakan meñ hai badī qadr-e-sukhan
kaun jaa.e 'Zauq' par dillī kī galiyāñ chhod kar

—Zauq (Delhi, 1790–1854)

These days poets are respected a lot down south,
but O Poet Zauq, who can bear to part with Delhi's lanes?

Wolves, ghosts, marbles and kites

Popular folklore hails the childhood mischief of Lord Krishna. He is referred to as *makhan chor*—the butter thief. There are hilarious, and often moving accounts of his childhood antics and mother Yashoda's admonitions. The popular *bhajan* (hymn) '*Maiyaa mori main nahin makhan khaayo'* is soul-stirring. God acts as a child and children are a manifestation of God. The story strongly reminds humankind of how to deal with children and their playful, adorable, loving mischief.

We lived near Gole Market, close to Birla Mandir, at the edge of the forested ridge. *Gole* means 'round' in Hindi and this market still stands in the middle of a crossing. The area next to the jungle and adjacent to Gole Market was known as the Birla Mandir ridge. My elder brother, Kirti Kumar, and I studied in DAV School, Gole Market. We used to walk to Talkatora Garden, opposite the President's Estate and near famous Willingdon Hospital (now known as Ram Manohar Lohia Hospital), to play local matches of football and cricket.

Gole Market was the area where the *babus* or clerks of the Govt. resided. It has its own character and charm. It is next to both the Connaught Place (a business district) and the Lutyens Delhi (the seat of the government). In pre-partition India, the British Government had employees sourced from across the country. The area also houses some of the most beautiful churches, *gurdwaras*, mosques and temples, apart from government quarters and markets. Anybody who has grown up in that area would be sure to imbibe love and respect for all cultures, religions and languages. In the same area there was a Kali Mandir, built in the 1930s by the pre-partition Bengali diaspora of Delhi, mostly employees of the British central government. It is a famous landmark in the area. For a Punjabi child, the Bengalis seemed to be from a distant planet. They dressed differently and had an unfamiliar language and culture. They seemed much less aggressive than our Punjabi folk. The *saree* and *dhoti* and the use of the sound 'O' were distinct.

Near to the Baird road crossing and Jesus & Mary Convent school there was a small Kali Mata mandir. The devotees would place *diyas* (small earthen lamps) and a few *paise* alongside in the veranda of the mandir. As the Bengali devotees concluded their elaborate *pooja*, a small band of mischievous kids on route to school observed them from a distance. Once everybody left, the horde would descend on the *mandir* and consume the *prasad*, then pick up and pocket the pennies. We would prematurely extinguish many lamps in the process. It was not long before we were caught by the priest and hauled up.

Apart from regular playground sports, all kinds of mischief were planned and executed. Some of us were fascinated with ghosts. We found it intriguing that many grown-ups were terrified of ghosts and performed elaborate rituals to ward them off. Many people wore amulets to be safe. We children wanted to see an actual ghost. We visited graveyards at night to catch a glimpse of them. We did not find them, though, and narrowly escaped a beating. We were once hauled up for playing marbles near a tomb by the caretaker. We apologized and bowed our heads with respect. As I mentioned above, children's antics must be forgiven with a laugh.

Maybe unknown to the leader of the band, perhaps Maa Kali was observing his every childish antic. Little did he know that Mother Dhakeshwari would summon him one day and the circumstances would ensure that he learned the great language and be a part of them, as well as become part of the liberation forces of Bangladesh. Maybe the Sufi peers and gurus had blessed the young child and gave him strength and luck to survive against all odds.

The 1950s—Patel Nagar

DAV School was about one kilometre from my residence at Baird Road. In 1951, my parents shifted to East Patel Nagar just three months before my final examinations of fifth standard. Our new house was over six kilometres away from the school, so to reach it one had to go through a forest ridge and a new semi-occupied colony, Rajender Nagar. There was no organised transport system except for one DTC bus. Its timing was at 6 a.m., and it returned in the evening. Therefore, my elder brother Kirti and I had to catch that bus to reach school on time, even though the school timings were 8 a.m to 1 p.m.

The route of the bus was from West Patel Nagar Depot to East Patel Nagar to Willingdon Hospital to Gurudwara Bangla Sahib and onward. We used to catch the same bus and get down at the Gurudwara. Those days, it was not as big, and had a small pond. We used to visit the Gurudwara to pray and to get the prasad of *halwa* and *puri.* In fact, that used to be our breakfast. There was a garden with trees of dates and jamuns outside the Gurudwara. At times, we would pluck them for our friends, children of the peon of the school, and ourselves. We would often partake food in the community kitchen *"Langar"*. Today, the Gurudwara is a sprawling complex with ornate buildings surrounding the main temple.

The wolf in the jungle

My school was about one km. away from my brother's school. The real challenge for me was when I had to go back home alone, as my elder brother had to attend sports and other activities during the afterhours. I had to walk a long distance and cross the thick forest ridge before I could reach the main road to hitchhike. In pre-partition days, the road was known as Lover's Lane, as it used to be desolate. The name is self-explanatory. It still is desolate in the wee hours of the night. The forest watchman had told us that there were wild animals like bears, wolves, monkeys, foxes and reptiles in the forest. Once, he had given me his stick with an iron head, shaped like a spear, for protection, especially from reptiles.

One day, my elder brother did not accompany me as he had gone for a football match. Therefore, I had to walk through the forest ridge alone. I was in the 5th standard. While going through the forest, I saw a fully grown wolf at a distance of about 30 yards, staring at me. Vulnerable and shocked, I did not know how to get out of that dangerous situation. I remembered my maternal grandfather's advice. He was an expert hunter, and though he was my grandfather, I used to address him as '*Pitaji*'. *Pitaji* used to take us children for various hunting expeditions. During one such excursion, he had remarked, "When you face an opponent, just look at the opponent with your piercing eyes and furious expression to kill his will to fight." I did the same, and after a few minutes, the wolf moved to one side, halted and looked back at me. I stood still, matching his gaze. The wolf slowly moved away from me. I changed my route so that I could reach the road as quickly as possible. Once I was on the road, I saw two forest officials and told them about what I had gone through. They were surprised at how I had survived. On reaching home, I told the entire episode to my family. They did not believe me and thought I was fooling them. Later on, they realised the truth. My eldest brother asked me why I had not thrown a stone and tried to run away. I reminded him of our grandfather's advice to not provoke the opponent if he withdraws. Any provocation would hurt him, and he might attack with a vengeance. Therefore, I did not react.

That day I had learned that 'Fear is a state of mind', which my father, an army veteran of World War II, used to believe in. Since then, I kept this approach and implemented it during my army service. That 'DARE' remained with me throughout. The wolf had unwittingly trained a young child for eyeball-to-eyeball confrontation and fear management. Years later, when I was taken as a hostage in armed rebellion (UP police), I could look calmly into the eyes of my captors.

Playground

In the 1950s, the digital age was almost half a century away. Children across the world would pour out of their homes in the evening and sweat it out. We played a host of games apart from the institutional or regulated games like hockey, football, cricket, volleyball, etc. The traditional games remained great favourites. These were passed on to us by the earlier generations, most of whom had not played regulated games. Some of these games had rhymes that all the kids would sing. I remember the names in Punjabi—*Kokla Chapaaki* accompanied with the rhyme *'Kokla Chapaaki jumme raat aaye je, jehda aage picche vekhe ohdi shamat aayee je', Lukka Chippi, Maaram Pitti, Kho-Kho, Kabaddi, Kanche, Gulli-Danda,* and the king of all traditional games–kite flying or *patang baazi*. It required a great degree of skill and finesse. We would look with awe at the senior children, who would cut or mop up other kites flying in the skies. Red, blue, green, orange… the kites would light up the sky in the evening with all hues. Some furious, some gentle, some high, some low, some regally airborne, some struggling to get off. From Delhi to Jalandhar to Firozepur to Lahore to Rawalpindi to Gujranwala—there was an army of children who was deeply involved in this art. There were many activities involved apart from actual flying - selecting the right kite as per the weather and wind speed, preparation of a kite, selection of the right thread which could ruthlessly sever the enemy kites, rolling the thread on or off the spool. The summer and monsoon evening breezes were ideal. However, the occasional *junooni* (addicted) could be seen at this craft at any time and day of the year. One day I and my brother were playing in the street when there was a commotion. A man was running with a crowd following him shouting – *Chor Chor* (Thief Thief). We were quick to respond and tripped him. He fell down and was caught. Elders were full of praise for our courage and quick thinking despite our young age.

The Tara family

We were three brothers and a sister. Childhood was full of fun for us. Mother being a teacher was a disciplinarian. Father was very loving but a man of few words.

The eldest Ashwani was five years older than me. Then Kirti, two years elder to me. Sister Upma was 5 years younger to me. Kirti was very handsome and had an artistic bent of mind. He tried his luck in Bollywood and did odd roles in various films. My sister Upma was very bright right from childhood, unlike us brothers she was very quiet and reserved and devoted to studies. After performing exceptionally well in school she did her MSc. (Physics) from Pilani. After working in Naval School Chanakya Puri Delhi she went on to become Principal of the Golden Jubilee Air Force school. Upma married an Airforce officer, Shiv Chopra who later retired from Indian Air force as a Group Captain. They have been blessed by two daughters and are living a peaceful retired life in Vasant Kunj, New Delhi. Unfortunately, both my elder brothers Ashwani and Kirti are no more. I miss them and fondly remember those carefree days of fun and frolic with our wonderful parents.

A shock and a dutiful mother

It was the summer of 1954. My elder brother Kirti was trying to retrieve a kite entangled with an electric pole. The kite was perched atop the pole and dangerously near to the cable. He decided it was worth the risk. The kite was swinging furiously like a cobra—bright and attractive with a 'dare you to catch me' attitude. He was about 13 years old and an expert at retrieving kites from the most difficult of situations, whether a tree, a building or a pole. I was stationed at the bottom of the pole while he climbed it steadily. The kite swung furiously. As he reached out to the thread, the gang of children looked at him, mesmerised. The *manjha* (thread) broke free at the last moment and my brother lunged at it.

The worst happened – he got stuck to the electric wire. As he convulsed, we shrieked. A person in the vicinity reacted in time and hit him with a wooden stick to free him and switched off the electricity meter. I ran back to the house to tell my mother. My mother rushed my brother to the hospital at once. On the next morning, she left for her job. She was a teacher at Lahore Montessori School, a famous primary school of those times. While many people were surprised at how she could leave her son at that juncture, she was a firm, duty-bound lady. She said her duty was to bring an ailing child to the hospital. The doctors were more qualified than her to treat the ailing child. She said she would not let her pupils wait for her. My mother seldom took a day off. It was a lesson to all of us in terms of sense of duty.

Generation Gap – Geeks vs Enid Blyton Kids

Enid Blyton was a famous children's author and very popular in the second half of the last century. Children were thrilled to read her books. My childhood was a page straight out of her books. Today's internet generation of kids is very smart, but sadly books and book shelves have disappeared from their rooms. Tablets and TV have replaced them. Parks and playgrounds no longer buzz with activity and the same vigour, footballs and hockey sticks have an endless wait while marbles and kites lie in a dusty corner to be discovered. We had spent our childhood closer to nature. Enid Blyton and her children's adventure series are all but forgotten.

Sheikh Mujibur Rahman Road

The jungle where I, as a child, faced a grown-up wolf, still exits, but the surroundings have much more traffic. A major road now cuts through the same jungle and it is named as Sheikh Mujibur Rahman Road. I am amazed at the uncanny coincidence it has with my life. As I drive past that road amid the woodlands, I relive my life from an almost petrified but brave child confronting a wolf, to a young army officer locked in a confrontation with the trigger-happy enemy in Sheikh Mujibur Rahman's house. My eyes well up every time I see the sign 'Bangabandhu Sheikh Mujib Marg'. My youth and childhood memories come rushing in, and the globe swirls around me. All I can see is a small child walking through the jungle and having many adventures. As we move further, I tell the driver to stop on Baba Kharak Singh Marg as I bow at a masjid, the Hanuman temple, Gurdwara Bangla Sahib, and the magnificent Church at the end of the road. I have to thank my parents, my teachers, and of course one of the greatest armies in the world—the Indian Army—that taught me the essence of humanity without bothering about the details of caste, creed and colour.

❑

CHAPTER 4

Goal, Century, and Drill

Crabbed Age and Youth cannot live together;
Youth is full of pleasance, Age is full of care;
Youth like summer morn, Age like winter weather;
Youth like summer brave, Age like winter bare.
Youth is full sports; Age's breath is short;
Youth is nimble, Age is lame;
Youth is hot and bold, Age is weak and cold;
Youth is wild, and Age is tame.
Age, I do abhor thee; Youth, I do adore thee.

—William Shakespeare, 'The Passionate Pilgrim', 1599

2020—Dhaula Kuan, Delhi

Dhaula Kuan is an important junction in Delhi. While driving into the city from Indira Gandhi International Airport, past the Delhi Cantonment towards South Delhi on Ring Road, one encounters an imposing name embossed on the edge of the Metro Rail ramparts: Atma Ram Sanatan Dharma College; or ARSD as it is often called. This is the beginning of Delhi University's South Campus.

Sometimes, I ask my driver to take me to the college. It is a sprawling complex with excellent lawns, well-appointed cricket and football grounds, and basketball courts, freshly painted in eclectic colours. The whole college buzzes with youthful enthusiasm. I can see young college kids with unbounded energy all over the place. I see a dozen boys engaged in net practice—two teams in striped t-shirts and crisp shorts, vying for control of the football. A young girl leads a group of sprinters around the large field in practice for a marathon. Bookworms, under the shade of the trees, along with multi-hued spring-time flowers, are busy revising their economics, electronics, physics and commerce books. Keeping them company are various birds, butterflies, squirrels, friendly mongrels, quaint insects, bees, and giant ants going about their daily chores in the benign presence of green trees, shrubs and grass. Spring is in full bloom in multiple hues, the sun imparting a youthful glow to the landscape, and a gentle breeze wafts with the scent of nature's bounty. Large rocks with thorny bushes stand on one corner like proud old monarchs, trying to remind everyone that they were bosses of this jungle once upon a time. There is a cosmic discipline in all the chaos around me.

Gulon mein rang bhare baad-e-naubahaar chale
Chale bhi aao ke gulshan ka karobaar chale

(Let there be colours in the flowers, and the breeze of new spring would come.

Come, so that the daily business of garden can go on.)

Jo hum pe guzri so guzri magar shab-e-hijraan
Humaare ashq teri aaqibat sanwaar chale

(What has happened to me has happened, but on the night of separation, my tears made your future better.)

—Faiz, 29 January 1954, Montgomery Prison, Rawalpindi

As I turned towards the office building, I could see a boy walking up to the administrative staff with a form. Memories flooded my mind and I was transported back in time, to the summer of 1959 when a tall and strapping young man had walked into the admission office of the Sanatan Dharam college situated in Ramjas School No. 2 building at *Kala Pahad* (Anand Parbat), with a form in his hand, to join the institution.

The shrill josh-filled roar of an NCC cadet broke into my thoughts. I saw an NCC column conducting a drill at the far edge; the boys were giving the salute. I stood mesmerised as one of the boys shouted, "*Salami dega*," and it took me almost 60 years back into a sepia-tinted time frame.

"*Savdhan, vishram, savdhan, vishram* (Attention–Stand at ease) Left, right, left, right, salami dega, about turn, stop." I could hear the usual sounds of a typical drill clearly.

Prof. Grover shouted, "Ashok, practice the salute one more time. I want you to be the best NCC cadet this year. Come, let us go to Principal Dr Rai's office."

I was standing in the corridors of my alma mater. I was part of the first batch of SD College, now known as ARSD. A small sapling had blossomed into a large banyan tree.

1959—Sanatan Dharma College, Kala Pahad, Delhi University

The transition from school to college is a wonderful phenomenon. One is shedding childhood and adolescence and stepping into youth. Youth brings with it physical and mental changes. As you stare into the mirror, you see a different person. It is as if a child peeps into the mirror one moment as an awkward young person, but a confident one ready to conquer the world stares back from the mirror. The feeling that an 18 or 20 year-old gets while he or she is alone with the mirror is matchless and unparalleled. The feeling probably comes back again when one is falling in love in their 20s.

Sanatan Dharma (SD) college was founded in 1959. It was founded by the Sanatan Dharm Sabha which was originally established in 1882 at Rawalpindi. After partition the Trust established a college and a couple of schools for the community. SD college was initially located at Anand Parbat, next to Ramjas School Number 2, in a well-maintained, modified army barracks. In the beginning, the office of the college was at Ramjas School complex until the classes started in August 1959. Anand Parbat is at the far end of the Aravallis. It is a hillock that stands about 160 feet from India Gate level. At the top of the mountain, one gets a 360-degree view of Delhi. It was earlier known as Kala Pahad (Black Hill). The army has a considerable presence in the area and they occupy one end of the hillock. The location of the college was very scenic—being on top of a hill; the surrounding area was open with some big rocks and small boulders strewn all around. It was away from the hustle and bustle of the city. However, because of haphazard growth and nearby industries, the place is now highly congested. Since the college was operating out of temporary premises, it had to shift to a permanent location.

The Hon'ble Home Minister Shri G. B. Pant laid the foundation stone for the present building at Dhaula Kuan in 1960. A noted philanthropist of Delhi, Mr. Atma Ram Chaddha, became the chairperson of the society in 1967. It is after him that the college was renamed Atma Ram Sanatan Dharma College. It is a co-educational college.

The college did not attract many students in the beginning on two counts. One, it was not known that much, and second, it was away from the old North Campus of Delhi University. The South Campus was under construction back then. It was mostly a rocky extension of the ridge with thorny shrubs.

Those days, there used to be a very dignified distance between the teachers and the students but the situation was quite reversed in our college. There was a great deal of camaraderie and cordiality between the teachers and students at ARSD. This was because the number of students was less compared to other colleges in the far-off North Campus.

The principal and lecturers of the college were very dedicated and sincere. I still remember the names of some of my lecturers. Dr. Rai was the first principal of the college. Mr. Yudhister and Mr. Prem Nath, both English lecturers, were excellent. Mr. Rudra Dutt and Ms. Kumud, both taught Economics, and Mr. Grover was a commerce lecturer and was also the in-charge of NCC.

As the numbers of students was less, some of us became very close friends. Out of the above- mentioned lecturers, Mr. Prem Nath and I became good friends because although I was not too good in studies, I once saved him from humiliation. Those days, many of the colonies near Anand Parbat had become notorious for rowdies.

A professor's honour

I remember one day during Mr. Prem Nath's class, two boys were talking loudly. They were disturbing both him and the class. Mr. Prem Nath tolerated them for some time and then politely asked them not to talk but they continued nonetheless. A visibly upset Prof. Nath told them to keep quiet or leave the class. Both the boys were local ruffians. They misbehaved with the professor and used offensive language. There was a loud gasp from the students as suddenly, one of the ruffians whipped out a knife and pointed it towards Mr. Nath. The entire class was stunned. In our culture, a teacher is known as guru and is revered because he imparts knowledge. Guru is akin to god. Prof. Nath was a sincere teacher. It would have been a shocking moment for him to face his own delinquent students foul-mouthing and threatening him with a knife in front of the entire class.

At school and college, there are always people who are throwing their weight around, bullying the weak. Even in the personal life, there are several instances when one is forced to take sides or just stay quiet. Choosing between good or bad and standing up to wrong requires courage and conviction. The motto of our nation is Satyamev Jayate, i.e., Truth Shall Prevail. The righteous shall ultimately triumph. It was probably the first test that life was going to subject me to. As the entire class and Prof. Nath stood frozen, I looked into the eyes of my friend Vinay Dar.

I would later learn in army life that in times of difficulty and peril, just a look can suffice to plan action or next move. At that moment, I do not know what possessed me—whether it was my grandmother's fearlessness, my mother's sense of duty, my nanaji's sense of righteousness, my father's acute sense of right and wrong, the sportsman in me, the raw courage that a young child had acquired while looking into the eyes of a menacing wolf, or the community and society that had groomed me. Vijay and I locked our eyes and the action plan was planned and executed without uttering a word. In a split second, Vinay and I acted in tandem and surrounding the duo, snatched the knife from them. The rest was easy. The entire class sprung up to support. Till we stood up to them, the bullies may have gained a sense of false superiority, but dharma was not on their side. We gave them the option of either leaving the room or being thrashed by the entire class. The bullies were outnumbered—they left the class without a murmur and Prof. Prem Nath heaved a sigh of relief.

A bully is inherently a coward. In his heart, he knows he is not on the right path. Both the boys left the class. Life has its own amazing ways of teaching lessons. Years later, I would witness the mighty West Pakistan Army that had unleashed unspeakable horrors in Bangladesh, leave with their heads bowed and their exaggerated sense of superiority biting the dust.

Since that day, Prof. Nath and I became very good friends. In a lighter vein, this was despite the fact that I was an average student. Normally, the toppers are the blue-eyed boys of the teachers. I take this opportunity to emphasise the point that in life's battles, it is not only the mark sheets that decide a winner. There was also a very charming young lecturer in the college from South India and we too shared a great bond. She would get home cooked Idlis and dosas for me ; a rarity and sought after delicacy in Delhi during those days. I lost touch with her after I left college.

One day as I was playing cricket in the college sportsground as usual, one of my friends came running to me and said that a girl was enquiring about the sportstar of the college who had fought for Prof. Nath's honour. Little while later, a vivacious girl approached me and asked, "Are you Ashok Tara?" I stammered "yes". She said " I am the trustee's daughter." She wanted me to contest the student union elections. It was an awkward moment for me, I was a bit hesitant. She offered me a lift back from the Anand Parbat hillock on her car. Owning a car during those days was a privilege reserved for the ultra rich.

My friends persuaded me to contest the post of Supreme Councillor in Delhi University Student's Union. I won by a huge margin. The credit went to my colleagues and friends, not to mention the girls, all of whom voted for me. A combination of youth, good looks, a sense of humour, a bit of dash, love for sports, and uprightness can be irresistibly charming or charmingly irresistible. (pun intended!). But no compromise on honour and character. My friends and supporters had run an energetic and committed campaign for me.

In college, I started taking a very active interest in sports. I was in the college cricket team as well as the football team. I was the captain of both in 1961 & 1962. I also earned the Monogram of the college in both games. Some of the matches are still fresh in my mind. In cricket, I was an all-rounder. In football, I played centre forward. Prof. Grover was in-charge of NCC and took a keen interest in grooming me. I always tried to excel and got many prizes, in the year 1961, I got the best student award. I was an enthusiastic NCC cadet in both my school and college. I was selected to attend 'Advanced Leadership course' at Manali (H.P). I had the honour to lead 'National Cadets Corps Rifle' (NCCR) Contingent on Republic Day Parade on January 26, 1963, at Jan Path road, India Gate, New Delhi. On 29th January 1963, I had the honour to give 'Guards of Honour' to the then Prime Minister, Jawahar Lal Nehru, and led him to inspect the parade, at Safdarjung Air Port, New Delhi.

From humble beginnings, the ARSD College has come a long way. Recently, it was adjudged as one of the top colleges of the country in many disciplines. Prof. Saruchi Tandon who teaches electronics in the college is a dear family friend, and one of the motivators to write this book. I call her Guruji. I believe I have a kinship with every student and teacher and other employees of the college. They are like my family.

An active, naughty child had unwittingly gate-crashed into youth with aplomb and elan, and it was Delhi University and SD College that took him under their wings and groomed him for the bigger challenges of life.

My friends, my life

A person who will listen and not condemn. Someone on whom you can depend. They will not flee when bad times are here. Instead they will be there to lend an ear. They will think of ways to make you smile. So you can be happy for a while. When times are good and happy thereafter. They will be there to share the laughter. Do not forget your friends at all. For they pick you up when you fall.

Do not expect to just take and hold. Give friendship back, it is pure gold.

– Gillian Jones, 'A Friend'

Life is incomplete without friends. A man can be judged by the number of friends he has and how long he has maintained that friendship. As I look back, I cannot imagine a life without some of my friends. Some went away a long time ago, but the times that we have shared are still fresh in my mind. Though the list of my lifelong friends is long, but I wish to mention some of them.

Colonel Vinay Dar, VSM.

He was my friend from college, NCC, and the army. He was born on 17th November 1942 in Jaipur (Rajasthan) and had a twin sister Vinita, a professional musician. He did his schooling from Anglo Sanskrit School, Daryaganj, Delhi and graduation from SD College, Delhi University. He was a talented singer and won many awards in singing competitions. He was always cheerful and popular among his friends.

He decided to join the army in his school days. Therefore, he joined NCC in both school and college. He had an excellent record in NCC. Vinay Dar and I jointly led NCCR (National Cadet Corp Rifle) Parade on Republic Day at Rajpath, New Delhi, on January 26, 1963.

He was commissioned in 1964 into the Kumaon Regiment. He got married to Nidhee on February 14, of the same year. He fought both the Indo-Pakistan wars, in 1965 and 1971. He was wounded during the 1965 war and also awarded the Vishisht Sewa Medal (VSM). He commanded 12 Kumaon. In 1993, he was posted as Deputy Brigade Commander of 35 Brigade, located at Delhi Cantt. After retirement, he worked at a private firm. Unfortunately, he passed away in July 2005. He left behind his wife, son, and a daughter.

Satinder Mehra

Satinder and I studied together in SD College. He was one year senior to me. Satinder played in the college cricket team as a wicketkeeper. His residence in West Patel Nagar, was on my way to college. We used to go together, both of us riding one bicycle. While going and on our return, there was always a hot cup of tea waiting for us, prepared by his mother. He was good at studies and debates. He was soft-spoken and popular among his friends. We were grouped together during debates in the college. In 1962, he was elected as office bearer Prime Minister of the college union while I was elected as supreme councillor.

He did his B. Com and joined a chartered accountancy firm. Later, he set up his own CA office in Daryaganj. His family later shifted to Punjabi Bagh from West Patel Nagar. He did very well in his professional life. Unfortunately, he passed away due to heart failure at the age of 77.

Kailash Duggal

He also studied in the same college as mine. He was a bold, happy-go-lucky person and a friend of friends. He also joined NCC in the college for the sake of his friends—Vinay and myself. He was from a business family. His father had a flourishing business of leather goods, which he joined after college. Though he was busy with work, he regularly used to be in touch with his friends. He was blessed with a son and daughter. Later, his son also joined the family business. He settled in Punjabi Bagh, near Rohtak Road, New Delhi. Later, he became unwell and passed away at the age of 78 in Delhi.

Anoop Singh

He was born on February 1, 1945 at Gujranwala, now in Pakistan. His father, Gurcharan Singh Lamba, worked in 505, Command Work Shop, Delhi Cantonment. He was my neighbour in Rajouri Garden, New Delhi and studied in the same school at that time. Both of us played cricket and used to do other activities together, which brought us very close.

After schooling, he joined ITI (Industrial Technical Institute) Pusa Institute, New Delhi, and was in NCC of the institute. On 26th January 1963, Republic Day Parade, which was led by Vinay Dar and myself, Anoop was also selected, but being a Sikh cadet with a *pagari* (turban), he needed to be placed at an appropriate spot. He was detailed to be the Right Marker (right side of the first row of the marching column), where the rest of the cadets of the column were to coordinate marching as per his pace. Every one appreciated his position and drill.

After the completion of his ITI automobile course, he started his own business of spare parts of agriculture equipment and machines at Karol Bagh. He did very well in his business, 'Sprayers India', and later his brothers also joined him. He was a well-mannered and dependable friend. He played an active role in planning my marriage. He is like a younger brother to me. At times, Abha and I used to sit on Anoop Singh's motorcycle and go to different places. His elder son has gone to Canada and has settled there. His younger son has opened his own restaurant at Rajouri Garden, and his daughter is married too. He is leading a comfortable retired life.

Om Prakash

Om, Anoop, and myself used to play cricket and other local games together and remained very close to each other, though we studied in different schools. After college, he joined his family business, at Anand Parbat Industrial Area. He became even dearer a friend to me when he was studying in Delhi University. We often used to go in the same DTC bus together.

After a few years, he established his sales office at Arya Samaj Road, Karol Bagh. Later, he was allotted an industrial plot where he built his own manufacturing unit. He also manufactured gas stoves and did a roaring business. He also started laying cables for companies like Airtel, Vodafone and more. During those days he used to live in Janakpuri and has not shifted to Mayapuri, New Delhi.

He is General Secretary of Mayapuri Small Scale Industries and General Secretary of Shri Sanatan Dharam Seva Sangh. He is actively involved in many social activities. He still maintains his childhood friendships with the same fervour.

Parvinder Singh

A school and cricket mate, he was my friend since the 5th standard. His parents were in a high position in the Ministry of Home Affairs, Government of India. They settled at East Patel Nagar. They were four brothers, and all were good cricketers. He was the best amongst them. He captained his school cricket team. In college days, he played for the Khalsa College team, and represented Delhi University team as well. He got a job in State Bank of India, Parliament Street, New Delhi, and was captain of its cricket team, too. He also joined the local Gymkhana Club and taught cricket to many young boys.

He played a very active part in my life, as a good friend being in same school and same class from junior school days. We played cricket, flew kites, and spent most of our time together. He played an important role during my marriage as well. He got married in 1972, against his parents' wishes. He did not stay with them, for reasons best known to him. Unfortunately, he died because of heart failure at a very young age of 55 years. It was a sad day for me, as I lost one of my best friends.

❑

CHAPTER 5

Army Life Beckons

Brigade of The Guards 'First Always First' (*Pahla Hamesha Pahla*)

It is the Soldier, not the minister
Who has given us freedom of religion.

It is the Soldier, not the reporter
Who has given us freedom of the press.

It is the Soldier, not the poet
Who has given us freedom of speech.

It is the Soldier, not the campus organiser
Who has given us freedom to protest.

It is the Soldier, not the lawyer
Who has given us the right to a fair trial.

It is the Soldier, not the politician
Who has given us the right to vote.

It is the Soldier who salutes the flag,
Who serves beneath the flag,

And whose coffin is draped by the flag,
Who allows the protester to burn the flag.

—Charles M Province, 'It is the Soldier'

Army service

Being a Punjabi, warfare is in my veins. As a child, my nickname was '*Fauji Beta*' (army lad). I was born in a military hospital and loved imitating army personnel; hence the nickname. One of my earliest childhood memories is seeing my father in the uniform. My father had taken part in the Burma campaign of World War II. I have mentioned earlier that my father hailed from Rawalpindi District, which was a major recruiting ground for the British Army. I grew up to excel not only in sports but also in the NCC.

A cricket match in Allahabad that never was

1962 is a year that India will never forget. It was the year when China attacked India. The war lasted from October 20th to November 21st, 1962. I was in the final year of graduation. During the Indo-China war of 1962, a national emergency was declared. India identified the need to expand the number of officers in the army. This was an emergency commission. The Ministry of Defence had allowed final year students to appear for the interviews. NCC cadets were preferred over others to join the Indian Army as Emergency Officers.

One of my friends saw the vacancy advertisement in a newspaper. I applied and was required to appear before the Service Selection Board (SSB) at Allahabad, Uttar Pradesh, for an interview. I did not want to tell anyone about it at that stage. So, I told my parents that I had to play a cricket match in Allahabad and left. The interviews were conducted in March 1963. My interview went rather well. I had NCC certificates, excellence in sports, and was blessed with a six-feet tall, strong, and strapping physique for the army. I came back from Allahabad while my family still remained unaware. It was in April 1963 that a letter came from the Army Headquarters, New Delhi. My father received it. He understood the reason of my visit to Allahabad and casually asked about the match that I had gone to play. 'How was the adversary team?' or 'who won?' were some of the questions, while pretending to be engrossed in his work. I was perplexed as to why he was so fixated on that match. My earlier concocted story led to another one. I blurted out that the other team was better than us, and so they won. Father laughed at this and said, "Umpires have made you the man of the match and here is the congratulatory letter."

There could not have been a prouder moment for my father and myself. After all, he was an army man, too. The news took my entire family, including my mother, completely by surprise, but they were all thrilled. They asked as to why I had not disclosed the facts earlier. All I could say was that I wanted to give everyone a pleasant surprise. The family distributed sweets to relatives and friends. I was instructed to join the Officer Training School (OTS), Madras (now OTA, Chennai).

Officers Training School

Officers Training School (OTS) was established in Poona and Madras (now known as Pune and Chennai) to train officers for emergency commission into the army. The school in Madras was inaugurated on January 15th, 1963, with Brigadier Ram Singh as its First Commandant. It was later rechristened as OTA and has a sprawling campus of over 750 acres. I was in the second batch of OTS. I appeared in my final year exams in March and joined the training school in April for a six-month training. I was probably the first NCC cadet, from SD College to become a commissioned army officer. Major Gaurav Arya who is also an alumnus of OTA Chennai has prepared a insightful documantary on the academy which is available on the YouTube.

An army officer never forgets his date of commissioning. Mine was October 13th, 1963, as a Second Lieutenant in the Brigade of The Guards. Initially, I was moved to the Training Centre, Brigade of The Guards, Kota, Rajasthan. Young officers were posted to training centres to give them more practice in firing all types of small arms. They also lived with *jawans* to know their way of life, tactical training, and so on. The motto of the brigade is 'First Always First' (*Pahla Hamesha Pahla*).

Traditionally, infantry regiments of the Indian Army derived their names and troop compositions from region, religion or sub-caste. The Brigade of the Guards was raised in 1949 as the first mixed-class Indian regiment to be raised after the independence. It was raised as the first all India, all-class infantry regiment of the army where troops from all parts of India served together.

It was the brainchild of Field Marshal Kodandera Madappa Cariappa OBE, who was the first Indian Commander-In-Chief (C-in-C) of the Indian Army. He raised the Brigade of The Guards and coined the phrase, 'The Guards, The Elite'. The regiment was formed on the lines of the elite foot guard units of the world, such as the Coldstream Guards of the British Army's Guards Division.

Though the Brigade of The Guards is only 70 years old, its constituent battalions go back as far as 225 years. Three of the army's oldest and most distinguished battalions were converted as Guards Battalions in 1949:

- 2nd Battalion, Punjab Regiment (India), became the 1st Battalion
- 1st Battalion, The Grenadiers became the 2nd Battalion
- 1st Battalion, Rajputana Rifles became the 3rd Battalion

A year later, 1st Battalion, Rajput Regiment became the 4th Battalion.

Amongst them, they share over 93 battle honours earned around the globe. Continuing the glorious tradition of its constituents, the Brigade of The Guards distinguished itself by being awarded the maximum number of battle honours after independence.

The Brigade of The Guards was the only regiment of foot guards in the Indian Army. It consists of 19 regular battalions and 2 territorial army battalions and 1 Rashtriya Rifle (RR) Battalion. The Indian Army, in the 1980s, increased the number of mechanised infantry battalions. As part of this programme, the battalions of the Brigade of The Guards were eventually converted to mechanised infantry.

Posting to Nagaland

In the middle of 1964, I was posted to the 3rd Battalion, Brigade of The Guards (3 Guards) situated at Nagaland . I proceeded to Nagaland to join my brigade, where I was to spend the next two years, i.e., 1964 and 1965.

North-East India was a different world then, especially for an army man. Nothing, absolutely nothing, prepared a person from the plains of Delhi, Punjab, (incl. Haryana) and UP to serve in the hills of the North-East. From the comfortable Delhi climes, I was suddenly in the middle of dense jungles & hills.

It was a period when Naga insurgents were very active and the entire region was considered extremely sensitive. We had to go for patrolling in the jungles for 10–15 days at a stretch to look out for the insurgents. We also had to interact with the local population and civilian authorities. It was quite an experience for a 23-year-old. I was bubbling with energy. As a part of intelligence gathering, I had to develop cordial relations with the locals as well as the head of the villages to keep a tab on insurgents' movements and other troublemakers active in the villages. I also had to be close to the civilian authorities for smooth administration in the area. I was a young man with pleasing manners. My excellence in sports, especially in football, made me a popular person with the locals. I used to play football with the local teams and soon became a regular invitee. At times, I was invited to their functions, generally musical evenings. In fact, my overall personality gelled well with the native folks whom I found very simple and fun-loving. Punjabis like their food, a hearty laugh, a dance, and an evening peg. I found the two cultures though thousands of miles apart, were yet so much alike. I had won their hearts and trust and hospitality. I had acquired a taste for Naga cuisine, which is predominantly non-vegetarian. I used to have meals, liquor and tea regularly with the locals. Such initiatives soon made me popular. I became very friendly, especially with the young folk. I was in regular touch with the village heads, teachers, the Father (priest) in the church and other elite of the area. My young Naga friends taught me the famous 'Bamboo Dance', which was very popular amongst them and an integral part of their culture. I was presented with several Naga artefacts made by them. I cherish my time spent with the Nagas, whom I consider amongst the most wonderful people in the country. My Naga friends realised that I had a great liking for fish. Whenever I was invited to a social gathering, there was always a specially prepared fish dish for me. As is my basic nature, I was always extremely polite and courteous to them.

I am thrilled to see peace and progress coming to Nagaland and the North-East. Their warmth, love and affection have not left me even after 55 years. I still consider myself as one of them. I feel elated when I see young boys and girls from the North-East doing so well in various walks of life across the country. I am deeply hurt when I see any news story wherein they are wronged. They are proud Indians as much as anybody else. While I was friendly with them, I knew my limits and duties as Post Commander.

In January 1965, I had to leave the post and Nagaland to attend the Weapon Course, at Mhow, Madhya Pradesh. After three months, upon the completion of my course, I returned to Nagaland but to a different post. I was now posted at Kerong, located on the Nagaland–Manipur highway. My task here was to ensure the security of army and public transport.

Imphal

I had barely started at the Kerong post when I got the message that I had to move to Imphal (Manipur), to take part in the 'Inter Battalions Football Championship.' After the practice and the matches, there was adequate time to meet the army and civilian officers concerned, as well as visit the local markets and places of interest and to collect intelligence about the insurgents. Here, too, I became friendly with many locals. I felt at home in the North-East as I got along with the locals, especially the sportspersons. During one of my visits to a civilian officer along with another army officer, I overheard the residents talking about some suspicious activities in Churachandpur. I found out that it was a hub of insurgent movements and smuggling. This area was located at the junction of the international border of Burma–Manipur and Mizoram. It was known for insurgent infiltration route to Manipur, Mizoram and further ahead. Some people also used to facilitate smuggling of drugs and other foreign goods.

I decided to visit the said village to explore, collect intelligence and other information, which could be useful for the army. I had a friend in the village whom I had befriended during a football match in Imphal. Visiting the village without security was like entering a lion's den. That day, to hide my identity and purpose, I wore civil clothes and travelled in a civil transport (contrary to army formation orders), with no security. On reaching the village, I contacted my local informer. My friend and I moved around the village and met a few of his close associates. I also visited three to four shops and purchased a few items and talked to the shop-owners to know more about the activities in the area. I got late and there was no public or private transport to take me back to Imphal. My friend advised me not to stay in any civil accommodation, as it could lead to a dangerous situation. Moreover, I had come to the village without permission and security. He suggested that a church would be least likely to be visited by the insurgents. I spent the entire night in the church. Very early, the next morning, I left the village. No one came to know about my visit to Churachandpur. However, I had passed the vital information to the higher authorities for their action. They were surprised as to how one could go to Churachandpur without any security.

While I was still in the Imphal unit, I was allotted the commando course at Mhow. This course was compulsory for young officers. During the same period, our unit received the orders to move to Ahmedabad, Gujarat. This was the end of a wonderful and first chapter of my army life. It was going to be a while before I would come back to the North-East. I completed the course in July–August 1965, and joined my unit at Ahmedabad. From the far eastern borders of the country, I was now in the far west—3,000 kms apart. That's the romance, thrill, adventure, and beauty of army life. When you're in the army, and that too in the Indian Army, no other vocation or job even remotely competes with it, in terms of the sheer adrenaline-pumping drama, high-voltage action, and opportunity to see and live in the most diverse locales, climes and cultures found anywhere in the world.

I had had a very hectic and eventful year and was longing to be with my family, especially my parents. I had never been away from them for such a long time. I longed to have my favourite homemade Punjabi cuisine, meet my friends, zip around Delhi roads with my friend Anoop Singh on his scooter, go to college and meet my professors, laze around the pillars of Connaught Place, and tell my friends about my adventures. Within days of joining duty in Ahmedabad, I went on two months' annual leave to home in Delhi. Everyone was overjoyed. All were eagerly hanging on to my every word and listening to my adventures with awe. But it was only a few days of bliss, as the leave was soon to be dramatically cut short, thanks to Gibraltar.

❑

CHAPTER 6

Gibraltar Rock Slammed by Mountain of Steel

Agar firdaus bar roo-e zameen ast,
Hameen ast-o hameen ast-o hameen ast.

If there is a paradise on Earth,
It is this, it is this, it is this.

—Amir Khusro

In the past 70 years, India and Pakistan have clashed several times over Kashmir. In 1965, Pakistan attacked India again over Kashmir.

The 1965 Indo-Pak War

It was 1st September 1965. While on my annual leave, I had gone to watch the movie *Waqt* along with my mother, sister, and a relative. There was an announcement on All India Radio. Pakistan had declared war on India and all leaves of armed forces personnel were cancelled and they were asked to report to their units. Anoop, my dear friend, heard it and went to our house looking for me. When he learned that I was at the cinema hall, he came straightaway to inform me about the news. There was hardly any time. I knew I had to join my unit that night itself. Father was out of town. Mother helped me pack my usual army trunk, holdall and haversack. A train left for Jodhpur at midnight from Old Delhi railway station. Delhi was under blackout. Panic had set into the city. I still remember that journey from Rajouri Garden to the railway station, like it would never end. My mother accompanied me and stayed till the end. "Discharge your duties sincerely as a committed and brave soldier. We shall all be fine. Do not worry about anyone here. I know how to cope with wars. Your father had gone through a more furious one in Burma sector during World War II when you were born. The moment you were born, I called you *'Fauji beta',* my mother said. This is how I came to be known by the nickname '*Fauji Beta'*. She wished me luck and said she was proud that her son was going to war. A 23-year-old son kept on waving at his mother as long as she was in sight. She stood on the platform like a rock, without a tear in her eyes lest her son forget his duty by becoming emotional. After all, whenever a mother sees off her son in uniform to a war or a strife-torn area, deep down in her heart she knows that anything can happen—he may or may not come home to eat *rotis* from her hand. In the 1965 War, India lost about 3,000 men and Pakistan about 3,800. I can only surmise it in my mother tongue: "*Shaheed hon wala har fauji apni maa da putt si, jo maa de hath di roti khan vapas nahi aaya.*" It means, none of the martyrs returned home where a loving mother was waiting to feed him homecooked food with her own hands.

The narrow-gauge line steam engine billowed out smoke as it chugged on furiously towards the heart of the Thar Desert, in the direction of the Indo-Pak border. That distinct and repetitive pounding of heavy metal with an eerie siren tore into the thick of the night. The train was full of soldiers and a few anxious civilians. Its memory is perhaps lost forever in the fog of time.

The 1965 War was thrust upon India by Pakistan. It is also an example of how localised, misplaced adventures can escalate into a full-blown war.

August 1965—Kashmir

Pakistan Army's Operation Gibraltar sparked the Indo-Pakistani war of 1965. The last time these two countries had engaged each other was in 1947. That war culminated in India, retaining its hold over two-third of Kashmir, including the prized Kashmir–Srinagar valley. Pakistan considered Kashmir as an unfinished agenda of partition left behind by the British, to the extent of a fatal obsession. There was another area disputed by Pakistan, though not as dear to them as Kashmir—the Rann of Kutch. It is a huge barren salt marsh in the Indian state of Gujarat, bordering the Sindh province of Pakistan. In January 1965, Pakistani troops infiltrated into the Rann of Kutch, set up a post at Kanjerkote, and established a track of 20 miles. Indian paramilitary force, CRPF, established a forward post at the border and named it Sardar Post. Pakistan routinely shelled the area, aggressively using artillery guns and mortars. There were casualties, too. India took up the matter with the United Nations (UN) as well as launched vehement protests with the Pakistani Government. Sardar Post was once again attacked on April 25, 1965. Initially, the border police of both the nations were involved but later there were skirmishes between the countries' armed forces. The British Prime Minister successfully persuaded both the countries to end hostilities and an international committee was set up to resolve the dispute. Both the countries agreed to accept the report of the committee. Ceasefire was declared at 6 a.m. on June 30, 1965. India had a better claim than Pakistan over Rann of Kutch, backed by historical and other facts. The award that came in 1968 was accepted by both countries, wherein almost 90 per cent of Kutch i.e., 9,100 sq. km was awarded to India, and 10 per cent to Pakistan, which is 910 sq. km.

Pakistan had tasted blood through the Kutch skirmishes. The Pakistani war machine took two major takeaways from that conflict—first, that Indian politico-military system could be easily outfoxed, and second, that following a similarly deceptive modus operandi on Kashmir they could either win it over or internationalise the issue to bring India on the negotiation table. The hawks in Pakistan did not waste time. Sane voices, if any, were silenced or side-lined or simply not taken into confidence. Before I take you to the Rajasthan front, I will summarise what many experts and analysts have deduced.

As I mentioned earlier, the 1965 War is a classic example of how a clumsily-planned localised strategic infiltration can escalate into a full-fledged battle, consuming over seven thousand precious lives.

Pakistan's assessment before launch of Operation Gibraltar and Grand Slam:

1. Martial Race Concept—Pakistan top brass sold to its country the idea that one Pakistani (read Pakistani Punjabi) soldier was equal to ten Indians. This was the superior martial race concept of fighting against inferior and timid people, later used mercilessly to haunt the East Bengalis.
2. Chinese Aggression of 1962—Pakistan perceived that India was decidedly weakened after the debacle in Sino-Indian War of 1962.
3. Political Vacuum—Nehru's death in May 1964 and his succession by Shastri was also seen as favouring Pakistan. Shastri was regarded as a weak leader. He turned out to be a giant.
4. Internal Dissent—Language riots in India in 1964–1965 gave Pakistan hope that India was crumbling internally.
5. Hazratbal Riots—Kashmir riots after the disappearance of a holy relic from Hazratbal convinced Pakistan that Kashmiris would support its infiltration and the world would be convinced that it was an internal revolt and not external aggression.
6. Indian Military Revamp—The Western powers had promised military aid to India after the Chinese aggression of 1962. The Indian military was undergoing massive changes both in personnel and equipment. This was likely to make India way too strong to overcome militarily. Pakistani generals believed that it was now or never.
7. Pakistan's Technical Superiority—Pakistan had better guns with longer range than India (155 mm, versus the old Indian 25 pounders), better tanks (Patton versus India's Sherman/Centurions). They had better aircraft than India. The Pakistan strategists wanted to hit before India matched its hardware/technological edge.
8. Kutch Conflict—In the summer of 1965, Pakistan had tested Indian political and military response with its unwarranted Kutch aggression, and concluded that its superior armour and artillery,

and deft international diplomacy could overwhelm India, militarily and politically.

9. Kashmir Confined Conflict—President Ayub, though initially reluctant, was convinced by his young hot-headed civilian Foreign Minister Zulfikar Ali Bhutto that India would not cross the international border, and that the entire action would be localised in the Jammu and Kashmir sector.

The above were some of the reasons that several experts had pointed out regarding Pakistan's miscalculation, leading to its decision to attack India in 1965.

What India achieved in the war:

The answer to the Pakistani assumptions and perceptions, as listed above, lie in the Indian achievements in the war:

1. 5th–28th August—Rout of Gibraltar force. Approximately 30–40 thousand Pakistani raiders (army regulars and a few *jihadis* in local dresses) were captured, expelled or killed by the Indian Army with information and help from the people of Jammu and Kashmir. Pakistan's aim of an uprising in Kashmir flopped miserably. Pakistani generals were surprised at the outcome.

2. 28th August—Operation Faulad and Operation Bakshi (named after the legendary Brigadier Zorawar Bakshi, CO of the Ops) captured Haji Pir Pass along with other important peaks in Uri, Thithwal and Poonch sectors. India captured the entire Haji Pir bulge. Major Ranjit Singh Dayal, 'Lion of Haji Pir', was awarded the Maha Vir Chakra for this operation.

3. 1st September, Chamb Sector—Pakistan launched Operation Grand Slam to capture India's jugular vein 'Akhnur' (Ayub Khan's statement) in order to cut off Kashmir from Jammu and the rest of India. This move was checkmated as Shri Y B Chavan, the Indian Defence Minister, authorised IAF to give air support to the Indian Army in the Chamb sector. IAF's Vampires and Mystere fighter planes unleashed havoc on Pakistani advance forces—13 tanks, 2 artillery guns, 62 motor vehicles destroyed. Pakistani attack flounders at 4 kms from Akhnur. It remained a town too far for the Pakistan Army for the rest of the war. There

was some loss of territory for India. India's politico-military planned the next move to take Pakistani pressure off Kashmir and succeeded.

4. 6th September, Lahore—Indian politico-military establishment bit the bullet. Indian Army launched Operation Riddle and crossed the international border in a three-pronged offensive. It was knocking on the doors of Lahore. 3 Jat Regiment, under Lieutenant Desmond Hayde (awarded Maha Vir Chakra), crossed Ichhogil Canal and captured the town of Batapore in a lightning strike, later fell back only to come back with a vengeance. Pakistan Army was caught napping. Pakistani ruling establishment was surprised at India's tactical move and they were forced to commit troops to protect Sialkot and Lahore instead of attacking Jammu and Kashmir.

5. 7th September, Munabao Village, Barmer District, Rajasthan—A company of 5 Maratha Light Infantry was sent to hold the post at Munabao—a strategic hamlet about 250 kms from Jodhpur. Pakistan made gains in Munabao, but was stalled after that.

6. 8th September, Gadra, Rajasthan—India opened 3rd front in Rajasthan to tie down Pakistani forces in Sindh. 11 Infantry Division carried operations on Barmer–Hyderabad (Pakistan) axis of this sector. Gadra was occupied in the first sweep on 8 September and Pakistani rangers were driven out from many more areas of the desert. Pakistani forces were tied down at Munabao.

7. 8th–10th September, Battle of Assal—Uttar Village, which means 'real answer', in the Khem Karan sector, was where the much-hyped M47 and M48 American-made sophisticated Patton tanks of Pakistan's 1st Armoured Division were decimated by a handful of infantrymen and a single Indian cavalry regiment, armed with Centurion Tanks of World War II vintage. Pakistan lost 99 tanks against India's 10. The village is littered with the remains of the mighty Patton tanks. Company Quartermaster Havildar Abdul Hamid was awarded Param Vir Chakra, India's highest gallantry award.

8. 9th–16th September, Sialkot (Pakistan)—India's 1st Armoured Division launched an offensive towards Sialkot. The fearless

commanding officer Lieutenant Colonel Tarapore and his men had gone into Pakistan and captured Phillora, Chawinda, Wazirwali, Jassoran and Buttar Dograndi. In the Battle of Chawinda, he led the tanks twice into the middle of the enemy's killing ground. In the Battle of Phillora, 23 enemy tanks lay scattered, mauled and burning. The biggest tank battle since World War II was fought in the Sialkot sector of Pakistan in 1965. 60 enemy tanks were destroyed or stalled at Chawinda. Lieutenant Colonel Tarapore was awarded the Param Vir Chakra (posthumously). India held about 518 square kms of Pakistani territory in the Sialkot sector, including the towns and villages of Deoli, Bajragarhi, Suchetgarh, Pagowal, Chaprar, Muhadpur and Tilakpur south-east and east of Sialkot City.

9. 11th September, Battle of Burki—15th Infantry Division of the Indian Army crossed the Ichogil Canal over the bridge in the village of Burki, just east of Lahore. Indian infantry captured Burki and held it throughout the rest of the war.

10. 21st September—Dograi was recaptured by 3 Jat Regiment for the second time, thus bringing the city of Lahore within range of Indian tank fire.

11. 23rd September—At the time of cease fire, the Indian Army was in possession of 1,920 sq. km of Pakistani territory, and the Pakistan Army held 550 sq. km of Indian territory. The territory occupied by India was mainly in the fertile Sialkot, Lahore, and Kashmir sectors, while Pakistani ground gains were primarily in the desert opposite Sindh and in the Chumb sector near Kashmir. Further, India had flattened the Uri-Poonch bulge and had a jewel in the crown—the Haji Pir Pass, which overlooked Muzaffarabad and Neelam and would have plugged one of the favourite routes of terrorists forever.

12. January 10th, 1966, Tashkent—Prime Minister of India, Sh. Lal Bahadur Shastri and Pakistani President Ayub Khan signed the Tashkent Agreement, agreeing to withdraw to pre-August lines.

13. January 10th, 1966, midnight—Lal Bahadur Shastri, India's diminutive Prime Minister but a giant among men, died of a heart attack.

4th September 1965—Thar Desert, Rajasthan

Thar Desert, Rajasthan, was the third front of the war after Jammu & Kashmir and Punjab. It covers an area of 200,000 sq km. Situated in the north-western part of the Indian subcontinent, it forms a natural boundary between India and Pakistan. About 85 percent of the Thar Desert is located within India, with the remaining 15 percent in Pakistan. Almost 60 percent of the desert lies in the Indian state of Rajasthan, rest of it extends into Gujarat, Punjab, and Haryana, as well as Sindh (Pakistan).

Munabao–Gadra Sector (Rajasthan–Sindh)

On 1st September, my unit was ordered to move out of Ahmedabad to Rajasthan. My unit reached Jodhpur on September 3rd, and then Barmer on September 4th, where I was able to join them on 6th September. From Delhi, the total journey was approximately 900 kms. I took a train till Jodhpur, and an army convoy from Jodhpur to Barmer. From Barmer, I took my unit vehicle to the location near Gadra Road Railway Station. Munabao, the last point, was still 41 kms away.

From the lush green jungles of the North-East, I was in the middle of the vast sand dunes of Thar, where life struggled every moment against nature. Every once in a while, a thorny shrub standing stoically would prop up and wave at me after a visibly heroic struggle with the mighty desert. The overall mood was sombre if not glum. It was a half-broken gravel road, partially covered by sand. The craters on the road could rival those on the moon. Suddenly, our jeep got stuck in the sand. We all got down and pushed the jeep, and started our rough and bumpy journey. I could see a scorpion scurry away into the sand. The jungle trail was no cakewalk either but the misty, flowery, oxygen-infused air of Nagaland and Mizoram had not gone out of my lungs, just yet. A sandstorm blew into my face, but my shades protected me from its wrath. It felt like I was on a different planet.

My Rajasthani driver said in his heavy Thar dialect, "*Sahbji, hai koi dunya ma iss se khobsorat jagah?*" (Sir, is there any other place as beautiful as this in the whole world, eh?) I took off my shades and looked around, amused. He was right. There were golden sand dunes for miles with amazing patterns, as if god himself had drawn them. But the painter seemed to be whimsical. One moment he would draw a pattern, but dissatisfied, he would disturb it the very next moment and draw another. Sand gleamed like gold dust as the sun rays bounced off it. This was definitely among the most beautiful places on Earth. My thoughts were broken by the familiar artillery fire. I could see the dark clouds of war on the golden sand dunes.

Our unit was told to move to an area close to Gadra city in Pakistan, keeping the impending attack by India in view. On 6th September, Pakistan had reinforced their posts at Gadra City. Indian troops were also reinforced with one squadron of tanks (Sherman MkV) and one regiment of artillery troops. We were now ready to attack and capture Gadra City. I was a lieutenant, a platoon commander in "B" Coy, which was part of the operation. Under the threat of an attack, Pakistani forces had thinned out but kept on firing artillery from the tanks. Even under that fire, our unit kept on moving forward.

Before attack, on 9th September, on order from higher HQ, the Unit was asked to move towards Munabao Rly Station via Jaisingder Rly Station. Unit had to reinforce the troops deployed there to counter enemy advance from Munabao direction, as Munabao had fallen into the hands of the enemy. The Defence of Gadra Road was very important from strategic and administration point of view. I was one of the Platoon commanders with the advancing troops of the unit.

Before the attack, on 9th September, on order from HQ, the unit was asked to move towards Munabao Railway Station via Jaisingder Railway Station. They were to reinforce the troops deployed there to counter the enemy advance from Munabao. The defence of Gadra Road was very important from strategic and administration point of view. I was one of the platoon commanders with the advancing troops of the unit. However, I was ordered to bring the rear party from Gadra Station to the advance base, Jaisingder Railway Station.

Early morning on 10th September, I left Gadra Railway Station with the rear party in 3×3 ton vehicles. After some time, I heard the noise of the enemy aircrafts which were flying very high in the sky but couldn't be seen. Those days aircrafts used to fly high to be out of reach of observation and firing range of anti aircraft guns, Most of the equipment being used in war was of WW2 technology. Troops were having 303 Rifles, with 5 rounds in the rifle magazine. Aircraft had to fly very high and then dive down towards the targets to fire/drop bombs and then fly back straight to its maximum height. I immediately informed the concerned HQ, but was instructed to keep on moving and not to be very apprehensive. To save the troops from aircrafts, I told the drivers to move close to high dunes and troops to walk through broken areas along the road. Soon two enemy aircrafts came down towards my column and strafed but could not harm either the men or the vehicles. The vehicles were away from the road and close to high dunes and men could hide in broken areas. This well thought timely action was highly appreciated by the Higher commanders. Unfortunately two vehicles got struck in the sand dunes. Therefore, a third one was also left behind for their security and help them to pull them out from the sand dunes. Essential items were taken out from these vehicles and the advance was resumed. Later I brought everyone on the road and moved towards Jaisingder railway station. The forward troop party had already reached Jaisingder railway station and secured as an advance base to move to respective areas on high sand dunes.The Troops were deployed to dominate Rail- Road Munabao-Jaisingder-Gadra, Axis.

1 Garhwal Rifles (6 Mechanised Infantry) had also reached Barmer from Gujarat on 4th September. On 6th September, the battalion launched an attack on the border town of Gadra City at 3 a.m. and by 2 p.m. on the same day, the city had fallen. A week later, the battalion captured 'Jessa Ka Pat' to tie up the enemy there. In Rajasthan sector, the Pakistan Army succeeded in capturing Munabao Railway Station and made an incursion up to Myajlar. On 18th November, Sangram Force, under Lieutenant Colonel Krishna Prasad Lahiri, launched a coordinated attack for the capture of Myajlar, taking the enemy by surprise. A number of enemy soldiers were killed or captured. Lieutenant Colonel Lahiri was awarded the Vir Chakra for the Gadra battle.

The war was being fought on three fronts: Jammu & Kashmir, Punjab, and Rajasthan. While Punjab and Jammu and Kashmir can be termed as extremely hot borders, the Rajasthan border can be termed as a relatively cooler one. The effort to capture the strategic towns in Thar would have required a phenomenal effort on part of both the armies. Further, the stakes were very high in Jammu and Kashmir, and Punjab. Densely populated cities of Amritsar and Lahore are just 40 kms apart, where both the armies were locked in an eye-to-eye confrontation.

Forward troops reached Jaisingder railway station and secured it as an advance base to move to respective areas on high sand dunes. Troops were deployed to dominate the railroad Munabao–Jaisingder–Gadra axis.

Desert warfare is a different ball game as compared to warring on the plains. The vehicles, i.e. jeeps, trucks, and other armoured personnel carriers, were not as sophisticated as they are now. Thin tyres would often burst or wear out. Sand worn gravel roads would appear and disappear at will. Hot sand pouring into shoes like molten lava is something one has to start enjoying. An army man's boot is amongst his most important accessories. It accompanies him wherever he goes till his last breath or until he hangs them. From Siachen Glacier to the marshes in the North-East, from river slush in the downstream Ganga to the thorny snake-infested jungles, to rocky barren mountains, to salt-cracked Rann of Kutch—they are a part of the adventure and the danger. They indulge in deadly romances with the snakes, scorpions, crocodiles, and ghariyals, and harmless flirtations with the leeches, frogs, earthworms, porcupines and whatnot? Today, one has an amazing quality and range of boots available to the army to suit every terrain and weather. The arms and ammunition, vehicles, dresses and overall infrastructure are much more advanced as compared to those days.

Gadra Road Station and Garuda 'The Eagle'

While we were driving towards the Gadra Road station, a BSF *jawan*, who was a local chap, was accompanying us. He gave me a small commando refresher. "*Janaab*, you are aware this is *Marubhoomi*, the great desert. There are different kingdoms at different times of the day. As the sun bows down, the temperature cools off and a different kingdom takes over. The desert day belongs to the mammals but the night belongs to the reptiles." He was right. Thar is home to some of the most venomous snake species such as vipers, kraits, and rat snakes, who like to come out at night when it is cooler. However, other genteel reptiles like our dear monitor and desert lizards and geckos like to avoid them and prefer the daytime company of mammals. Camel is the king of the desert.

The seasoned Rajput pointed towards a spotted eagle soaring high in the skies. The desert eagle, also called the Indian spotted eagle, with its massive wingspan, is one of the biggest predators of the desert. Even the mighty snakes fear it. One of my boys remarked, "Sir, what a good omen. The patron of our regiment is here to bless us." The insignia of our regiment was 'Garuda' which is known as the king of birds and enemy of all snakes. Snakes can be interpreted as death and Garuda as birth. I led the men in unison in greeting the awe-inspiring eagle by shouting our war cry "*Garud ka hoon bol pyare.*" (I represent the eagle king). We looked at the lord of the skies soaring majestically as if he was guiding us to our destination safe and sound.

The unit was told to harass the enemy by aggressive patrolling and organising raiding parties. The enemy brought heavy artillery fire when troops were under deployment. My 'Company' being forward, had to bear the maximum brunt.

In the desert, it is difficult to mark the exact border between two countries, since sand dunes keep on shifting. Sand dunes can be very deceptive, too, as they can hide innumerable men and machines in their bosom, and you can be just metres away without anticipating their presence.

During one of my night patrols, I took about seven to eight men near the border and spent a night there. In the morning when we got up, we found out that there was a Pakistani patrol almost at an arm's distance. They were equally surprised to see us. The Pakistani patrol beat a hasty retreat. There were a couple of fires in the air from both sides. Straight firing is useless in the sand dunes as the bullets get trapped in the sand. it may be a wastage of ammunition. Artillery fire is an effective way to pound the enemy in such terrains. Further, one has to be careful as land mines may be planted.

Once, during a night patrol, I got too close to an enemy recce patrol. They fired two-inch mortar at us. Unfortunately, I could not chase them as we were very close to the mine fields. Even though the enemy had also fired 81mm mortar from the main position on my patrol, it was not very effective as the sand dunes offered natural protection. While withdrawing, my left foot got twisted and swollen.

Later, I was moved to the advance base at Jaisingder Railway Station. At this place, I had ensured security by preparing fire trenches around the station. In coordination with HQ, we had moved a train with lights on and some non-combat civilians were made to travel to create high volume noises, to make the enemy believe that more reinforcements had arrived. It was possible that this deceptive reinforcement made the enemy reluctant to move further towards the Jaisingder–Gadra Railway Station. The objective was to stop the enemy from coming anywhere near the crucial road and rail link to Barmer and Jaisalmer.

By the end of September, offensive action from both the sides was limited. In fact, there was more emphasis on patrolling and artillery fire than any major attack.

United Nations Organisation (UNO)

During October, the process of peace treaty had started as Soviet Union intervened and asked both the countries to come to a peace resolution. Later it was called the Tashkent Treaty.

Under this treaty, the officials of UNO had arrived at Gadra railway station guesthouse to use it as their residence cum office. I was the detailed liaison officer to coordinate their movement, meeting with the army officers, and the translator with the civil authorities and the locals. I had also been to a few troubled areas to ensure ceasefire and peace. I being with UNO officials and White Flag had managed to evacuate Capt. Ranbir to Bn. HQ for medical aid. who was fired and wounded by Pak fire. Both sides were attacking each other's posts to claim more captured areas to show to the UNO officials for better bargains before the final Tashkent Treaty was signed.

In January 1966, I was posted as an instructor at Commando Wing, called the Infantry School during those days, at Mhow, MP. It was a great war experience for a young officer like me. Our unit carried out its tasks successfully, that too with minimal casualties. As I was coming back from the front, I again saw the great desert eagle with its outstretched wings, soaring high into the skies over me. Just like the last time, his direction was the same as mine. I take all superstitions with a pinch of salt, let alone omens, good or bad. But I knew that my men believed them. I smiled at the eagle and whispered under my breath, *"Garuda ka hoon bol pyare."*

War Summary

On September 22nd, the United Nations Security Council unanimously passed a resolution that called for an unconditional ceasefire from both the nations. The war ended the following day. The Soviet Union, led by Premier Alexei Kosygin, hosted ceasefire negotiations in Tashkent, now in Uzbekistan, where Indian Prime Minister Lal Bahadur Shastri and Pakistani President Mohammed Ayub Khan signed the Tashkent Agreement, agreeing to withdraw to pre-August lines no later than February 25th, 1966.

Some believe that there was a stand-off at the time of the ceasefire but Pakistan's strategic, moral, and political defeat in the 1965 War was beyond doubt. The figures were heavily in favour of India. Some experts even predicted the complete rout of Pakistan had the war continued.

Pakistan celebrates September 6th as Defence Day (*Yaum-e-Difa*). The admission of truth would've been very embarrassing, if not suicidal, for the ruling elite who brought up generations of Pakistani people on the invincibility of Pakistani forces. Remembering the countless martyrs from both sides who needlessly died to pander the political egos of few men of the ruling Pakistani elite, it would be appropriate if they can name September 6, as 'The Day of Self Realisation' or 'Yaum-e-Khud Ahsas'. I will let the quotes of a few neutral experts summarise:

> *"India won the war. It held on to the Valley of Kashmir, the prize Pakistan vainly sought. It gained 1,840 sq. km (710 sq. mi.) of Pakistani territory: 640 sq. km (250 sq. mi) in Azad Kashmir,*

Pakistan's portion of the state; 460 sq. km (180 sq. mi.) of the Sialkot sector; 380 sq. km (150 sq. mi) far to the south of Sindh; and most critical, 360 sq. km (140 sq. mi) on the Lahore front. Pakistan took 540 sq. km (210 sq. mi) of Indian territory: 490 sq. km. (190 sq. mi.) in the Chhamb sector and 50 sq. km (19 sq. mi.) around Khem Karan."

—David Van Praagh
(*The Greater Game: India's Race with Destiny and China***)**

"A brief but furious 1965 war with India began with a covert Pakistani thrust across the Kashmiri ceasefire line and ended up with the city of Lahore threatened with encirclement by Indian Army. Another UN-sponsored ceasefire left borders unchanged, but Pakistan's vulnerability had again been exposed."

—William M. Carpenter and David G Wiencek
(Asian Security Handbook)

"...though Pakistan 'lost heavily' during the 1965 war, India's hasty decision to call for negotiations prevented further considerable damage to the Pakistan Armed Forces.

"India's chief of army staff urged negotiations on the ground that they were running out of ammunition and their number of tanks had become seriously depleted. In fact, the army had used less than 15 per cent of its ammunition compared to Pakistan, which had consumed closer to 80 per cent and India had double the number of serviceable tanks."

—Jeremy Black, Historian
(War in the Early Modern World)

"Pradhan writes, 'On September 20, when the prime minister asked Chaudhuri whether India could expect to gain if the war continued for a few days more, he informed the PM that the army was coming to an end of its ammunition holdings and could not sustain fighting for much longer. Chaudhuri advised acceptance of the ceasefire proposal. It was later discovered in overall terms only 14–20 per

cent of the Indian Army's ammunition stock had been used up.' In contrast, Pakistan had expended 80 per cent of its ammunition. It had also lost 250 of its latest US-supplied tanks. This time, India's victory was nearly total: India accepted ceasefire only after it had occupied 740 sq. mi. though Pakistan had made marginal gains of 210 sq. mi. of territory. Despite the obvious strength of the Indian wins, both countries claim to have been victorious."

—Arif Jamal
(*Shadow War*)

In 2015, the marshal of the Indian Air Force Arjan Singh, the last surviving armed force commander of the conflict, gave his assessment that the war ended in a stalemate, but only due to international pressure for a ceasefire, and that India would have achieved a decisive victory had hostilities continued for a few days more.

"For political reasons, Pakistan claims victory in the 1965 War. In my opinion, the war ended in a kind of stalemate. We were in a position of strength. Had the war continued for a few more days, we would have gained a decisive victory. I advised the then Prime Minister, Lal Bahadur Shastri not to agree for a ceasefire. But I think he was under pressure from the United Nations and some countries. India's leadership frittered away on the negotiating table what the soldiers won on the battlefield."

Pradhan writes, "In a way, India's leadership, out of its sense of restraint, fair play and endeavour to seek enduring peace and goodwill with the neighbour, seems to have missed opportunities to solve the problem."

There was another reason for Pakistan's eagerness for talks. According to Pradhan, "The continued presence of Indian troops on the east side of the Ichhogil Canal, facing Lahore City, was hurting Pakistan's pride. The heat was clearly on Islamabad. Haji Pir pass, which if India had kept, would have forever nullified Pakistan's advantage in Kashmir."

—R. D. Pradhan, Former Maharashtra Chief Secretary
(*1965 War: The Inside Story*)

"The myth of 'victory' was created after the war had ended, in order to counter Indian claims of victory on the one hand and to shield the Ayub regime and the army from criticism on the other. Most observers agree that the myth of a mobile, hard-hitting Pakistan Army was badly dented in the war, as critical breakthroughs were not made. Several Pakistani writers criticised the military's ill-founded belief that their_'martial race' of soldiers could defeat 'Hindu India' in the war."

—Haidar Imtiaz, Pakistani commentator

"In three weeks the second Indo-Pak war ended in what appeared to be a draw when the embargo placed by Washington on US ammunition and replacements for both armies forced cessation of conflict before either side won a clear victory.
India, however, was in a position to inflict grave damage to, if not capture, Pakistan's capital of the Punjab when the ceasefire was called, and controlled Kashmir's strategic Uri-Poonch bulge, much to Ayub's chagrin."

—Stanley Wolpert, American author.

Pakistan lost more than it had gained during the war. It failed to achieve its goal of capturing Kashmir. Indian Army was sitting across Lahore and Sialkot. Uri bulge had been flattened and Haji Pir was in the control of India. The aura of invincibility of the Pakistan Army and the concept of racial superiority lay shattered. The war led to economic slowdown in Pakistan. Defence spending zoomed from approximately 5-10 per cent of its GDP. By 1970, defence was spending an unsustainable 56 per cent of total government spending. The discontent in East Pakistan (today's Bangladesh) increased even further. Bangladesh leaders accused the central government of taking out money from Bengal to finance the war without providing adequate security to the region.

Sheikh Mujibur Rahman was critical of the disparity in military resources deployed in East and West Pakistan and called for greater autonomy for East Pakistan. The 1965 war exposed chinks in the armour of Pakistan. On hindsight, the war accelerated the formation of Bangladesh. President Ayub could never recover from the blow—

the war was the major reason for his downfall. Zulfiqar Bhutto, the wily civilian foreign minister who convinced Ayub that India would not cross the international border, was an astute politician adept at running with the hares and hunting with the wolves. He resigned after the war and launched an agitation against Ayub. It is said that Ayub was initially sceptical about the plan but later agreed on Bhutto's animated counsel. However, as an army man, Ayub should have had better sense. Further, he had been part of the same British Army just 19 years ago. He was up against his own erstwhile colleagues and Sandhurst batchmates who were now leading the Indian Army. Experts point out that Ayub knew very well that he would not be fighting an inferior army but some of most decorated and brave regiments of the world—Sikh, Punjab, Maratha, Gorkhas, Hodson Horse, Poona Horse, Rajput Regiment, Jat, Dogra, Madras. Not to mention my regiment, the Brigade of The Guards which had some of the oldest and most decorated battalions of the world as constituents. Perhaps the Pakistan hawks did not fully study the reasons of the 1962 debacle; it may have been everything but Indian Army's bravery. Ayub and General Moosa should have known that the Indian Army fighting in the Northern Indian plains and Jammu and Kashmir would be a different ball game altogether. They underestimated the Indian leadership and the revamp of the army in the intervening period. This was a very costly war for Pakistan, as it lost on all fronts be it be military, diplomatic, economic, moral or political.

Though Rajasthan front was not as active as Punjab or Jammu and Kashmir, I still had an amazing experience. If '65 whetted my appetite, my plate was to be full in '71. I had no clue that '65 would only be a trailer for me. *Picture toh abhi baaki thi* (The action was yet to begin). The next blockbuster action would be almost six years away.

After the war, I did a number of Army courses - Weapon and Commando courses, at Infantry school Mhow., Junior Commander (JC), pre staff and Senior Commander course, Mhow. Intelligence and Field Engineering courses at Pune, Para Jump course at Agra and Jungle Warfare Course at Warangte (Mizoram). I excelled in the courses. Later, I got recommended for being an Instructor in Commando Course.

In January 1966, I was posted as an instructor in Commando Wing, then at Infantry School, Mhow. Once, during commando course, a demonstration to cross a gap of 30 feet+ between two rocks was to be shown to the team of officials from Army Headquarter (AHQ), Delhi. They came to inspect/ assess the standard of training of Commando Course.

A commando student was detailed to demonstrate the crossing of the gap between two big rocks with the help of a parallel rope. While crossing from one rock to other, the safety belt of the commando student fell down and he got stuck with the main rope. It was a very sensitive and dangerous situation to move on single rope without safety rope/belt. Everyone was worried on the unexpected vulnerable situation as the student's life was in danger. I volunteered to go on the rocks, despite knowing the vulnerability of the situation. I moved up to the top of the rocks and reached the student with the safety belt. I did not have any safety for myself either of rope or belt as I was on a different rope. I had to pull up to the student and fix his safety belt to his main rope. In case, either of us slipped or lost the grip, it could be disastrous for both. However, I brought him down safely. Everyone was relieved. But, AHQ team was told that the action/ demonstration and initiative of Ashok Tara was intentionally planned to show them the standard of Training given to students in Commando Wing, Mhow (MP). After completion of my tenure as instructor in Mhow, I was posted to 9 Para Commando Unit.

9 Para Commando Unit

It was First Para Commando Unit of Indian Army. It was raised under command of Lt. Col. Megh Singh,VrC, at Gwalior (MP). Officers and Jawans with a Commando aptitude, physically and mentally robust, were selected from other army units irrespective of any Faiths, Caste and Creed. After completion of initial Commando (Cdo) training, Unit (9 Para) was moved to Danasa, near Udhampur (J&K). While in 9 Para I had also completed my Para jumps at Agra and took part in operational oriented Para drop near Udhampur (J&K) and Heliborne exercises at Chamba (HP).

I was also the member of selection team, which was ordered to visit army posts at Rajouri, Poonch, Uri and other areas of J&K to select jawans for 9 Para Cdo and also to familiarise with army operational areas. Survival of the fittest was always kept in mind. Commandos had to prepare for every scenario in the battles, therefore, a proper training in all types of weapons, unarmed combat (Judo) and psychological warfare to make them mentally and physically robust was given to them. Commandos had to operate behind enemy positions and in jungle for a long period. They must know, how to survive off the land. A Commando Pit (Circumference appx 50 ft to 60 ft and 2 ft depth) to train commandos in unarmed combat was dug.

Jungle warfare

They were also taught to recognise the edible plants, fruits in jungle and lay traps for small wild animals, capture of reptiles, specially snake and make it edible. To catch a snake one has to carry a stick/ branch of a tree with V shape in it's front. The V should have 4 inches to 5 inches arms with an approx. 3 inches gap between the arms. On seeing the snake one must move close enough to put the V of the stick on the neck from behind the snake. Press it hard towards the land and ensure that snake would not be able to take out his head from V of the stick. After making severe movements, it would cool down. Then from the rear, hold it's neck strongly, near the head. Snake's poison is always in the mouth-teeth. Chop off from the neck and 4 inch tail and remove the skin. Rest of the body of snake is ready to be cooked and is to be eaten like any other animal flesh. I, personally had many times given this demonstration, even eaten cooked snake, also Cobra, to make young commandos believe.

Mizoram Posting - 1970-1971

While in 9 Para, I did Operational Oriented Heliborne and Para drop exercises at Samba (HP) and near Udhampur (J&K) respectively. After completion of my tenure in 9 Para Commando, I was posted to 2 Para battalion (now special Force). In 1970, I took part in a major and an important Operational Oriented Exercise, as a part of Para Brigade. Unit (2 Para) was air dropped in Bikaner (Rajasthan) to carry it's task to capture Nal air field. It was a successful exercise.

In November 1970, I was posted to 32 Bn Brigade of the Guards (counter – insurgency unit) in Mizoram. Due to political turmoil the then East Pakistan (now Bangladesh) 32 Guards was redesignated as 14 Guards and converted in to a regular Infantry Battalion (Bn).

Dear readers, before the next war i.e. '71 war, the young soldier in me had to fight a 'wholehearted personal war' in the heart of Delhi (pun intended).

❑

CHAPTER 7

Operation Rose Bouquet—An Explosive Bloom in a Soldier's Heart

क्यूँ जवानी की मुझे याद आई
मैंने इक ख़्वाब सा देखा क्या था
Kyun Jawani ki mujhe yaad aayee
Maine' ek Khwaab sa dekha kyaa tha.

(Did I reminisce about my youth
Or was it just a beautiful dream)

—Asrar-ul-Haq Mazzaz (Majaz Lucknawi) (1911–1955)

The 1960s—A new dawn and a transformational decade

The Indian counterpart of baby boomers was the new and confident post-partition generation. 1960s was a transformational decade for the World, India, and of course my generation. For the west it was the post WW2 generation and for us it was the post partition generation coming of age. Nothing captures its spirit better than the famous song of a 1960 movie—Hum Hindustani starring an energetic Sunil Dutt moving around newly-built industries, dams in the making, marching columns of soldiers and historical monuments with a wonderful song in the backdrop—Choddo kal ki baatein, kal ki baat purani, naye daur mein likhenge, mil kar nai kahaani, hum Hindustani.

As I broke into my teens in the 60s, it was a new dawn for India. The earlier, post-partition 15 years were spent in building and stabilising the nation. Of course, the wounds were still raw for the older generations. The new generation had grown up in a budding nation with new ideas and opportunities and infrastructure. The 60s was a burst of new energy on the Indian landscape. Partition had thrust urban living and modern education on a large number of people. The children of partition had come of age in this decade. A new generation was sprouting.

The 60s heralded a new era in the society. There was a visible new wave in everything, be it architecture, music, art, films, education, or infrastructure. New colonies were springing up in Delhi. There was action all over the country—new university campuses, schools, dams, factories, large steel plants. The seeds of green revolution were being sown. India was on the move.

As India was trying to forge ahead and transform itself, there was a spanner in the works. The Chinese aggression of 1962 jolted the country. India knew that it could no longer neglect its defence. After years of inattention, defence became the main focus of the nation. India started recruiting, training and reinvigorating one of the finest armies in the world. After all, the same army had distinguished itself in all previous wars, including the two world wars.

There was a renaissance in the films too. The Punjabi refugees were making a mark in the Hindi film industry based in Bombay (now Mumbai). There were some excellent films with war themes. The suave army man was the hero of new India. If we were being groomed as fighters, para commandos, we were also being groomed in our soft skills. We used to have special screenings of the movies at our Saturday evening get-togethers in the mess.

Some of the notable war films of that decade were *Hum Dono, Sangam, Haqiqat and Aradhana.* Each of these films showcased its protagonists as brave and glorious army officers with a passionate romantic streak. My own love story and subsequent marriage was no less than a Bollywood potboiler. A typical Bollywood film story goes like—hero woos his lady love with various antics—some funny, some silly, some daredevilry, some dance, some music, some romantic meetings in the parks and colleges. Then comes either a villain or the girl's father or the hero's family, which is against the match. There are a lot of twists and turns, and obstacles, after which the hero and the heroine get married and live happily ever after.

Indians are emotional people with strong family ties. There is deep respect for elders and their wishes. During those days, most of the marriages were arranged by families and the couple got married without much personal interaction. The institution of arranged marriage still survives and is thriving, but the opposition to a love marriage is far lesser. Earlier, it was common for a couple in love to part ways, heartbroken simply because the elders did not agree to the match. Marriages where a girl and a boy choose each other on their own were rare back then, though not entirely uncommon.

By 1966, I was already four years into the army and had been part of a major war in 1965. All my elder brothers and sisters were married by then. Like all parents and grandparents of those days, mine, too, started looking for a match. There were a number of ways to do that—giving the particulars of the prospective groom in the local temples, asking the busybody neighbourhood aunts trying to fix matches, finding eligible matches within the friends and extended family circles, etc. People tended to stick to their communities. Today, one has a number of matchmaking sites where young boys and girls scout for prospective life partners. Those days this facility was not available. Sunday editions of leading newspapers would carry matrimonial advertisements of brides and grooms. People would then correspond with the suitable matches and try to finalise one.

A typical advertisement could read like:

"Wanted a suitable Punjabi beautiful girl for a Hindu, very handsome and fair Army Major, Height 6'1", Well known and progressive family with modern outlook from Rawalpindi now settled in Delhi. Caste no bar. Boy in Delhi on leave till Feb 28, 1968."

Punjabis like to celebrate. Most Punjabi weddings qualify for the tag of 'big fat weddings'. They are amongst the most colourful nuptials in the subcontinent, maybe even the world. With passage of time they have become even more pompous and fancy. However, the weddings of those days were less ostentatious. They did have a lot of rituals, and of course, the now world-famous Punjabi music and dance. After days of ceremonies and celebrations, the groom, in full finery with a turban and *sehra*, would arrive at the doorstep of the bride on a white mare, with a customary sword in hand and accompanied by a *baraat*. With hundreds of guests in attendance, the marriage rituals would normally take anything between 2–3 hours, including the ceremonial seven rounds around the holy fire. Father of the bride gives her hand away to the groom in a ritual known as *kanyadaan*.

The festivities and rituals would continue for the entire night. In the morning, it would be time for the girl's family to send off the married couple in a *doli* with tears in their eyes. The total festivities would span many days for which relatives would come from all over the country and stay put. The festivities at the bride's end are equally loud and joyful. There is a henna night (*mehendi ki raat*), a ladies' *sangeet* night (for music and dance) before the marriage, the *haldi* (turmeric) ceremony and the *chuda* ceremony, where the maternal uncle gets *chooda* (red and white ivory bangles) and *kalire* (golden metallic tassels to be tied to the bangles) for the bride.

Those days, most other communities had simpler wedding celebrations. Now, I find almost all communities going for big, fat and loud weddings. After my years in the army, I have no fancy for big, pompous weddings.

The ladies' *sangeet* ceremony before any Punjabi wedding is the liveliest of functions. Women, young and old, would sit with basic musical instruments like *dholki*, *chanakna*, a spoon to beat the *dholki* with, and belt out folk songs. Some romantic, some emotional, some funny, some bawdy. There's also *'tappe'* which is a delightful limerick war between two singers, at times between ladies and gents. Bachelors are known to flock to the *sangeet* ceremony to find love. Cupid is notorious for lurking there.

You can see many of the things like ladies *sangeet* that I am referring to in Yash Chopra movies like *Kabhi Kabhie, and Chandni*. Years later, I read the story of how Yash*ji* met his wife, Pamela. He had first seen her singing at a Punjabi ladies' *sangeet*. They were married in 1970. I have often found his films like *Waqt* (1965) tugging at my heart. It was so similar to our homes, our struggles and our lives.

Aren't you wondering why am I describing a wedding in detail? The mystery shall unfold in the coming paragraphs.

15th June 1968, Rajouri Garden, Delhi—A soldier and an ace batsman is clean bowled

My heart melts thinking of that evening. The fragrance of that day is still fresh in my heart like it was yesterday. I was a captain with 9 Para Commando and posted in Kashmir at the time. I had come home for my annual leave. We were living in Rajouri Garden, Delhi. My *Maasadji*, K. K. Sharma, was a professor in Dehradun at that time, and *Maasiji* Kulwanti was living in E Block with her children. It was my cousin Kanchan's *sangeet* ceremony. She was getting married to Omi Chopra. The whole house was filled with people, rushing in and out, laughter pouring from all sides. Everybody seemed to be busy or pretended to be busy. It was a merry-go-round. A starry-eyed 26-year-old young army captain on his leave, somewhat lost, perhaps waiting for an order from someone to do this or that. At a sister's wedding, everybody has to be useful. Here I was with sleek pants, well-stitched shirt, hair gelled back, perfume—an army officer sure knows his grooming. Somebody came running and addressed me by my nick name in Punjabi,

"Shoki, Dholki uthe fadaaeyaa, ladies sangeet shuru karna haiga."
"Shoki, take this little drum and give it to the ladies to start the singing."

As I ventured into the area where the *sangeet* was taking place, which was now swarming with women and children, I nearly collided with a young girl. A simple but a very charming girl. She gave me a shy smile and took the *dholki* from my hands. I could not take my eyes off her for the rest of the evening. She took an active part in the celebrations. It took all my espionage skills to find her without eliciting any suspicions. I tried to follow her and find her but was unable to know much about her. The cupid was lurking around and both of us were unaware. It was almost impossible to communicate in that melee, everyone would have noticed plus I had been assigned duties. My heart flutters as I fumble for words to describe her smile—genuine, natural, innocent, and enchanting.

I met the girl again on the wedding day. Late night weddings are fun with various rituals like hiding the shoes of the bridegroom. It is time for light-hearted banter and mild flirtations between young girls and boys. I greeted her with a broad smile. She smiled back. I asked her how she knew my *maasi's* family and tried to strike a light conversation with her. She was both confident and shy at the same time. Her parents and family were there, too, so we could not interact much. The festivities wound up next day and all the guests went back. I lost touch with her. There were no mobile phones, no WhatsApp, no Facebook in those days. There was no way I could have contacted her. My leave came to an end and for the first time, I was melancholic when I left for the station. As I touched my parents' feet to leave, my mother said, "We will like to see you settle down by your next annual leave. I will arrange for some more prospective matches." The matter of my marriage was the most important task at everybody's hand. Once a soldier's family decides to find a match for him, leave become a very precious commodity. My parents and grandparents were also looking for girls for me to get married to. I had met some girls but nothing materialised. None of the girls I met were able to overshadow the impact that simple, charming smile had left on me. A soldier was either undecided or was probably in love. Even as my leave came to an end, that magical evening never came to an end in my heart. I somehow managed to coax my family into leaving the issue till my next visit. I left for my place of posting but her smile had not left my thoughts.

1967, Srinagar—9 Para Commando Unit

I was posted at the Paradise on Earth—Kashmir. Many films were shot in Kashmir those days. Especially the Shammi Kapoor romcoms with breezy romantic songs on Dal Lake S*hikaraas*. For me, it was a different man who was going back after the leave. I was not sure who was I waving at when the steam engine train chugged out of Delhi station on route to Jammu—my friends and a brother, or a mysterious girl. The train had a lot of army men, but I kept to myself; sat beside a window reminiscing about the memories of the vacation. Somebody was singing a soulful melody. The siren and the rhythmic sound of the iron wheels provided the music.

A jeep was there to receive me in Jammu. Those days, we would halt in the officer's transit camp house in Udhampur and proceed to Kashmir the next day. The evening haunted me in my dreams. Next day, we drove down to the picturesque valley of Kashmir. En route, I asked my driver to halt the jeep. I told him to step aside and took the wheel. The sun beat down on my shades as I swerved left to right and right to left. As I whistled and took off my beret, my military-puff locked horns with cool Himalayan winds. The same beautiful face smiled at me at every turn. A battle-hardened soldier blushed for the first time since he was commissioned. I landed on one of the most beautiful places on Earth with beautiful memories. I was jealous of every honeymooning young couple floating down the Dal Lake in fancy S*hikaraas*.

The Indian Army was in a sweat mode. We were playing or planning war games. The first bugle would sound at 3:45 a.m. Each night, I would crash into my tent, bunker or barracks, tired. Romantic thoughts, if any, dissipated quickly. An army that sweats during peace saves up on its blood during war. While the Indian Army commanders were busy planning their strategic moves and war games, the Pakistan Army commanders were also busy doing a lot of things, mostly political, and trying to crush the spirit of their own countrymen in East Bengal. The rigorous schedule was intense enough for me to forget everything else back home. Everything took a back seat, including the fond memories of that day.

At weekend mess parties, the bachelors were in demand, and we would groove to one song or another, both from Hollywood and Bollywood. Tunes like 'Come September' and Shammi Kapoor hits were hot favourites. I had, by now, almost gotten over the wedding episode. After all, life was not a Hindi film where unexpected things like lost and found happen in every other reel.

I came home on leave again a few months later. Mother told me to drop something at my maternal aunt's residence. My heart missed a beat as memories of the last time flashed back. *Maasi's* house was about two kms from mine. I drove on my Lambretta scooter from Rajouri Garden to her place, the tune of Come September playing in my sub-conscious. Last time I was there, it was during my cousin's wedding. I remembered the charming girl and smiled to myself as her name cropped up in my thoughts. Love stories have happy endings only in films. Many a times one would go back on holidays only to be told that the girl that we suggested last time is already married or engaged. "So be it," I said to myself.

Upon reaching, I yelled like any other exuberant lad, "*Maaaasi jiiii.*" I knocked and entered the drawing room, and just then, I was almost knocked over. At the slightest hint of danger, I could dive a couple of feet, duck enemy fire, take position, aim and shoot before the adversary could react. I was a football forward who could duck and tackle the roughest of defenders. An all-rounder cricketer who would smash the fiercest of bouncers for a six. Had it not been for my commando training and impeccable sports record, I would not have been able to hold on to the parcel in my hand and, yes, of course, my expressions. There was one thing out of control—my heartbeat. Now this was pure serendipity, mimicking a romcom movie. The girl of my dreams was right there in front of me. Dozens of invisible artistes and dancers had surrounded us with a Dmitri Shostakovich symphony, and the modest room lit up and swooned around me in a waltz.

At this point, I have to take you back almost a century ago to North West Frontier Province (NWFP), Undivided India.

1933, Nowshera cantonment on the banks of River Kabul—NWFP

In 1933, Bhupinder Nath Pal, son of Head Master Kan Chand Pal, had stood first in the entire NWFP in his matric examination. He was given a gold medal and a scholarship to study in Lahore. Head Master Kan Chand, apart from being an excellent teacher, was an expert astrologer too. His predictions were very accurate. Even British officers would consult him. Struggles came on early in the life of young Bhupinder. He was born on 19th October 1919 in Punjab, the year of the Jallianwala Bagh massacre. In 1927 his mother died, leaving him and his five-year-old younger sister Anand Lata behind. While Anand was given the care of her maternal aunts in Gurdaspur, Bhupinder continued his schooling in Nowshera.

1935—Lahore, Punjab University (Dyal Singh and DAV College)

After matriculation, he joined Dayal Singh college in Lahore (now in Pakistan) on a scholarship. He had the knowledge of Hindi, Urdu, Sanskrit, Punjabi and English. Economics and Astrology were his passion. He would get up early in the morning and go to DAV School hostel to give tuitions on borrowed cycles. Bhupinder got his younger sister admitted into the prestigious Foreman Christian (FC) College, Lahore. Bhupinder started writing for Urdu magazines, *Cinema* and *Chitra* as a critic. His brilliant academic record secured him a seat in MA Economics in Punjab University, Lahore, in 1939.

Pals were originally from Batala, Punjab. On 1st October 1946, Bhupinder married Shanta in Batala, Punjab. Before his marriage, he had solemnised the marriage of his sister Anand Lata to Vidya Bhushan, a noted film director from Minerva Movietone (a film studio created by the legendary Sohrab Modi).

In 1947, Bhupinder joined B.M College, Shimla as Professor of Economics. His first book *"Principles of Agricultural Economics"* was published in 1957. He wrote two more books on Economics later on.

Bhupinder and Shanta had three children—Bipan, Abha and Nipun. Abha was born on 12th November, 1948. He gave his children education in the best known institutes both in school and colleges. Some of the most loving days of the family were spent during Prof. B.N. Pal's posting Shimla.

Abha – Shimla to Delhi; A new phase of life

Abha was the girl I had met on that night of *sangeet* held for my cousin Kanchan's wedding. My maternal aunt Kulwanti and her husband Prof. K. K. Sharma were posted in Shimla during the time

Pal family was residing there. My *masaad ji* used to teach English. They became close family friends. My *maasiji* and Shanta ji were close friends and so were both the professors. My cousin Kanchan was three years older than Abha. Both the families continued their close ties once they shifted to Delhi.

Abha joined the prestigious Auckland House School, Shimla for her initial schooling. The school was founded in 1866 by the British church related ladies' group, most notably Mrs. Cotton, wife of the legendary academician Mr. Bishop Cotton. The school had some of the best staff and students of that time. It had a profound impact on Abha's personality. It is still a leading school in Shimla. She joined the reputed Presentation Convent in Delhi, when the Pal family shifted to Delhi.

Abha completed her schooling at Presentation Convent (Estt.1924). Abha had inherited her father's genes when it came to academics. She, however, pursued a career in science instead of economics. After completion of her schooling, she joined Miranda House college of Delhi University to pursue her BSc.

December 1968, Rajouri Garden

It felt like an eternity as our eyes were locked in a mesmerising gaze, only to be interrupted by my *maasi ji. "Changa ae Shoki, tu aa gaya. Hanera pean 'ala ae, tu Abha nu ahede' ghar Model Town chaad-aenga."*

("Good that you have come, Shoki. It is getting dark. Can you drop Abha at her place in Model Town?")

I bit my lip as my heart leapt with joy. Abha had come over to my aunt's house for a visit. She had gotten late in the evening and her place was far away. I was too happy to drop her. I had a scooter and readily complied. The winters had set in & the weather was pleasant. Those days, wearing a helmet wasn't in vouge. The journey took about 45 minutes on the Ring Road and we kept talking ceaselessly, as I drove the scooter at a leisurely pace. It seemed like we had known each other for ages. That journey laid the seed of roses for us. The wily cupid had managed to pierce the commando's heart with his arrow. When we reached Abha's house, it felt like we had come to our destination too soon. After a few days, I left for my unit as my leave was over, but on a very happy note this time. I was in a slightly different mood as I boarded the train this time. I was smiling to myself and planning to come back as soon as possible.

My name 'Ashok' in Sanskrit means one who has no sorrows, and her name Abha means luminous beauty. Though I was not superstitious, I did not fail to notice that we shared 'A' as the first alphabet of our names. A good omen for believers of Indian zodiac sign system, which follows the first letters of names. But neither my family nor I had any belief in horoscopes or astrology. However, for Abha's father and family it was a sacred requirement, passed on from generation to generation.

Life sure was difficult for people in love or intending to fall in love. One had to come up with ingenious ways to meet. It would be a couple of months when I came back to Delhi again for some work. I wanted to meet her. I could not go to her house, nor could I write letters, as there was the problem of getting them to her. But I knew she was studying in Miranda House college.

1968–1971—Tempest, The Storm Cometh

Miranda House is a prestigious girls' college in University of Delhi. Sir Maurice Gwyer, the Vice Chancellor of Delhi University from 1938 – 1950 is credited with founding Miranda House in 1948. Abha joined there in 1966 and I met her when she was in her final year. The Latin meaning of Miranda was 'worthy of admiration'. It is believed that in a magazine published in 1952 by Sir Maurice Gwyer, he gave three reasons to name the college as 'Miranda'—his favourite actress was Carmen Miranda, his daughter's name was Miranda, and a character named Miranda in William Shakespeare's play *The Tempest* was his favourite. As per Sir Gwyer, Shakespeare's Miranda was a perfect example of what a lady should be. In the next few lines, I discuss Shakespeare's Miranda of *The Tempest*. Why? That too in a *fauji's* book?

The Tempest—Shakespeare's last play

Miranda, the protagonist in William Shakespeare's final play, *The Tempest*, is the daughter of Prospero. She is loyal to her father and does whatever he says. Miranda grows up and matures on a deserted island with her father and a servant. She is a naive but charming girl who is innocent and timid, yet strong when necessary. She immediately falls in love with the first strange man she sees on the island, Ferdinand. Ferdinand, too, after having a near-death experience, falls in love with Miranda. Despite her naive and simple nature, at times Miranda is strong and speaks up for herself. She dares to stand up to her father whom she otherwise adores. Love blossoms between Miranda and Ferdinand despite vehement opposition by her father.

Prospero is a complex and contradictory character. He loves his daughter dearly whom he considers to be naive. He is an expert in magic and presumes that he can control the destinies of his family and county. He opposes Miranda and Ferdinand's love.

Prospero is very harsh and rough on Ferdinand and imprisons him. Prospero comes across as a scheming, manipulating and unforgiving man. He punishes Ferdinand both physically and psychologically for daring to love his daughter. In an act, he warns Ferdinand not even to smile. The play ends on a happy note as Prospero blesses the couple.

Like the play, life too is about storms, misgivings, intrigues, love and forgiveness. Unfortunately, in my case, this was not to be the case—Neither my 'Miranda' nor I was forgiven.

September 1968—Delhi

After a few days, I came on casual leave and wanted to meet Abha. In those days, communication system was limited to scarce local telephones or the postal service. It was very difficult to contact someone or to pass on a message. I was unable to contact her, but I knew where she was studying. The soldier in me had to move forward. On the spur of the moment, I decided to go to her college, a girl's college, where young men dare not enter. Many young Romeos were known to have been mauled outside the ramparts of the college. I knew it was almost impossible to venture into the strict convent-like girls' college. The steely 9 Para commando took his position alongside the somewhat shaky Romeo inside. I entered the gate without disturbing the sentries at the gate. Neither did they dare to interrupt the confident, well-built intruder, nor did the six-feet tall young man spare them a glance.

It took guts to enter an all-girls college those days for a bachelor, even for a battle-hardened soldier. The army parades give you an enviable swagger. I entered the college but did not know her class room. I strutted around the corridors like a peacock prancing around in a garden, sticking out like a sore thumb. I was attracting a number of raised eyebrows from the fairer sex—both students and lecturers alike. I moved ahead on my mission with courage and dedication. In my heart of hearts, I dreaded the thought of a professor questioning me about my presence. I was looking for my love in an alien territory. I kept on moving without any hesitation, and finally, saw her sitting in a classroom. She looked stunned to see me. It was impossible to exchange words, but our eyes met and everything was said. There was a concealed exchange of signals between our eyes and subtle smiles. As I turned, I bumped into a lady professor who was our neighbour in Rajouri who was a friend of my mother. She wanted to know, why I was there. I mumbled something incoherent and scooted. I waited impatiently outside the college and she came out to be with me after the class was over. I drove her to the nearest café in Kamla Nagar on a Rajdoot motor cycle, borrowed from my dear friend Anoop Singh. We met again a couple of times clandestinely during that brief vacation.

There is an Urdu metaphor '*Ishq aur mushq chupaye nahin chupta*'. (Despite all efforts, love and fragrance cannot be concealed). Her younger brother Nipun was studying in the Ramjas Junior College in Delhi University. Our little secret was bound to come out in the open. It was a very conservative society back then. Courtship, even in family arranged betrothals, was rare. Love marriages were even rarer in middle-class families.

After the Miranda House meeting, as I left for my unit, I knew that life would never be the same for me. I had found my soulmate.

We continued to be in touch with each other. Her letters were like a breeze of fresh air every night as I crashed into my modest army bed and read them. I would meet her whenever I came to Delhi. Abha was very close to her younger brother who studied in the same university and was a year junior to her. He got a whiff of the affair and she later confided in her mother. She was very close to both of them. I took my mother into confidence as well.

September – November 1968

Kulwanti, my *maasiji* and Abha's mother Shanta were close friends. My maasi broached the prospect of our marriage with Abha's mother who then spoke to her husband. Abha's father did not favour her early marriage but wanted her to continue her studies. When I came to know about it, I was disappointed. We had no option but to wait till the summer of 1969 when Abha would complete her graduation. Unlike today, communication was a major problem those days. Telephone was a scarce commodity. There was a landline telephone in the house of her neighbourhood friend, Guddo. During our courtship I would call at Guddo's landline to get in touch with Abha. I would call at pre-decided times to talk to Abha. This would be a high point in our lives.

One day Abha told me that her parents were aggressively searching for a match for her. I was shocked. Her studies was just a ruse, to avoid me. It was not clear to both of us as to why her father would be against our match. Abha could have been married anytime to anyone without me coming to know about it. We were both very young and it seemed as if we were in middle of a storm of emotions. My heart was on fire. Kashmir valley glowed like embers as nature's autumn palette painted deep green Chinar leaves into blood red to pave way to cold winters. Our little love story was all but over. However, an urdu couplet from eminent poet Iqbal aptly sums up my state at that time.

Jis Khaak Ke Zameer Main Ho Aatish-E-Chinar,
Mumkin Nahin Ke Sard Ho Wo Khaak-E-Arjumand!

The dust that has in its conscience the flame of Chinar,
It is impossible for that celestial dust to cool down.

– Allama Iqbal

December 1968— On Leave to give one month notice for Civil Marriage

My December annual leave was now a major mission. The only people we could confide in were our friends. I spoke to Parvinder, my best friend, one of our friends was an advocate in Tis Hazari courts. A consensus built up amongst a bunch of 20 somethings – Court marriage was the only solution to pre-empt forcible marriage of Abha. A year or two down the line we could convince her parents to allow us to get married in traditional way. The plan although juvenile seemed great at that time. There was hardly any time as I had to report back to my unit. Abha, Guddo and Raseel were a group of three friends, all living in the same neighbourhood of Model Town. Guddo & Raseel were to be from the brides side. Our advocate friends took care of the court and other formalities. On 5th December, 1968, her friends and my friends, all gathered at Tis Hazari courts and the marriage was solemnised. Only my sister Upma was present from my family's side. Someone got the sweets and someone got garlands. I had bought a beautiful ring for her and another one that she could give me. There was no one from our families, the entire operation was top secret. All possible problems or conspiracies coming in the way of two hearts were pre-empted. We went back to our respective homes after a sumptuous lunch at Connaught Place.

But there was twist in the tale as life seldom goes as per script. In the evening when Abha's friend Raseel went back home, her mother questioned her and she spilled the beans. It seemed someone had seen her in the courts and had told her mother. Both her parents were lawyers. Her mother promptly went to Abha's home which was next door and told her mother. Abha's mother was a simple lady devoted to her family. She confronted her daughter. A tight slap followed the confession. All hell broke loose when her father came back home. Next few days were very tough on her. Her father had stopped talking to her. She was not allowed to step out of the house. I had joined my unit in Kashmir and oblivious to her suffering. I tried calling her many times but could not get through.

One day Abha's father came home and told her that I was a married person and had a child. He told her that the debauched Army captain had tricked her. My father-in-law was a film buff and critic from his Lahore university days. Apart from books on economics, he wrote film stories too. He had woven a perfect tale to paint me as a villain and Abha was convinced. Meanwhile, oblivious to the sinister plot, the beautiful Kashmir locales were puncturing my heart, I wanted Abha to be with me. I envied the young couples on their honeymoon. I wondered if I did a right thing by not involving my family. I needed to talk to my wife and beloved.

Like in the past I called up at Guddo's residence and requested her to call Abha. It was a conservative society those days, our friends too would have faced their parents wrath. Guddo went to Abha's house to call her. By now, Abha was convinced that I had tricked her and I was a married man with a child. She had withdrawn from the world. She is a very sensitive and introvert person. A pall of gloom and sadness had engulfed her. As decided with Guddo, I called up after half an hour. It was my mother-in-law on the phone. "Abha doesn't want to talk to you, leave her alone and never call up again." I was speechless as the phone was slammed down. The dead tone of the phone kept buzzing in head till someone behind me in the line reminded me that my time was up. I knew instinctively that something was amiss. I was getting very worried and restless in Srinagar. I had to go to Delhi to meet her. My commanding officer allowed me to go to Delhi. There was a strange pain in my heart all through the journey. I reached Delhi. Parvinder was waiting for me. I washed at the army rest house and went to her house. Only her mother and *buaji* were there. I asked her, "Why are you not talking to me?". She replied, "You know better."

I was taken aback, oblivious to the plot that my father-in-law had woven. Her mother brought the ring that I had so lovingly bought for her. I reluctantly removed my engagement ring and held it out towards her. She did not extend her hand, her mother took it from me. There was a piercing pain in my heart as I came out of her house. It was hardly the walk of a fearless commando. Dal lake had started to freeze and chinar was in autumn mode, turning leaves from crimson to yellow and ready to fall from grace.

One day my commanding officer called me to his office. He asked me if everything was alright in my personal life. I just nodded. He gave me a letter to read. I was taken aback at the contents of the letter. It was an anonymous letter stating that I was an enemy spy and other nonsense. I was dumbstruck and looked at the CO in disbelief. My commanding officer took it from me and tore it into pieces while smiling. I could guess it was my father-in-law behind it. The letter was posted to make my life difficult. The unit was under transfer to Agra Cantonment.

Summer of 1969—Jamia Millia Islamia, Delhi

I wanted to know what had happened; we were so much in love. Abha finished her graduation in the summer of 1969 and her father got her admitted in B.Ed course in Jamia Millia Islamia. Those days, reaching Okhla was quite a task from West Delhi. Only an occasional bus would go there. It was sparsely populated. Okhla, today, is teeming with life and adjacent to the now-famous township of Noida, Uttar Pradesh. After retirement I made Noida my home.

Abha's admission in the B.Ed course served two purposes—one, she was getting admission into one of the most prestigious institutions in the country and could pursue a career in the teaching world, and secondly, she had to stay in a well-protected girl's hostel. Her father opted for this as it practically meant an end to our meetings and our relationship. Her father meanwhile got divorce papers prepared and held them out to her. She agreed as if in a stupor. The papers were sent over to me. I was aghast.

My CO sent me on a assignment to Delhi. I wanted to talk to Abha come what may. I straightaway went to Sushma's house, who was my (uncle) *mamaji*'s daughter, and Abha's classmate in Presentation Convent. I asked her to accompany me to Jamia. I had to meet Abha. Sushma met her in the college as I stood outside. Abha refused to meet me. That was it. I was heartbroken. I did not want to spoil her life so I decided to move out of her life. It was a sombre morning when the same friends who had arranged the wedding signed the divorce papers as witnesses. I wanted to set her free of the legal bonding, but had secretly hoped against odds that she would not sign. In a not so smart move I sent the papers to the Principal's office. I had not wanted to send it to her parent's house because they would have surely persuaded her to sign. The Principal sent the head boy and head girl to Abha with the papers. A 21 year-old girl in a very conservative era would have been very embarrassed about her personal life in public glare. She signed the court papers in the principal's office in extreme embarrassment. The love story was over. I told my mother to stop looking for a suitable bride. I was disenchanted and did not want to do anything with both love & marriage. The Army drills and sports are rigorous and I immersed myself in it.

The unit had moved to Agra in 1969 in the city of Taj – The monument of love. But there was no love in my life. I had immersed myself into sports in my free time and made my fitness regimen even more stringent. I had been an ace commando and had also been a trainer.

Come September – 1970

I was in my office in Agra cantonment one day when an armyman came and told me that an elderly lady is looking for me and she was currently in 2 Para Officer's Mess. It was September of 1970.

Abha was a good student and had immersed herself in her studies and completed her B.Ed. degree. But a pall of gloom too had descended upon her. It was September 1970, as she sat sadly in her house, her mother asked her whether they should look for a suitable match for her. Abha told her that she did not want to get married. Mother asked, "Have you not forgotten that boy?" Abha kept mum. Abha's mother was a simple lady devoted to her family and confined mostly to the house where her father's writ ran large. There is a cosmic bond between mothers and daughters. No one knows a daughter's heart better than a mother. She knew both her daughter and her husband well. All this while she had been a silent and abiding spectator to her domineering husband's machinations, till her deep love for her daughter gave her courage to step out and take matters in her hand. Knowing her nature, it was both unexpected and unbelievable. She asked Abha once again, you want to marry him, Abha nodded. Abha's mother was not fully convinced with her husband's concocted story that I was a married man with a child. My *Maasiji,* her friend had vehemently denied it to her. She asked her "Where is he now." Abha knew through common friends that I was now posted in Agra cantonment.

Her mother told my father-in-law that somebody had suggested a good match for Abha and she wanted to meet the family in Agra. My father-in-law had no idea that I was now posted in Agra and he agreed. For him it could be anybody but me. Next morning Nipun, Abha's younger brother dropped his mother at the Delhi Railway station to take the early morning train to Agra, Taj Express. She somehow reached the cantonment. All she knew was my name. She went to the sentries on duty and asked whether they could take her to Captain Ashok Tara. She knew nothing about army. It was like looking for a needle in a haystack. They guided her to the officer's mess. Luckily there she met a 2 Para army man. It was he who came to me and told me that an elderly lady is looking for me.

I was surprised to see her. As customary to greet elders in our culture, I bowed down to touch her feet. She raised her hand to bless me. The conversation was in Punjabi. After pleasantries, she asked "Are you married." I said no. She asked if I wanted to marry Abha. I said, "Yes, if Abha has no objection." The monsoons were just over, many a dead saplings had sprouted and scorched plains were buzzing with green cover. Mother nature ensures that life continues despite all odds.

"If you can come to Delhi next weekend, Abha will meet you near Jamia bus stand after the college hours." I still remember that day vividly. I ordered food for her and dropped her at the Railway station in an Army Jeep. It was like a bolt from the blue. A most unexpected turn yet again in our love story. I smiled after ages.

On Saturday, I started off early on a Lambretta scooter from Agra to travel to Jamia. It was a difficult and risky drive as there were no highways at that time. The roads were in bad shape and mostly two-lane. It was time to repeat the daredevilry that I had carried off in Miranda House. In a lighter vein, the scene from iconic film 'Come September' starring Rock Hudson & Gina Lollobrigida on their Lamby scooters and signature tune can be conjured up by the readers. I reached Jamia after about 4 hours of driving and waited patiently for her. Her mother had played the cupid this time. My mother-in-law told Abha to be there and had also taken her brother *(mamaji)* into confidence. I have no words to describe the turbulent sea of emotions in our hearts that day. Abha's maternal uncle *(mamaji)* Mr. Ram Nath Sharma was a big support to both his sister and niece. Abha would occasionally stay with them every Friday or Saturday. It was a big hassle to commute from that far in Delhi, as Jamia was at the fag end of Delhi. I met Abha and it was like before. I dropped her at her mamaji's place in Kidwai Nagar – a government officers' colony. The entire operation was kept secret from my father-in-law.

4th October 1970—A marriage is solemnised despite all odds

Abha's *Mamaji* stood by us like a rock. In late September, the prospect of our marriage was brought up again in front of my father-in-law. The entire family including *Mamaji* was there. My father-in-law was surprised to see the entire family in support of our marriage. Her mother and brothers were in favour of the match. My father-in-law was a firm believer in astrology. His books told him that our marriage would not last long. Further, he thought that I was still in Srinagar. He agreed to the marriage dates on the condition that it should take place on 3rd or 5th October as they were auspicious dates. There was only a week's time left. He was under the impression that I was still in Srinagar and it would be impossible for me to reach in time. Led by his wife - the conspirators were determined to outfox him. However, I proposed 4th October as the date, as most of my army batchmates and seniors could it make to Delhi on a Sunday.

This infuriated him further. Neither me nor my family was concerned about the auspicious timings and dates. For us every moment was auspicious. It was practical for me to get married on 4th October. Her father oblivious of my current posting, thought that I would not be able to come so fast from Srinagar. But, I was there on the due date. My family was supportive of my decision. They hurriedly made arrangements.

It was a simple low-key ceremony in Arya Samaj Mandir in West Patel Nagar, New Delhi, attended by a few close family members and friends. This was unlike the ostentatious night-time weddings that were a norm during those days. Some 40–50 people from both sides attended the wedding held in the afternoon. My mother and sister had arranged for a customary *sehra* with a silver crown and a ceremonial sword, which a bridegroom is supposed to carry at the time of marriage. There was a small band and a white mare. In line with the custom, my friends and family danced ahead of the band, but all in all it was a low-key affair.

Prof. Pal did come to the venue for a few minutes but neither attended the marriage ceremony nor blessed the newly-married couple. I have to thank my mother-in-law and my brothers-in-law for their wholehearted support. Abha's brothers Bipan & Nipun performed all rituals from the bride side including the important 'Kanyadaan' (Giving away the bride) which was supposed to be performed by their father.

My brothers organised a lavish reception next day at the Constitution Club of India, Parliament Street, New Delhi. It was attended by almost 150 guests. My father-in-law, came to the party but kept himself aloof and did not meet any of my relatives. He turned away as I bent down to seek his blessings. My colleagues who were looking forward to our marriage came in from Agra and other places. I was exalted, even though our marriage was simple, but it was like conquering Mt. Everest. It was a match made in heavens and our love was genuine. It was a relationship that had to stand the wrath of a conservative father against a determined army man.

Unlike these days when couples go to exotic locations abroad for their honeymoon, the most popular destinations those days were Kashmir, Shimla, Mussoorie, Nainital, Ooty, etc. Since I was posted in Kashmir and she had grown up in Shimla, we decided to visit a different destination. We went to Jaipur and Udaipur in Rajasthan, which both of us had not visited earlier. Both the places were sheer magic. I was coming back to the romantic Rajputana after four years. The last time, I was there in the fierce Thar Desert during the 1965 War as a young captain of the Indian Army. Rajasthan, with its magnificent palaces and lakes appearing in the desert, is probably the most romantic place in the world. I would suggest to all young couples to add Indian destinations to their honeymoon plans in addition to other exotic locations that travel agents recommend. You will help the local tourism industry in addition to experiencing pure magic, and of course, love.

I had planned to take her to the famed Taj Mahal as I was posted in Agra, but I received orders to proceed to Mizo Hills (now Mizoram) to join 32 Guards, a counter-insurgency unit. There was turmoil on the Eastern front due to Mizo and Naga insurgents and especially political turmoil in East Pakistan (now Bangladesh) and other adjoining areas. I had an intervening leave of about a month and a half. Abha and I had moved into our joint family house in Rajouri Garden, Delhi. In December, I had to leave for Mizoram to join for my new posting. I took a train to Siliguri. This time, it was my newly-wed wife with sadness in her eyes who waved good bye to me as I boarded the train from Delhi. The train was full of *faujis*. It was very difficult for me to leave Delhi. I felt a tinge of sadness. I wanted some more time with her and my family. Mercifully, my commanding officer understood my wish and sanctioned my casual leave in January. I came back into the arms of my loving wife and overjoyed family. This was in the beginning of 1971 when the turmoil in the entire eastern part of the subcontinent had just started. In early 1971, as many young army men and I waved good byes to our families en route to the North-East, none of us knew who would come back. I had managed to take a transport aircraft from Delhi to Siliguri this time. The rest of the journey to Mizo Hills was by road. When we stopped at the famous village, Vairengte, an entry gate to Mizo Hills, I got down from the jeep and strolled for a while remembering my family and wished Abha was with me in this picturesque journey.

We celebrated our golden marriage anniversary together and home-alone during the COVID pandemic. The memories of those days are still fresh in our minds. I raised a toast to our togetherness with my wine and with a smile, and she probably with moist eyes. She probably reminisced those emotionally surcharged days when she was torn between the love of her father and me. And I was torn between her love and my duty to my unit and my country.

Musings on the past—A doting father becomes vindictive

In the play *The Tempest*, Ferdinand and Miranda are able to get married with the blessings of their fathers and lived happily ever after. We, too, got married; however, unlike in *The Tempest* wherein Prospero forgave Ferdinand, I was not so lucky. Abha's father never forgave me for the temerity to steal his beloved daughter. Neither did he forgive her or our children. His attitude remained vindictive towards us. Abha's father had declared that he would not meet her. Many a times my mother in law would meet Abha without telling him. We would visit her house only when he would not be there. Anshu my daughter was born in 1970 in the Army hospital when I was posted in the North East, my mother in law visited Abha alone in the Army hospital. Abha survived those tough days of extreme emotional trauma with dignity and courage. His astrology had told him that the marriage would not last. We have been married for 52 yrs. He came to my house at the time of my son's marriage for the first time in 30 years.

Even after half a century I have not been able to decipher her father's strong opposition to her marriage with me. He remained indifferent to us as long as he lived. It is customary for us in Punjab to greet our elders by touching their feet whenever we meet them, and in return they shower verbal blessings on us with raised hands.

The youngsters utter the words '*Paeri pauna'* (I bow on your feet). I would touch his feet whenever we met in family or social gatherings without any response from his side. He would barely acknowledge me or his daughter or our children. It did not matter much to me as I was by disposition a jolly, happy-go-lucky chap. Plus, I was too busy in service for otherwise bothersome family problems. In parties where my father-in-law was also there, I would melt somewhere in the crowd, often nursing my drink or striking a small chat somewhere, but it would have been really hard on Abha. She had been the apple of his eyes.

In the later days of his life, he was struck with Alzheimer's disease and could not even eat on his own. In one of the family functions, I saw my mother-in-law feeding him from a plate as he was unable to hold it. He was only a pale shadow of himself. Abha was feeding our children, and suddenly they asked her who that old man was. I could feel her pain as she held back her tears, struggling to tell the young ones that he was their grandfather. For the rest of his life till his death in 2002 at the ripe old age of 83, Abha, my children and I were persona non-grata for him. In 1985, he had written an amazing astrological poem in English for all his grandchildren predicting their future lives, except, of course, our kids. On hindsight, I feel it was his loss as he deprived himself of so much love and affection of his only daughter and his lovely grandchildren—Anshu and Ashish. Even after 50 years, I still do not have the answer as to what triggered his anger against us. My being an army officer with my life on a razor's edge, or his beloved daughter daring to fall in love and choosing her own life partner, or his inability to fathom and sniff out a love story blossoming right under his nose.

My father-in-law retired as a Reader from NCERT Delhi. He expired on 4th June 2002. My mother-in-law Shantaji was a simple lady devoted to her family and was always thinking of their welfare. Generally she remained silent and an abiding spectator to Mr. Pal's domineering machinations, but she also had her inner strong courage to step out to take matters in here hand. She also bequeathed same qualities in Abha. It was her inner strength and cooperation of her younger brother Mr. Ram Nath Sharma that she was able to get our marriage solemnized. She kept the family united even during low periods when either Mr. B.N. Pal was without job/out station. She was pious soul and breathed her last on 5th June, 2012.

As I come to an end of this chapter that talks about our courtship and marriage in the backdrop of college education and our careers, I wanted to reiterate some things. We and our parents were lucky to go to some of the best educational institutions in the subcontinent, which moulded and prepared us for our future lives. Abha was good in academics and distinguished herself wherever she studied, and I had a successful career as an army officer and distinguished myself. We never neglected our studies or duties. Our story was from another time, another generation. We never disrespected our elders in family or in school and colleges. Today's life is much more fast-paced and competitive. I want to advice my young readers that come what may, they should never neglect their studies and career goals, everything else is secondary. To close this chapter, I scouted for the right advice to sum it up. What better than listing the mottos of the institutions that have been mentioned in this book. They are listed at the end of this book.

Un kaa jo farz hai vo ahl-e-siyaasat jaanen
Meraa paigaam mohabbat hai jahaan tak pahunche

Jigar Moradabadi

❑

CHAPTER 8

Mother Tongue, Massacres and a Mail Soaked in Blood

Motherland, mother tongue, and the mother herself are essential to epitomize a person's life. The importance of these in the overall development of an individual is immense. Without the proper identity of these in life, a person is like a wingless bird. The mother tongue is like the wind under the wings. It is the medium through which self- expression takes place in its highest form.

The Daily Star (Bangladesh)

Before I narrate my story as young major on the front lines in Bangladesh, it is important to recall the events that led to this fratricidal war which involved officers and soldiers who were once brothers in the same army.

It is a story of a remarkable struggle and sacrifice which must be recounted to each generation lest they forget.

1947 – Creation of Pakistan – East & West Wings

The genesis of the Bangladesh crisis had its origins in events of 1940s. The British left its Indian dominion in the middle of August 1947 and the country was partitioned, resulting in the creation of Pakistan.

The newly formed country, comprised of two geographically and culturally separate areas to the East and the West with India in between. The western zone comprising of Punjab, Sindh, Baluchistan, NWFP was popularly termed, West Pakistan and the eastern zone (now Bangladesh) was known as East Bengal or East Pakistan. The political and administrative power was concentrated in West Pakistan, in contrast to the numerically superior East Pakistan. It was decided that Urdu was to be the official language of Pakistan. None of the provinces, on either side of the newly formed country, had Urdu as their mother tongue. The chiefly spoken languages of Pakistan were Bangla, Punjabi, Seraiki, Balochi, Sindhi and Pashto.

The bonhomie between West and East Pakistan was short-lived. Linguistic, cultural and political differences between the two wings came to the fore almost immediately after independence. Bangla was disallowed in the Constituent Assembly. Bengali script, in vogue since the British Raj, was removed from currency and stamps. Bangla civil society protested the removal.

It is said that Bangla and French are amongst the most beautiful and sweetest languages in the world. Bangla is the fifth most spoken language in the world with a history of over 1000 years. In modern times, its rich literature was further enriched by poet-writer-philosophers like Gurudev Rabindranath Tagore and Kazi Nazrul Islam. Gurudev got the Nobel Prize for Literature in 1913 and since then the prize has eluded the sub-continent.

Mohammad Ali Jinnah, the founder and first Governor-General of Pakistan, visited East Pakistan from 19th-28th March 1948, which was his first and last visit to the East Wing. On 21st March 1948, Jinnah addressed a huge public rally at Ramna Race Course Maidan (currently Suhrawardy Uddyan). Apart from sending warnings about conspiracies and crushing of quislings and traitors, he said something that East Pakistan could not have appreciated:

"Let me make it very clear to you that the state language of Pakistan is going to be Urdu and no other language. Anyone who tries to mislead you is really the enemy of Pakistan. Without one state language, no nation can remain tied up solidly together and function. Look at the history of other countries. Therefore, so far as the state language is concerned, Pakistan's shall be Urdu."

It was, however, a different matter that anglophile Mr. Jinnah, a leading Gujrati barrister and politician was probably proficient in English more than any other language, let alone Urdu. The West Pakistan ruling elite wanted the Bengalis to abandon their mother tongue as a state language.

They had underestimated the Bengalis love for their mother tongue. The reaction to Jinnah's speech is summed up in the following analysis of THE DAILY STAR (Bangladesh):

"Jinnah's abrasive remarks were severely condemned by Prof Abul Kashem who, on the same day, came down hard on the governor general's attempt to paint the advocates of Bangla as fifth columnists and communists and as enemies of Pakistan. Two days later, on 23rd March 1948, Sher-e-Bangla AK Fazlul Huq denied that there were any quislings, fifth columnists or enemies of Pakistan. He made it clear that Jinnah's language had not been polite and that his insistence on Urdu being the state language of Pakistan had been wrong."

The Bangla-speaking population took immense pride in their culture and language. The people of East Bengal demanded that their language be given federal status alongside Urdu and English and slowly the movement moved out of Dhaka and fanned to the entire East Bengal.

East Bengalis felt that there was a systematic attempt by West Pakistan to undermine their language and culture. The matters did not end at linguistics but went beyond. There was a perception in East Pakistan that they were being exploited economically by their western counterpart.

Punjabis had a dominant share in both military and civilian jobs in 1947. It is estimated that less than 20% of central bureaucracy was Bengali, despite being more than half of the then population of almost 75 million. The situation in military was probably worse with their representation in single digit. Very few Bengali origin officers were in command positions. The disparity and discrimination were too stark to miss. Today, Bangladesh has a strong and professional army, air force and navy.

There was massive disparity in the national budget and resource allocation and expenditure with West Pakistan taking a lion's share despite Bangladesh having a large impoverished population. FDI and International assistance were also directed towards West Pakistan. East was neglected in every socio-economic area – education, health, business, infrastructure. It is a remarkable achievement that today, in less than 50 years, Bangladesh has become a leading exporter with a vibrant economy and has out-performed its neighbours on many social parameters. As for Pakistan, the less said the better.

While Pakistan has relentlessly pursued fanaticism, nurtured terrorism and regional instability with disastrous results, Bangladesh has remained a secular country without losing focus of its socio-economic goals set by its founding father - Mujibur Rahman. My young readers may like to peruse a thorough comparison of all three countries with regard to various parameters in the 75th year of post-colonial existence. The results may surprise you. The success has come at a huge cost and sacrifice. The green landscape of Bangladesh was spattered with crimson and blood flowed through its beautiful rivers, instead of pristine water from the Himalayas. An entire generation perished to ensure a glorious future for their children and coming generations. They must never be forgotten as their memory is sacred and their story must be recounted and retold to generations to come.

"...Bengali salariat was deprived of its just share in power at the centre and even in East Bengal where the most powerful and lucrative jobs were controlled by the West Pakistani bureaucracy and the military. Moreover, the Bengalis were conscious that money from the Eastern wing, from the export of jute and other products, was predominantly financing the development of West Pakistan or the army, which, in turn, was West Pakistani (or rather, Punjabi-dominated.) The language, Bangla, was a symbol of a consolidated Bengali identity in opposition to the West Pakistani identity."

– Dr. Tariq Rahman, Professor at Quaid-i-Azam University

The protests and movements in favour of Bangla started almost immediately after independence. The central leadership chose to ignore, ridicule, and suppress it. They ascribed every possible sinister name, motive, reason and conspiracy to a movement that tugged at the heartstrings of every man, women and child of all classes in East Pakistan. Then came a day in the winters of 1952 which would immortalize itself.

The population of East Bengal saw a glimmer of hope of fulfilling their aspirations when an ethnic Bengali Khawaja Nazimuddin was appointed as Governor-General of Pakistan. Their hopes were albeit dashed in January 1952 when Nazimuddin as Prime Minister gave a speech in Dhaka, defending the "Urdu only" policy as the national language and this stirred up emotions across East Pakistan. On 31st January 1952, a committee was formed under the leadership of Maulana Abdul Hamid Bhashani to lead the protests. A demonstration was announced for 21st February 1952. The government banned gatherings of more than three persons in one place and imposed Section 144 in Dhaka. Undeterred, students gathered at Dhaka University. Police resorted to baton charge at slogan-shouting students. Even female students were beaten up mercilessly. The police resorted to tear gas and later opened fire, killing four students and wounding many others.

The world took notice of Dhaka University and its students and professors; unfortunately, it would not to be the last time. The pavements, classrooms, staff-rooms, and hostels would be spattered with blood again and again.

Abdul Gaffar Choudhury, journalist and Freeman of Tower Hamlets, wrote the famous gut-wrenching Martyr's Day song '*Amar bhaier rokte rangano ekushe February*'.

History was created almost half a century later when 21st February 1952 was remembered and recognized by the world. On 17th November 1999, UNESCO declared the historical day as 'International Mother Language Day' thereby, honouring the immense sacrifice and martyrdom of countless young men and women. The day is revered in Bangladesh as the Language Movement Day. There is a "Shaheed Minar" at the spot where the students were martyred. I recommend a visit to Dhaka University to spend a moment of silence in front of the awe-inspiring sculpture of the struggle. It was one of the most remarkable movements in the history of mankind.

On 16th February 1956, Pakistan Constituent Assembly bowed in front of the movement and unanimously adopted both Bangla and

Urdu as state languages of Pakistan. It was perhaps too late in the day as seeds of a revolution were already planted. As I write this chapter, I can feel the pain in the hearts of those determined young men and women who took on the might of a determined and brutal leadership, just out of love for their mother tongue.

A series of important events took place between 1956 and 1969 in the tumultuous history of the then Pakistan. During this period, the Pakistan Army under Gen Ayub Khan usurped the power and crushed democracy.

Meanwhile, Sheikh Mujib continued his struggle for the rights of the people of East Bengal and emerged as one of the tallest leaders of the country. In 1966, Sheikh Mujib launched a six-point movement aimed towards greater autonomy for East Pakistan. In early 1968, President Ayub Khan accused Sheikh Mujibur of conspiring with India and charged him with sedition, in what was known as the Agartala Conspiracy case. There were mass demonstrations in East Bengal and the government was forced to withdraw the case on 22nd February 1969. Next day, in a massive rally attended by almost a million strong crowd, at the Race Course Maidan, Sheikh Mujib was given his famous title 'Bangabandhu'. Zulfiqar Ali Bhutto, a one-time confidant of Gen. Ayub also put pressure on him as leader of Pakistan People's Party to harden his stand on East Pakistan.

Unpopularity and ill-health forced Ayub Khan to give the reins of the country to the Commander-in-Chief of Pakistan Army, General Yahya Khan on 26th March 1969. Yahya imposed martial law and abrogated the Constitution. Yahya later called for General Elections on 7th December 1970. The election was considered as the first fair general election held in Pakistan.

The main contest was between East Bengal based Awami League led by Sheikh Mujib and West Pakistan based Pakistan People's Party led by Zulfiqar Ali Bhutto. Huge crowds were drawn by both the parties.

Just a month before the elections, one of the deadliest cyclones in world history – Bhola Cyclone – struck East Pakistan, killing 300,000 to 500,000 people. The government's poor response to this major tragedy further widened the divide between East and West Pakistan.

Unfortunately, the angels of death had not departed after the natural disaster. They were lurking to witness one of the most brutal state-sponsored pogroms perhaps after World War II.

The election results were a rude shock to Gen. Yahya and the West Pakistan elite who did not expect the Awami League to win decisively. Out of 300 parliamentary constituencies of the National Assembly of Pakistan, Awami League won a landslide with absolute majority of 160 out of 300 seats. Bhutto's PPP got only 81 seats, mostly in Punjab and Sindh.

In the Provincial Assembly Elections of East Pakistan, Sheikh Mujibur Rehman led Awami League won 298 out of 310 seats. East Pakistan had almost completely backed Sheikh Mujibur Rehman and his party.

President Yahya Khan did not inaugurate the Assembly as most West Pakistani leaders led by Bhutto opposed Awami League to form the government. Bhutto's famous phrase "*idhar hum, udhar tum*" (We here, You there) was almost a prophesy of things to come. Bhutto proposed the formula of appointment of two Prime Ministers, one for each wing. It was a ploy to keep Sheikh Mujib from leading the country.

Decades of economic, cultural, and political marginalization had now completely alienated the East Bengal populace. The election results led to a chain of events which would ultimately lead to the war and independence of Bangladesh.

THE IRISH TIMES

DUBLIN, SATURDAY, MARCH 27, 1971

Declaration of independence by East Pakistan

FIGHTING "HEAVY"

A CLANDESTINE RADIO said last night that East Pakistan has been declared independent and that heavy fighting was going on between East and West Pakistani forces.

In response, Sheikh Mujib came up with six-point demand aimed at more autonomy. Predictably, Bhutto did not agree. Under pressure from West Pakistan leaders. President Yahya Khan postponed the National Assembly. On 3rd March 1971, President General Yahya Khan met both the leaders in Dacca.

However, the talks did not succeed. Sheikh Mujib demanded lifting of martial law and withdrawal of military to the barracks. He further demanded immediate transfer of power to the elected representatives of the people before the assembly meeting on 25th March.

On 7th March 1971, Sheikh Mujibur Rahman delivered a rousing speech at the Race Course Ground, urging people to turn every house into a fort of resistance. He summed up his speech with the clarion call, "Our struggle is for our freedom, our struggle is for our independence. Joi Bangla!"

"...Between March 1–15, 1971 Mujib played an unchallenged role in East Pakistan, controlling the entire machinery of administration. There is no other example in history where such a shift of loyalty emerged even before recognition of national independence."

– Nitish K. Sengupta,
Author of *Land of Two Rivers: A History of Bengal*

The Awami League launched a successful non-co-operation movement. The writ of the Pakistan government became non-existent in East Pakistan as civilians clashed with the Pakistani Army. The atmosphere was extremely surcharged. The local Bihari population, however, had sided with the West Pakistan establishment. An alleged anti-Bihari riot in Chittagong became the ruse for Pakistan Government to launch Operation Searchlight on 25th March 1971.

The Butcher of Bengal – Gen. Tikka Khan

Gen Tikka Khan, an ethnic Punjabi Muslim Rajput from Tehsil Kahuta, District Rawalpindi, had risen from being a sepoy to a three Star General. He had got his commission in 1940 from Indian Military Academy, Dehradun. He carried a reputation for being ruthless. He, along with Major General Khadim Hussain Raja, GOC 14th Division, and Major General Rao Farman Ali, was the chief architect and planner of Operation Searchlight. General Tikka Khan was flown into Dacca to become Governor and GOC of East Bengal. Sane voices like Lt. General Shahabzada Yakub Khan, GOC East Pakistan, and the governor of East Pakistan, Vice Admiral Syed Mohammad Ahsan, were relieved of their duties. Air-Commodore Mitty Masud, who refused to use airstrikes was also relived. The emotions in East Pakistan were surcharged and there was complete alienation. Pakistan government writ had ceased to exist in East Bengal. Chief Justice of East Pakistan Justice B A Siddiqui refused to swear in Gen. Tikka Khan and other judges of the East Pakistan High Court also followed suit.

Operation Searchlight - Humanity is shamed

The main areas to be covered under the operation were cities and towns like Dhaka, Khulna, Chittagong, Sylhet, Comilla, Jessore, Rajshahi, Rangpur, and Saidpur amongst others. Lt. Gen. Tikka Khan estimated that no resistance would remain after 10th April.

The crackdown was as brutal as it could get. The genocide started with Dhaka University in full ferocity as contingents from Pakistan Army's 18th and 32nd Punjab Regiments surrounded the University area. The flower of Bangladesh youth was targeted. Awami League members, students, intelligentsia, and minority communities bore the brunt of the crackdown. Young men were killed indiscriminately. Residential halls of Dacca University were particularly targeted. The only Hindu residential Jagannath Hall was destroyed. Its almost 700 residents were murdered in cold blood. The university massacre at Jagannath Hall and other nearby student dormitories of Dacca University, was secretly filmed by engineering Professor Nurul Ula whose residence was opposite to the student dormitories. Shaheed Minar, offices of The Daily Ittefaq, Daily People, and the Kali temple at Ramna were also destroyed.

In the pitch of darkness at midnight, a killer searchlight was tuned on in full intensity on the illuminated minds of students and professors of the ill-fated Dhaka University. Grounds swelled up with bodies. It is believed that Yahya Khan had said, "Kill three million of them, and the rest will eat out of our hands." This certainly seemed to be the intent of Operation Searchlight.

By the end of April, many Bengali officers and armed personnel were massacred in cold blood. These included officers of the rank of Lt. Col and Majors. Hundreds of JCOs and thousands of Bengali soldiers, mainly from the East Pakistan Rifles and Police Personnel were executed. Millions would perish or be displaced over the next few months.

Operation Searchlight was a meticulously planned crime against humanity. The world would perhaps never forget and must not forget the night of 25th March 1971. It had chilling parallels to the Nazi pogroms. Bangabandhu Sheikh Mujibur Rahman was arrested and taken to West Pakistan.

The Army locked up about 200 foreign journalists in the Intercontinental Hotel and later moved them out of Dhaka. A 27-year-old British journalist from London Telegraph, Simon Dring, decided to stay back by hiding on the hotel rooftop and kitchen for 32 hours. Entire night, he could hear blasts and see fires around the city. Once the curfew was relaxed, he ventured out on 27th March along with French photojournalist Michelle Laurent in a hotel bakery van. Simon hid his notes in his socks and Michelle hid her camera rolls in toiletries as they flew to Karachi. The Daily Telegraph front page of 30th March 1971 carried the infamous story 'Tanks Crush Revolt in Pakistan'. Simon had broken the story from Bangkok and the world took notice.

"In the name of 'God and a united Pakistan', Dacca is today a crushed and frightened city. After 24 hours of ruthless, cold-blooded shelling by the Pakistan Army, as many as 7,000 people are dead, large areas have been levelled and East Pakistan's fight for independence has been brutally put to an end."

He recalled the horrors…

"I found the bodies of students who had been shot to death in their dormitories and outside on the campus grounds; the rickshaw pullers, bullet-ridden and bloodied, lying by the roadside; whole families burnt alive in their homes when their street had been sealed off and the houses torched; bazaars in the old city burnt to the ground."

Simon was conferred the "Friends of Liberation War Honour" by the Government of Bangladesh in 2012.

Over the next fortnight, millions were massacred in cold blood. Thousands of ethnic Bengali soldiers JCOs and officers were segregated, disarmed and killed. Fuelled by misplaced notions of racial prejudice, East Bengal was soaked in blood – killings, arson, rape and pillage were carried out with clockwork precision. The state and its army were cannibalising its own citizens.

25th March 1971– The Genocide Day

A Telegram Soaked in Blood

An American couple stood on the balcony of their house on the night of 25th March watching fires burning all over the city and hearing the ringing of gunshots. In the next couple of hours, many of their friends and acquaintances would be killed along with hundreds of thousands other innocent Bengalis. They were no ordinary couple but the American Consul General in Dacca, Archer Blood and his wife Margaret. He was witnessing a genocide unfolding in front of his eyes. There was a major moral dilemma for him. President Richard Nixon of US and his National Security Advisor, Henry Kissinger had fully backed Yahya Khan and the marauding army. Arthur knew that the guns, bullets, and tanks unleashed on the hapless folk that night were all supplied by the US but his hands were tied. He was a rising star in the foreign services and hoped to become an ambassador one day.

In a telegram dated 27th March 1971, under the heading "Selective Genocide" Archer Blood wrote:

1. *Here in Decca we are mute and horrified witnesses to a reign of terror by the Pak Military. Evidence continues to mount that the MLA authorities have list of Awami League supporters whom they are systematically eliminating by seeking them out in their homes and shooting them down.*

2. *Among those marked for extinction in addition to the A.L. hierarchy are student leaders and university faculty. In this second category, we have reports that Fazlur Rahman, Head of the philosophy department and a Hindu, M. Abedin, Head of the department of history, have been killed. Razzak of the political science department is rumoured dead. Also on the list are the bulk of MNAs elect and number of MPA's.*

3. *Moreover, with the support of the Pak Military, non-Bengali Muslims are systematically attacking poor people's quarters and murdering Bengalis and Hindus.*

Blood and his staff repeatedly intimated the horrors to Washington. However, Capitol Hill ignored both the carnage and Consul Blood and continued to back Gen Yahya. The staff was horrified at the unfolding genocide. At the risk of their careers, the staff of the Consulate drafted the first "dissent cable" in the history of US Foreign Service on 6th April 1971. Blood's political deputy Scott Butcher drafted it and Blood added an addendum stating his agreement with the contents. Only three members of the Consulate staff did not sign it. The cable now famous as the "Blood Telegram" summed it all up.

"*Our government has failed to denounce the suppression of democracy. Our government has failed to denounce atrocities. Our government has failed to take forceful measures to protect its citizens while at the same time bending over backwards to placate the West Pak[istan] dominated government and to lessen any deservedly negative international public relations impact against them. Our government has evidenced what many will consider moral bankruptcy,... But we have chosen not to intervene, even morally, on the grounds that the Awami conflict, in which unfortunately the overworked term genocide* is applicable, is purely an internal matter of a sovereign state. Private Americans have expressed disgust. *We, as professional civil servants, express our dissent with current policy and fervently hope that our true and lasting interests here can be defined and our policies redirected in order to salvage our nation's position as a moral leader of the free world.*"

Blood had to choose between his conscience and career. He chose the former and had to pay the price. Nixon and Kissinger were livid. They had continuously ignored all his reports on the rapidly deteriorating events and ever escalating state sponsored violence. Blood was relieved by an officer who had not signed the dissent cable. Arthur Blood was later transferred to an insignificant position in Washington for the next 6 years. Arthur Blood retired from service in 1982 without realizing his ambition to become an ambassador.

Readers who want to know more can read the insightful book *"The Blood Telegram: Nixon, Kissinger, and a Forgotten Genocide" By Gary Bass.*

Declaration of Independence – 26th March 1971

Bangabandhu Sheikh Mujibur Rahman was arrested by the army but not before he had given a message to his people.

"This may be my last message. From today Bangladesh is independent. I call upon the people of Bangladesh wherever you might be and with whatever you have, to resist the army of occupation to the last. Your fight must go on until the last soldier of the Pakistan occupation army is expelled from the soil of Bangladesh and final victory is achieved."

This declaration of independence marked the beginning of the Bangladesh Liberation War and is observed as Bangladesh Independence Day.

Government in Exile – 10th April 1971

Many Awami League leaders crossed over to India after the military crackdown to escape the mayhem and carry on the struggle. People's Republic of Bangladesh Government, was formed in exile on 10th April. Bangabandhu Sheikh Mujibur Rehman was named as President and Tajuddin Ahmed as Prime Minister. Later, Colonel MAG Osmani was appointed Commander-in-Chief of Bangladesh Forces.

India, led by Prime Minister Indira Gandhi, on 27th March 1971 expressed full support for independence struggle of the people of Bangladesh. India took up the cause of Bangladesh on various international fora.

On 28th April 1971, the Indian Cabinet authorised Chief of the Indian Army General Sam Manekshaw to "Go into East Pakistan". India's Research and Analysis Wing (RAW) swung into action and started recruitment and training of Mukti Bahini guerrillas from the refugee camps.

The Bangladesh Forces including Mukti Bahini would later wage a successful guerrilla war against the Pakistani military. They harassed them extensively and liberated numerous towns and cities.

Misery Months – April to December

From April to December 1971, the people of Bangladesh endured untold misery and oppression. Lt. General Amir Abdullah Khan Niazi was posted as GOC East Pakistan Command on 11th April 1971. Gen. Tikka Khan remained Governor of the province till 31st August 1971.

More than 30 million civilians were displaced internally, another 10 million people took refuge in neighbouring India. As an officer posted on the frontlines in the North East, I could see the misery of refugees pouring into India. Impoverished men and women had just one burning desire - to fight for their motherland and their mother tongue, and to avenge their humiliation and torture. There was a fire in each eye.

During the entire period, there were massive uprisings. Bangladesh authorities estimate killings of over three million people, many of them women and children. Thousands of women were tortured, raped, and killed in cold blood. Moral depravities of the Pakistan Army had chilling similarities to medieval barbarians, in many cases even worse.

After the crackdown, India opened its eastern borders for refugees and started preparing for a possible war. On 15th May, India launched 'Operation Jackpot' to train, arm, and support Mukti Bahini fighters engaged in guerrilla warfare against the Pakistan armed forces. Outside the sub-continent, the world was not fully aware of the bloodshed perpetrated by Pakistan army and sufferings of the people of Bangladesh. The Pakistan army had almost achieved or thought that it had achieved the objective of the crackdown – to crush the nascent freedom movement and the spirit of Bangladesh. It was time to whitewash the sins. They nearly succeeded but for an article on a June Sunday.

A Horrific Headline and a Shocked World

Sunday, 13th June 1971 – The world woke up to widespread horrors inflicted by Pakistan Army in Bangladesh when The Sunday Times published an aptly titled article 'Genocide' by brave journalist Anthony Mascarenhas. The scale of atrocities committed by the military left the world in shock and dismay.

Mascarenhas, hailing from the Goan-Christian community, was educated and settled in Karachi along with his wife Yvonne and five kids. He had opted to remain in Pakistan on the eve of partition. He was a respected journalist and on good terms with the military and the ruling elite. The Pak army had expelled all foreign journalists at the beginning of the crackdown and had ensured that no news came out. A few weeks into the crackdown, the army brass was satisfied with the outcome – the Awami League and the freedom movement had been crushed.

The army wanted to publicise its own narrative; eight journalists were taken on a 10-day tour of the province. All but one wrote the establishment's view. Anthony was sure to be shot dead if he wrote the truth in Pakistan. On the pretext of visiting his ailing sister, Mascarenhas flew to London and landed in the office of Harold Evans, Editor of The Sunday Times. Anthony told Evans about the widespread and systematic killing spree. He had heard army officers describing the killings as a "final solution".

They decided that Yvonne and the kids had to escape from Karachi before the story was published. With just a suitcase each, the entire family fled to London, leaving everything else behind. Anthony himself had to escape via land route through Afghanistan. The family later reunited in London on 12th June and the very next day, The Sunday Times published his article, under the headline "Genocide".

Abdul Bari had run out of luck. Like thousands of other people in East Bengal, he had made the mistake - the fatal mistake - of running within sight of a Pakistani patrol. He was 24 years old, a slight man surrounded by soldiers. He was trembling because he was about to be shot.

I have witnessed the brutality of 'kill and burn missions' as the army units, after clearing out the rebels, pursued the pogrom in the towns and villages. I have seen whole villages devastated by 'punitive action'.

And in the officer's mess at night, I have listened incredulously as otherwise brave and honourable men proudly chewed over the day's kill. 'How many did you get?' The answers are seared in my memory.

BBC noted: "There is little doubt that Mascarenhas' reportage played its part in ending the war. It helped turn world opinion against Pakistan and encouraged India to play a decisive role."

As per Harold Evans, Prime Minister Indira Gandhi told him that the article had shocked her so deeply it had set her "on a campaign of personal diplomacy in the European capitals and Moscow to prepare the ground for India's armed intervention."

GENOCIDE

by ANTHONY MASCARENHAS

The truckloads of human targets

A pencil flick, a man 'disposed'

A friend in need is a friend indeed!

Pakistan elite had power and powerful friends and knew it could get away with anything. In the aftermath of Operation Searchlight, they believed they had killed the idea of Bangladesh. In reality, they had completely misjudged and miscalculated the courage and determination of the people and their leader Sheikh Mujib. The spirit and soul of Bangladesh was alive in every heart.

Albeit far and few, there were courageous journalists, diplomats, army officers, politicians and artists who stood by the people of Bangladesh in their hour of need. A few of them have been named here.

Senator Ted Kennedy in the United States led a congressional campaign to advocate the end of Pakistani military persecution while US diplomats in East Pakistan strongly dissented with the Nixon administration's close ties to the Pakistani military dictator Yahya Khan.

French minister Andre Malraux vowed to fight alongside the Mukti Bahini in the Liberation War.

The plight of Bangladesh moved several artists as well. George Harrison of The Beatles fame was made aware of the grim situation in Bangladesh by his friend and sitar maestro Pandit Ravi Shankar. Ravi Shankar had roots in Bengal. Married to Annapurna Devi, his father-in-law and guru, Baba Allauddin Khan was a noted musician from a family steeped in classical Indian music, hailing from Shibpur in District Brahmanbaria of Bangladesh.

George Harrison composed the song "Bangla Desh" and organised fundraising concerts in aid of the Bangladeshi people.

The concert was held on 1st August 1971 at Madison Square Garden, New York and featured a galaxy of stars – Harrison, Bob Dylan, Pt. Ravi Shankar, Ringo Starr, Ali Akbar Khan, Eric Clapton, Billy Preston, Leon Russell amongst others.

Harrison and Ringo Starr came together for the first time since the 1966 Beatles split. It was also Dylan's first major US concert in five years. 'The Concert for Bangladesh' was a runaway success, topping album charts in various countries. It won the March 1973 Grammy Award as Album of the Year.

The plight of Bangladeshi citizens caused worldwide outrage but the Pakistani generals and ruling elite were unmoved. They continued there diplomatic and military offensive and fed lies to the people of West Pakistan and to the rest of the world, including the UN. In West Pakistan cities of Rawalpindi, Islamabad, and Lahore 'Crush India' banners began to appear everywhere, especially on car rears. 'Hang the Traitor' stickers also appeared everywhere. Life of Sheikh Mujibur Rahman incarcerated in West Pakistan was under serious threat.

Admiral Mohammad Shariff, the commander of Navy of East Pakistan, in his autobiography 'Admiral's Diary' wrote:

"The initial military success in regaining the law-and-order situation in East Pakistan in March of 1971 was misunderstood as a complete success. In actuality, the law-and-order situation deteriorated with time, particularly after September of the same year when the population turned increasingly against the army as well as the government".

Murder Most Foul – Intellectuals are Killed in Cold Blood

On 3rd December 1971, Pakistan Air Force (PAF) launched strikes on the Indian Air Force bases. This was the beginning of the War. On 14th December 1971, just two days before the surrender, the Pakistan Army and local Razakar militia murdered hundreds of Bengali intellectuals. The lists were approved by top ranking Pak Army officers. 14th December is observed as Martyred Intellectuals Day. What started on 25th of March 1971, culminated on 16th of December. A new nation was born in almost nine months.

The liberation of Bangladesh is a story of people who dared to stand up and walk alone for their dignity, their honour, their mother tongue, their motherland, and faced the storm with uncommon resilience. They gained friends and admirers as they continued their heroic march on a blood-splattered road stoically. Extreme brutality and adversity were met with matching bravery. The enemy was a multi-headed hydra, but David won this round too and Goliath was humbled yet again.

Jodi tor dak sune keu na ase,
Tobe' ekla cholo re, ekla chalo, ekla chalo, ekla chalo re,

If no one answers your call,
fear not, walk alone,
walk alone, O friend.

Bangladesh did not forget them when the storm was over and the rainbows shined. The 'Friends of Bangladesh' and their families became part of the new nation's family for all times to come. It is a matter of great pride that my family and I are also a part of this Bangladesh family.

Kitne' toofano se guzrein hai toh jannat paayi hai

We have passed through innumerable storms to beget this paradise

{Pakistan continues with its Urdu-Only policy till date. It teaches Urdu to its 90% non-Urdu speaking population and looks down upon its native languages. Punjabi, a glorious language spoken by a large majority of Pakistanis is banned in its Parliament and Punjab Assembly. India, on the other hand, has more than 22 state languages which are accorded state patronage. Bengali is thriving on both sides of the Indo-Bangladesh border. One can hear soulful melodies of Gurudev Rabindra Nath Tagore, Kazi Nazrul Islam and other leading Bangla poets reverberating from Calcutta to Chittagong, from Delhi to Dhaka.}

An iconic poster by Quamrul Hassan on General Yahya Khan, representing the Pakistani military junta as demons

Advertisement for former Beatle George Harrison's "Bangla Desh" concert, released in July 1971 to raise international awareness and funds for the millions of Bangladeshi refugees.

Anthony Mascarenhas

CHAPTER 9

War Clouds Gather

Refugee Influx

Millions of fathers in rain
Millions of mothers in pain
Millions of brothers in woe
Millions of sisters nowhere to go

Millions of daughters walk in the mud
Millions of children wash in the flood
A million girls vomit and groan
Millions of families hopeless alone

Millions of souls nineteen-seventy-one
homeless on Jessore road under grey sun
A million are dead, the million who can
Walk toward Calcutta from East Pakistan

On Jessore road Mother wept at my knees
Bengali tongue cried mister Please
Identity card torn up on the floor
Husband still waits at the camp office door

—Excerpts from Allen Ginsberg (1926–1997),
'September on Jessore Road'

Ginsberg wrote the poem after visiting the refugee camp on Jessore road in 1971.

For the Indian subcontinent, December 1970–71 was a soldier's year, a refugee's year, a year of despair, death, destruction, tears, turmoil, blood, bullets, body bags but, in the end, it became a year of hope, a new dawn, and of smiles that could survive the mayhem.

November 1970—Demagiri Post, Mizoram–Bangladesh Border

In November 1970, Army headquarters had posted me to 32 Guards, which was a counter-insurgency unit. This was done keeping in view of my commando training and my earlier experience in Nagaland. Before the 1971 Indo-Pak War, 32nd Battalion of Guards was re-designated as 14th Battalion of Guards regular infantry battalion.

14 Guards was posted in the southern part of Mizoram. We were required to hold four village group centres viz Hawrang, Lunglei, Bunghmun and Demagiri, located on Lunglei–Demagiri road. It was during this time that I was promoted as a major and I was appointed as the company commander, Alpha (A) Company.

My company was deployed at the forward most post, Demagiri, on the Mizoram border. The Demagiri post was on the border opposite to the picturesque Chittagong track in East Pakistan, now Bangladesh. One of our main objectives was to operate against any cross-border movement of Mizo and Naga insurgents and their supporters. Further, any mischief from across the border was to be effectively neutralised. A lot of insurgency movements were active at that time. But NE insurgency is almost all but a matter of past. There has been tremendous progress in the entire North-East in the past few decades. I have remarked earlier in the book that it is the robustness of the Indian democracy and federal system that allows aspirations and growth of each group and community. Today, the North-East has left insurgency behind and there is new hope. After having spent so much time in various parts of this region, I identify myself with its natives and my heart swells with pride when I see them doing well in all walks of life. I have been associated with sports and army, so I will name a few of them who have excelled in these fields. I start with sports since it is my weakness: Mary Kom, Dipa Karmakar, Bhaichung Bhutia, and the list is ever growing. In the army, we find the examples of Lieutenant Ipupu Mena from OTA Chennai who became the first lady from the Idu Mishmi community of Arunachal, Lieutenant General K. Himalay Singh (retd.) from Manipur, and Lieutenant Colonel (Ms.) Ponung Doming, Captain Keishing Clifford Nongrum—a Kargil war martyr, to name a few.

On 26th March 1971, Bangabandhu Sheikh Mujibur Rahman declared Bangladesh an independent nation amidst political turmoil. Pakistan Army dominated by the Punjabi and Pathan troops scaled up its presence in the region. Pakistan junta let loose a reign of terror in erstwhile East Pakistan, the sordid details of which have been discussed in the earlier chapter. The refugees started pouring into India from East Pakistan (now Bangladesh) from March–April 1971 onwards. Mrs. Indira Gandhi, the Prime Minister of India, announced diplomatic, economic, and military support to Bangladesh in April 1971. The provisional government of Bangladesh in exile established its secretariat in Calcutta. The Indian Armed Forces were now providing substantial training and the use of its bases for the Bangladesh Liberation Forces. The Bangladesh liberation guerrillas had training camps in Assam, Arunachal Pradesh, Bihar, Meghalaya, Mizoram, Nagaland, Tripura, and of course, West Bengal.

Some of the refugees also started arriving in Demagiri after crossing over from Chittagong hill side for safe shelter. All of them carried tales of atrocities by the Pakistan Army. As an army major deployed to look after the Demagiri army post, I was ordered to provide shelter, medical aid, clothes and other requirements to the refugees. They were in bad shape. It was a major humanitarian crisis, building up across the entire Indo-Bangladesh border. I set up camps for the refugees and tried to make them as comfortable as possible. Demagiri was a beautiful small hamlet in Mizoram, located across River Karnaphuli. It was crowded with war refugees from Bangladesh[1]. The Indian post was at a position of advantage. There was a 'V' formation of the river with a hill. The refugees were hungry and in tattered clothes. Many had walked hundreds of kilometres to escape the wrath of the Pakistan Army. Most of them had just escaped with their lives. They were given food and shelter. Some of them were carrying old or basic arms like single- and double-barrel guns, suitable for farmers or planters. Many of the young and middle-

1 Bruce. W. Watson, Encyclopedia Britannica, Article Military Science Intelligence.

aged men and women refugees wanted to take up arms so that they could go back to fight the Pakistan Army to protect their people from atrocities. One of the JCOs came into my tent and told me that some of the young girls also wanted to learn use of firearms to be a part of the struggle. We all had heard enough stories about the sadistic and highly despicable atrocities by Pakistan Army on East Bengal women. But the girls were adamant. Some were educated and some illiterate, but all of them very hungry—hungry for revenge.

Part of my brief at the advance post was to facilitate movement of the Bangladesh Liberation Forces as well as training for those refugees who were willing to join the struggle. I cannot forget the burning desire in those anguished eyes to fight for their motherland, that would soon be known to the world as Bangladesh. I organised a basic training camp for the willing men and women. Some of them were poor and uneducated, but full of zeal. I remember there was a professor and two teachers among them. In hindsight, they would have been extremely lucky as Pakistan Army unleashed a targeted pogrom on East Bengal intellectuals, particularly on professors, doctors and engineers.

My men at the Demagiri post gave weapons and field craft training to these eager men and women. The enthusiasm of these brave people was admirable. In the ensuing months, these impoverished genteel folks seething in rage would soon blow the deeply-flawed racial superiority complex and doctrine of the West Punjab dominated Pakistan Army to smithereens.

After the basic training, they would venture out back into East Pakistan and conduct raids on the Pakistan Army. Their knowledge of the local terrain and topography was of immense use, putting West Pakistani troops mostly at a disadvantage. That area had a lot of Razakars. Sometime my men, in local disguise, would accompany them. The objective was to harass and demoralise the enemy as much as possible. We gave them cover whenever required. Four or five ladies were very active, and all of them became adept in firing and defending themselves when needed. They were mostly used in overground operations, recce, and to provide cover to menfolk wherever required. We took care not to put them at risk.

It was a similar story in many other camps. The Jodhas—men and women did a commendable job. Years later, when I visited Dacca, my guide took me to Dacca University campus where I was moved to tears after looking at the wonderful sculpture dedicated to Mukti Bahini, and aptly named '*Aparajeyo Bangla*' (Invincible Bengal). I was told that Syed Abdullah Khalid made it and finished on the 7th anniversary of the liberation of Bangladesh, i.e., 16th December 1978. The sculpture brought back a rush of memories and emotions long forgotten.

(A Sculpture of Mukti Jodhas at Dacca University circle.)

My company was happy that they were seeing some action instead of the routine guard duties. It was these adrenaline-pumping games that we had been training for long. It was as if the sword was unsheathed and was being sharpened. There were times when my boys would go along with the liberation guerrillas to help in accomplishing their tasks. They simply loved to harass the Razakars or Mujahids. There were at least two very daring raids involving Pakistani troops in which I had also accompanied them, disguised as a local Bengali. In one of the raids, a *jawan* was mildly injured. The boys extracted a more than suitable revenge. This sabre rattling continued from April till September. The sharpened swords of the unit were to soon taste blood.

During July 1971, my Coy was ordered to move to Agartala in Tripura. It was an emotional parting with the Jodhas. The Indian Army, under the leadership of legendary Field Marshal Sam Maneckshaw, anticipating the possibility of the war between India and Pakistan, was planning and preparing hard.

The battalion was stationed in Agartala for administrative command and control. The unit carried out training, exercises and briefing, keeping in view the possible war at Pratapgarh and Mahori, near Agartala. I was under the command of Lieutenant Colonel Channa. The IV Corps command was in the hands of legendary Lieutenant General Sagat Singh.

October '71— A Srinagar in North-East

Baptism by fire. Initiation of 'A' Company (14 Guards) In the last week of October of '71, my Coy was ordered to move down to South Tripura towards East Bengal border, where Pakistani troops had readied embattlements. I reached the border town of Srinagar in South Tripura. Our local intelligence sources indicated further consolidation of enemy troops near the area.

Intelligence, in military science, is information concerning an enemy or an area. Military intelligence is as old as war itself. These days, technology plays an important role in gathering intelligence. However, 'HUMINT', or Human Intelligence, has always been an integral part of both tactical and strategic operations. Many a battle have been swung with the help of intelligence. Thanks to the alienation of the East Bengal citizenry, Indian Army had credible information on the moves of the Pakistan Army. Lack of credible or inaccurate information can be very damaging. But overall, India had established an upper hand in terms of intelligence gathering over the Pakistan Army, thanks to the Jodhas and their network.

Srinagar (South Tripura) was strategically much more important to both Pakistan and India as compared to Demagiri. An upper hand in Srinagar by the enemy could lead to a tactical emergency. Further, the flow of refugees from this area was much more than in Mizoram.

Our intelligence inputs indicated a flurry of activity in the enemy ranks. It was deduced that the Pakistan Army wanted to dominate the area strategically for advance action, if any, as well as to stem the tide of refugees. While other companies of the unit remained put in Agartala, 'Alpha Company', under my command, was deputed to Srinagar 130 kms. away down south.

A company of BSF (Border Security Force) held embankments at the Srinagar outpost. About 500 metres away, Pakistani troops had occupied higher bunds on the opposite side. Some 300 metres from the international border was a gravel road running almost parallel to the border. It was on this slightly higher ground next to the gravel road that BSF was positioned almost diametrically opposite to the Pakistani post. The ground in between the two posts was a relatively lower plain with very little or no vegetation cover.

The order was clear: "Major Ashok Tara, Company Commander, 'A' Company, you are directed to establish defensive positions in between the BSF embankments and the Pakistani positions situated across the border."

The company cautiously moved along a gravel path, closer to the point of interest. Enemy troops became aware of this movement and tried to stall the approach. They opened fire with automatic weapons. The provocation was unexpected. One *jawan* was injured heavily in the crossfire. Our every movement was visible to the enemy. We were moving in a sparsely vegetated, relatively low-lying area with minimal tree or any other natural cover. This was hardly the ideal place to entrench the troops. To prevent any further damage to men and armoury, we decided to halt the operation. A more thorough reconnaissance and planning was vital to be strategically secure and ensure relevant stations for the MMGs (Medium Machine Guns), 81mm mortars and troops.

I had two excellent platoon commanders. Subedar Hoshiar Singh, a Jat from Haryana as the infantry in-charge, and Subedar Ajit Singh, a Sikh from Punjab as in-charge of the mortar unit. For the next two days, we carried out our recce during daytime and planned the deployment of men and guns. In the intervening two nights, we successfully deployed guns and troops in the cover of darkness.

Commanding Officer Lieutenant Colonel V. N. Channa, upon hearing about the wounded *jawan*, rushed to the BSF post from Agartala. He was inevitably aghast and wanted immediate retaliation against the enemy. The entire Coy was aware that the Pakistani post was sitting at a position of advantage in terms of numbers and battlement. I advised him to engage the enemy at a more favourable moment, to which he agreed. At this time, Major Prem Kshatriya, too, joined the company to encourage and extend moral support to the troops. We waited for an opportune moment to get even.

It was not long before a potential opportunity presented itself. I got an intelligence lead regarding a forthcoming religious festivity in the enemy camp on the next day. I figured out the high possibility of the enemy troops convening at a common place during the festivities, and letting down their guard to some degree. This had to be the vulnerable moment we could capitalise upon. I hastily convened a meeting and relayed the plan to Major Prem Kshatriya, Subedar Hoshiar Singh, and Subedar Ajit Singh. There was unanimity on the plan and the wheels of engagement were put into motion without any delay. Unknown to the enemy, Alpha Company, too, prepared for the festival that night.

Garuda, the Bravest of the Brave

Next day, all the troops were weapon ready and waiting patiently for the right moment, just like a tiger does for his prey. A tiger can stalk his prey for hours without the prey knowing, and attacks only when he is sure of the kill. Our intelligence and hunches were bang on the dot. We waited patiently in our trenches, in our positions with hands on triggers and mortars with bated breath, and finally the moment came when the enemy camp broke into festivities and let their guard down. They were celebrating after soaking the entire East Bengal in sorrow. Bangabandhu was imprisoned away from his home. Bengali homes, farms, schools, universities, and hospitals were destroyed. The stench of death, disease, destruction and dishonour was everywhere in East Bengal. They had a right to celebrate, too, but there was hardly a family that was not mourning the loss of near and dear ones. We were determined to not to let the enemy celebrate. They had to feel the same pain as the East Bengalis were feeling that day. And my boys had an axe to grind.

We were just minutes away from engaging the enemy when Subedar Ajit Singh, in-charge of 81 mortars, apprised me that his radio-set was not operational. This meant that a coordinated fire would be severely hampered and might not have the intended impact. A split-second decision was required. As captain of the football and cricket teams in the college, I had to change plans midway many a times for victory. It was now or never. Almost immediately, I came up with an innovative plan to daisy chain a handful of soldiers between myself, Subedar Ajit Singh, and the mortar positions to 'control direction of fire with voice'. Subedar Ajit Singh would position himself behind a big tree, close to the company commander, while a handful of other soldiers would station themselves in the safety of dug-outs, large rocks and trees, separated by approximately 50–75 yards, in a row till the last man was close enough to the mortar positions. Further, to ensure that the enemy did not easily figure out the scheme of things, it was decided that a code word of '*Kabootar ek... do...*' would be used to transmit instructions on when to fire and the number of rounds to be fired. Ajit Singh made full use of the solitary tree in the area as I dived into one of the trenches nearby.

The plan was firmly in place and there were no more foreseeable obstacles. I locked my eyes with Ajit Singh and ordered in a barely audible voice, "Fire." The indomitable Sardar with his eyes flashing, shouted in full throttle: "FIRE!" The compliance was deafening. 'A' Company orchestrated its fire, and all hell broke loose in the opposite camp. The enemy was caught off guard with MMGs and 81 mm mortars raining havoc on them.

There was no chance to escape and no time for the enemy to regroup and take their positions. It was only a matter of time before the Pakistani troops raised a white flag and relentlessly screamed out requests to stop firing. Not to mention that both the sides spoke and understood the same language: Punjabi. We had given the enemy a taste of their own medicine, and a befitting reply to their unethical and unprovoked firing on us a couple of days ago. Major Kshatriya and I mutually agreed to consider the pleas and ordered a ceasefire. This was followed by the Pakistani commander requesting a 'White Flag' meet, during which they notified the Indian contingent of significant casualties in their camp. They further assured us, in the name of Allah, of not initiating any escalations from their end. That night, there were discrete festivities at our end. The BSF company watched the entire drama unfold with glee. They had done a commendable job in terms of cultivating the intelligence network and coordination with Mukti Bahini. We celebrated the festival on behalf of the people of East Bengal.

'A' Company had accomplished the purpose and mission to set up a stronghold in the region. The Srinagar (South Tripura) experience had prepared the 'A' Coy for further action. Basking in glory, the men, guns and mortars were aligned, upbeat, ready and itching for more action. After a few more days, 'A' Company was ordered back to Agartala, having achieved their objective.

'A' company's sabres had tasted blood in Srinagar. Initiated and having had their first taste of success, our personnel were in high morale. Little did they know they were to create history in a few weeks and be immortalised forever. The same zeal, vigour, grit and courage would see them through the Battle of Dhalai, the Battle of Gangasagar, and engagements up till the triumphant march to Dhaka. It was *Nischay-Josh-Himmat-Hausla-Jeet*. (Decision-Enthusiasm-Courage-patience Victory).

A victory is twice itself when the achiever brings home full numbers.

—Shakespeare, *Much Ado About Nothing*

❑

CHAPTER 10

A Tea Garden Turns Crimson

Battle of Dhalai

'Our battle is more full of names than yours,
Our men more perfect in the use of arms,
Our armour all as strong, our cause the best;
Then reason will our hearts should be as good.'

—Shakespeare, *Henry IV Part 2*

1st November 1971—Sreemangal, Sylhet, East Pakistan

14 Guards, except 'A' Coy, was left behind at Agartala in Tripura, 'A' Coy had a swagger when they returned to Agartala in the later part of October 1971. The Srinagar action of Alpha Coy could, at best, be termed as a skirmish wherein we ended up having an upper hand. Nevertheless, the boys were very excited and had a lot to share with other the Coys. They had gotten the enemy under fire and compelled them to raise the white flag. Unknown to them, a huge storm was brewing on the Tripura border.

14 Guards had barely settled down when they got the orders to join the units already fighting battles at Kamalpur, a small border town north-east of Tripura on 1st November 1971, post-haste. I have maintained that often a supposedly small run-ins can escalate into a major crisis. One such border skirmish[1] at a tea garden in Dhalai

in Sreemangal, Sylhet, snowballed into a major confrontation with casualties on both sides. The skirmish started on 27th October and ended up as a major battle on 3rd November 1971. The full-blown war was almost a month away. In cinematic parlance, this was the hair-raising, nail-biting trailer to the forthcoming blockbuster.

Sreemangal is a border upazila of Moulvibazar District in the Sylhet division of Bangladesh, overlooking the Indian town of Kamalpur. The picturesque town of Sreemangal is also known as the 'Tea capital of Bangladesh' because of the number of tea plantations in the area. On 30th April 1971, Pakistan Army entered Sreemangal and started mass killings, violation of women, torture, and plunder. Many houses of the upazila were set on fire to terrorise people into submission. Mass graves in Bharaura are a chilling reminder of the horrors. Dhalai was a net of some tea gardens east of Sreemangal, with few labourers' huts. Pakistani troops took over the Dhalai tea garden complex bordering India, and this became their border outpost (BOP). This tea garden was to attain immortality as the centre stage of the 'the Battle of Dhalai.' The Pakistan BOP was on relatively higher ground and overlooked Kamalpur, which was approximately 900 metres away. The complex had overgrown tea gardens in the north and west, while the south and south-east areas were covered with paddy fields.

Though the war commenced on 3rd December 1971, the Indian Army, Mukti Bahini, and East Bengal Rifles (EBR) were already harassing and attacking the Pakistani forces. Lieutenant General J S Aurora planned to keep on attacking Pakistani troops in that area during the twilight period, before the commencement of formal hostilities. One such position was the Dhalai BOP. A pitched battle was fought for over three days between Pakistani forces and the Indian Army, EBR and Mukti Bahini on the other side.

Dhalai Tea Garden Complex

The entire action from the Indian side started on the premise that the Dhalai outpost had weak defences and lightly manned guns. The moves and countermoves from both sides just kept on escalating till it was a full-blown battle involving generals. The Battle of Dhalai set the tone, tenor and direction of the war just before the war.

The Pakistan Army was very well-entrenched in the tea garden complex. On hindsight, the entire complex gave them excellent cover. Apart from the main Dhalai border outpost, the other posts in the complex included the tea factory and officers' bungalows, Twin Hut post, Red Hut post, and Coolie Lines. The posts were well fortified by artillery withstanding concrete bunkers, wire and punjees (spikes made of wood / bamboo). The complex was roughly 1,100×1,100 mts. The initial assessment of the post being defended lightly proved to be wrong.

There was intermittent fire from the Pakistani side. A raid was conducted by Mukti Bahini in the tea factory area but they were unsuccessful. Unlike many other such raids across East Pakistan by Mukti Bahini, this raid yielded little information about the enemy's strength and their fortifications.

October 27th–28th, 1971

61 Mountain Brigade, under Brigade Commander S D S Yadava, now pressed 1st Battalion of the East Bengal Rifles to capture Dhalai on the night of October 27th–28th, 1971. Indian forces provided all the necessary help and logistics. Since there was no formal declaration of war, Indian Army, whenever required, would join the guerrillas disguised in local attire. Reverses were taken seriously and necessary help, cover, and reinforcements were readily provided to keep the morale of the Bangladeshi forces at a high.

EBR, despite being heavily outnumbered, fought valiantly, but the moderately equipped regiment could not match the superior firepower of the enemy. Hamidur Rahman, a young sepoy in East Bengal Regiment, took the responsibility of throwing grenades at the roaring machine guns. He crawled through the hilly canals and threw two grenades before being shot. Hamidur Rahman was posthumously awarded the *Bir Sreshtho,* the highest recognition of bravery in Bangladesh, for his act of exemplary courage. After the EBR attack was repulsed, Pakistani artillery opened fire on Kamalpur in retaliation.

This brought in the Indian Army. 2 Jat, one of the most decorated units of the Indian Army, was ordered to go forward to Dhalai on an emergency basis. The Indian forces were still convinced that the enemy strength at Dhalai was only one platoon.

28th-29th October—The first attack

Initial attack parties ran into trouble as there was heavy fortification from the Pakistan side. Indian troops could not make any headway at night through the unruly and uncut thick tea bushes. There was no labour to attend to the tea gardens as it was now an army embankment. It was later discovered that there were over 45 bunkers in the complex. Unknown to the attacking unit, Pakistan had also moved a unit on a counter-attack role and placed them in the Coolie Lines.

30th-31st October 1971—The second attack

A two phased attack was planned by the Indian unit, 2 Jat, from the east on the night of 30th-31st October as below:

- **Road Block—'**A' Coy established a roadblock behind Dhalai complex.
- **Twin Huts—'**C' Coy captured Twin Huts initially, but the enemy counter-attacked with artillery and MMG, and pushed the Coy back to Ganganagar. 2 Jat, with hardly any artillery support, suffered heavy casualties. The enemy cut off the Coolie Lines from the east.
- **Coolie Lines—'**B' Coy captured the Coolie Lines where each house had been fortified into a bunker.
- **Dhalai BOP—**Initially 'D' Coy was to attack the outpost but plans were changed midway after the counter-attack and upon seeing the Pakistani strength in the Coolie Lines area. 'D' Coy was ordered to capture the Red Hut area. This last moment change would prove to be costly again.
- **Red Hut—**Red Hut had a 3-tier setup of bunkers. Pakistanis had a Coy there, plus surviving defenders from the Coolie Lines had also come there. A portion of Red Hut area was captured after a stiff fight. 2 Jat had no weapons to destroy the bunkers, and the attack was not pressed further.
- **Factory Area—**Enemy was entrenched.

2 Jat had suffered heavy casualties. Brigade Commander S. D. S. Yadava and Lieutenant Colonel Devasan of 7 Rajputana Rifles were injured and had to be evacuated. Experts assess that it was a major intelligence failure and lack of coordination with artillery. The casualties on the enemy side were heavy, too. Despite fierce resistance by the frontier force, the Indians kept on attacking left, right and centre.

The situation at 9 am on 31st October was grim and bloody. If the total casualties and wounded were taken into account, there were only two Indian Coys in the tea garden complex to foil enemy counter-attacks and future battles. One Coy was permanently tied up with the roadblock; therefore cutting off the Command HQ of the Pakistan Army from the Dhalai BOP. The road block ensured that new reinforcements from Pakistan side could be blocked from the complex.

The Indian Army was fighting a battle that was going to be a game changer for 1971. It was in this situation that Lieutenant General Sagat Singh personally assumed command of the situation. General Singh, the indomitable warrior with roots in Rajasthan and known for his tough and aggressive attitude, knew that the stakes had become very high. A defeat or roll back in Dhalai could demoralise not just the Indian troops but also the allied Bangladesh Liberation Forces. The battle had become a do or die situation. In addition to 2 Jat and 7 Raj Rif already in the thick of the battle, 14 Guards was also summoned from Agartala. With Brigadier Yadav injured, Brigadier 'Tom' K. P. Pande was brought in. Meanwhile, as per Pakistan army's Colonel Mukhtar, Pakistan senior army brass gave orders that not an inch was to be vacated. The battle had now heated up and was at full throttle. The easiest option was immediate cease fire or retreat by the Indian side, any other commander might have dithered, but General Sagat Singh upped the ante. 2 Jat was ordered to dig into Coolie Lines and defend against any counter-attack by the enemy. Pakistan mounted multiple fierce counter-attacks on the Jats on 31st itself. The Jats defended their positions, inflicting heavy casualties on the enemy. On 1st November, 7 Raj. Rif. was given the task of capturing Dhalai BOP. Meanwhile, 14 Guards which had earlier moved from Srinagar to Dhalai, joined the battle on 1st November.

The brief of 14 Guards was to take a defensive position initially and then to undertake offensive at Dhalai. The objectives comprised Twin Huts, Coolie Lines and factory area.

14 Guards reinforced the defences of Coolie Lines and pushed deeper. 'A' Coy, which was under me, was tossed to capture one of the most difficult and sensitive objectives, the factory area. This was captured by my troops, and Twin Huts and Coolie Lines were secured by 'B' and 'C' Coys. The enemy launched a counter-attack, but was repulsed with casualties. During the counter-attack, JCO Kanhaiya Singh was injured. He later got a mention in dispatches. Another *jawan* was also wounded. When I walked into the factory area to organise the defences of 'A' Coy, Pakistanis had laid an ambush to one of our platoons, that was ordered to move forward to occupy an area ahead of the Coy location to give depth to the defensive position of 'A' Coy. The scouts of the patrol party had observed their movement and took position on the side of the track. On seeing that, Pak troops withdrew from the location. It was apparent that the enemy was retreating in a hurry. There were heavy casualties on the enemy side. They could now see the Indians coming from all directions and started thinning from various positions.

Entry of 14 Guards in the factory area completely broke the enemy's will to counter-attack or continue the fight. Pakistan Army started thinning out from the area. By 3rd November, their army had completely withdrawn from the tea garden complex. The war cries of our regiments reverberated in the picturesque hills. It was a well-deserved victory. Indian Army's grit and General Sagat Singh's steely resolve had paid off.

The strategic importance of Dhalai BOP and the tea estate was known to both Indian and Pakistani forces. The captured outpost was used as one of the many launch pads for the subsequent offensives. The fierce fighting in Dhalai and heavy casualties broke the morale of Pakistani forces and filled Indian and Bangladesh Liberation forces with enthusiasm. The Indians had sharpened their claws. IV Corps under General Sagat Singh would rain havoc on Pakistani forces during the war. IV Corps would redeem its honour again in the battle at Mynamati when the formal hostilities commenced. 14 Guards' morale was high and upbeat. It is believed that the success achieved in Dhalai had contributed immensely to the success of the battalion in its next attack during the war, which was to be known as the famous Battle of Gangasagar.

We must give a brave enemy his due. Bodies of 60 dead Pakistani soldiers of the Pak 30 Frontier Force Regiment were recovered. A Pak subedar, was killed just five metres from the Indian trenches. It was midway in the battle that from the Pakistani side, GOC Major General Abdul Majid Qazi and Brigadier Rana both moved into the tactical HQ (command post) of Lieutenant Colonel Mukhtar and conducted the battle on the other side. The HQ was at the rear of the road block established behind Dhalai complex.

Lieutenant Colonel Mukhtar of the Pakistan Army, who was the officer commanding the Coy that was at the forefront in Dhalai facing the Indian attack, mentioned in his sitreps of 26th–31st October '71- the casualties of the battle from Pakistani side as 4 officers, 3 JCOs, 61 ORs, 30 FF (Frontier Force), and 89 ORs EPCAF/Razakars. As per him, the Pakistan Army Eastern Command was not prepared to admit to its GHQ that an area of 3–4 sq. km was lost to the Indian Army. This battle was, therefore, shown as a minor skirmish. The hundreds of casualties suffered by 30 FF and troops under command were staggered to show a dozen or so casualties on odd days. Accordingly, none of the defenders were given any gallantry awards.

The Indian Army was gracious in victory to acknowledge the bravery of the Pak martyrs, Second-in-Command Major Raja Javed and a subedar whose body was found just 5 metres from the 2 Jat trenches. Colonel Mukhtar identified him as Subedar Amal Din. In sharp contrast to Pakistani stand, India and Bangladesh honoured its bravehearts with suitable awards.

14 Guards was to soon enter the thick of the war and wrap itself with glory in Gangasagar.

❑

Colonel Ashok Tara, VrC in 1994

Parents
Damyanti and Chattrapati Tara

Abha and Ashok with Darbari Lal (Nanaji) and Roopmati (Naniji) October 1970

Ashok Tara during his early Army Days
Indo-Pak War 1965

Ashok Tara 1968 Agra before para jump

Ashok Tara (2nd from right) at NCC Advanced Leadership Camp Manali(HP) 1962

Ashok Tara at un-armed combat training area (Unit 9 para commando in J & K 1968)

NCC Advanced Leadership Course at Manali 1962. Standing 4th from right

Marriage Ceremony at Arya Samaj Mandir Patel Nagar, 4th October 1970 L to R: Dr. Khatri (Raseel's husband), Madhu Bhabhi, Ashwani (eldest brother), Shiv Chopra (Upma's husband), Upma (Sister) Ashok & bride Abha. Standing behind Mohan (cousin). Parvinder Singh & Anoop Singh

Civil Marriage at Tis Hazari.1968, (L-R) Upma Chopra (Sister), Ashok, Adv. Singh, Abha, Parvinder, Raseel, Anoop Singh and Satinder Mehra

Abha's brothers Bipan and Nipun performing kanyadaan—Abha and Ashok's wedding cermony, 4 October, 1970

With Nani ji

Ashok Tara at Jaisingder railway station Rajasthan Indo Pak war 1965

Ashok Tara shaking hands with former Indian PM Smt. Indira Gandhi 1972

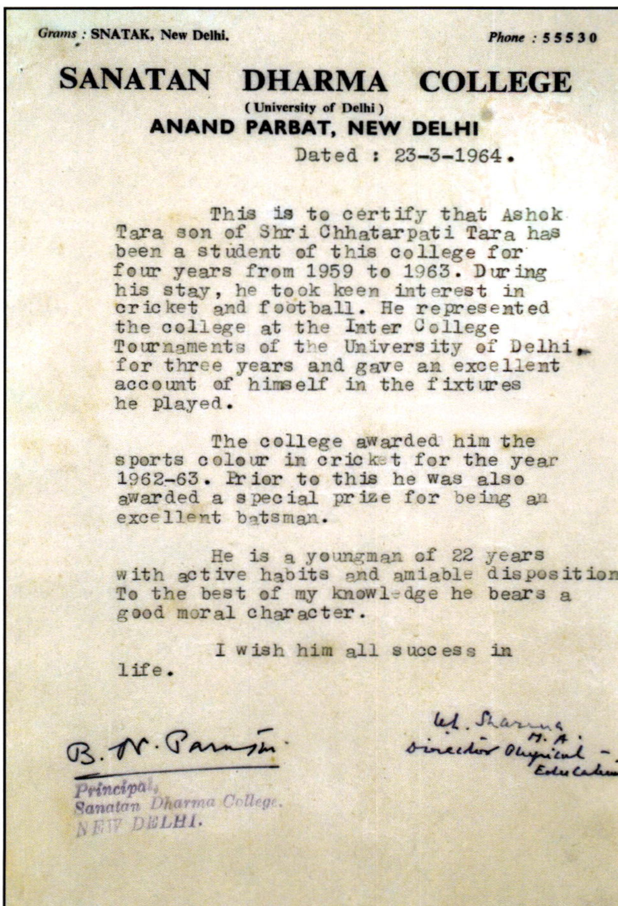

Grams : SNATAK, New Delhi. Phone : 55530

SANATAN DHARMA COLLEGE

(University of Delhi)

ANAND PARBAT, NEW DELHI

Dated : 23-3-1964.

This is to certify that Ashok Tara son of Shri Chhatarpati Tara has been a student of this college for four years from 1959 to 1963. During his stay, he took keen interest in cricket and football. He represented the college at the Inter College Tournaments of the University of Delhi, for three years and gave an excellent account of himself in the fixtures he played.

The college awarded him the sports colour in cricket for the year 1962-63. Prior to this he was also awarded a special prize for being an excellent batsman.

He is a youngman of 22 years with active habits and amiable disposition. To the best of my knowledge he bears a good moral character.

I wish him all success in life.

Principal,
Sanatan Dharma College,
NEW DELHI.

M.A.
Director Physical Education

Father Chattrapati Tara (Father), Kirti (Brother), Damyanti (Mother), Anurag (Nephew), Ashok, Abha, Madhu (Bhabhi), Anuj (Nephew), Ashwini (Brother)

Bangabandhu Family from L to R: Sheikh Jamal (eldest Son), Rehana (younger daughter), Sheikh Mujibur Rahman with Russel (youngest son), Mrs Mujibur Rahman, Sheikh Kamal (second Son) and Sheikh Hasina (eldest daughter)

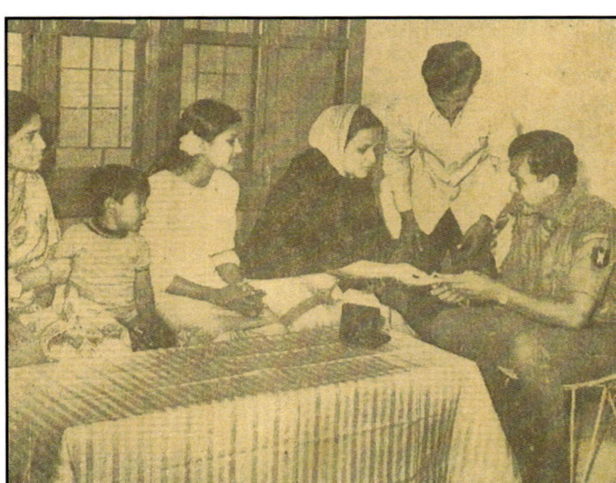

Courtesy "Patrika" R- L — Major Ashok Tara. Standing Mr. Khoka (cousin & aide of Sheikh Mujibur Rahman) Bangamata presented wrist watch 'Tissot' to Ashok Tara, Rehana and family of Mr. Khoka.

East Bengal Regt. Flag captured by 14 Guards during Battle of Gangasagar on 03 December 1971. Liberation War of Bangladesh

House on Road 18 in Dhanmondi Dhaka where Sheikh Hasina family members were held captive

Abha and Ashok with Mrs. and Mr. Sam Manekshaw

Sheikh Mujibur Rehman family with Ashok Tara L-R— Standing Mr. Khoka, Sheikh Kamal. L-R— Sitting Ashok Tara, Sheikh Mujibur Rahman, Russel, Sheikh Jamal and Mrs. Mujibur Rahman. Photo at their residence Dhanmandi. Dhaka, January 1972.

Major Ashok Tara receiving 'Vir Chakra' from Hon'ble President of India Sh V.V. Giri, 1972

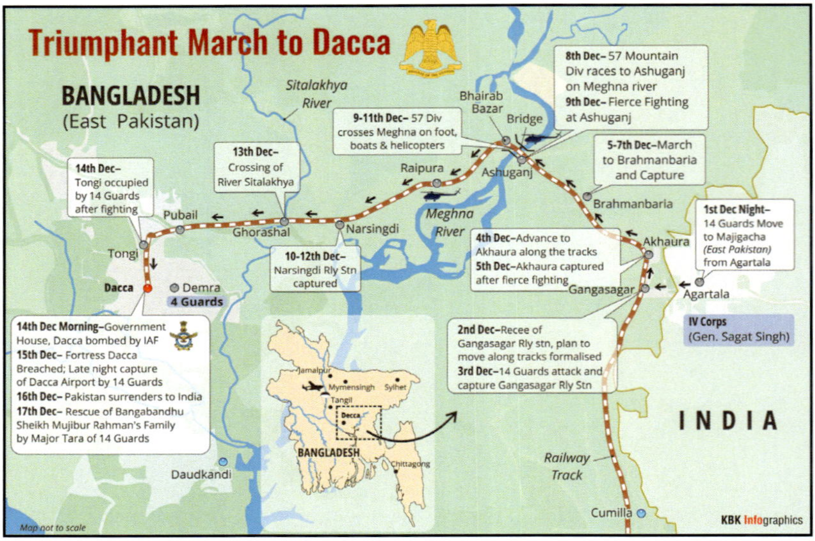

Train Ticket from Gangasagar to Akhaura

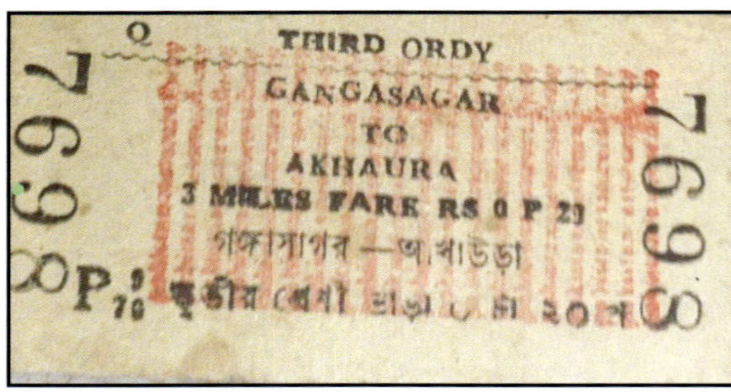

Pictorial Depiction of Battle of Gangasagar 3 December 1971

(L-R) PM Sheikh Hasina, PM Narendra Modi, Ashok and Abha Tara 08 April 2017, Manekshaw Hall, Delhi Cantt.

Photograph of Sheikh Hasina and her son, Joy, sent to Abha in 1972.

Abha and Ashok with Sheikh Hasina, Zayan Fida Noor- liaison incharge Bangladesh and Sheikh Rehana (October 2012) at their residence, Dhaka

Hon'ble Prime Minister of Bangladesh Sheikh Hasina conferring 'Friends of Liberation War Honor' to Col. Ashok Tara VrC on 20th October 2012 at Dhaka

Ashok Tara paying homage at Bangabandhu Memorial Museum in Dhaka

Gangasagar Railway Station after 42 years (From L to R) Lt Col. Sajjad Ali, representative of Bangladesh, Ashok, Balamdini Ekka, Vincent Ekka (Albert Ekka's wife and Son) and Abha, 22 October 2012

Receiving torch from Prime Minister Modi during Golden Jubilee celerations of 1971 Victory, 16 December 2020 at National War Memorial (near India Gate), New Delhi

Abha and Ashok with Prime Minister Sheikh Hasina during her visit to New Delhi, 7 April 2017

Receiving Veteran of the Year 2017 award from Former Gen. V. K. Singh by Veterans India next is Mr. B K Mishra (Founder And National President of ' All India Ex- servicemen'.)

ANZAC

Our gratitude and our pride

Anzac Day 2019: Indian veterans march again in Melbourne

BY GAURAV MASAND

This remembrance is equally significant to India's military history

Participation in ANZAC day Parade. 2019. courtesy Guarav Masand

Abha's Parents.
Mrs Shanta Pal and Prof BN Pal

From L-R- Abha Tara, Col. Ashok Tara, Kiran Pal, Bipan Pal (elder brother) Sarita Pal, Nipun Pal (younger brother).

Tara family. (L-R) Anshu (Daughter), Ashok Tara, Abha Tara (Wife), Sanyogita Tara (Daughter in law), Rhea Tara (Grand daughter), Ashish Tara (Son)

Anshuman Tandon at Bangabandhu Memorial, Dhaka

With family friend Ekta Gupta

L-R Dr. Ashok Singh & Dr. Deepa Singh (Dr. Sanyogita's Parents), Abha Tara and Ashok Kumar Tara, VrC.

*From L to R—
Dr. Sanyogita Tara (Daughter-in-Law), Ashish Tara (Son), standing in rear Rhea Tara (Grand Daughter), in front Abha Tara (Wife), Anshu Tara (Daughter), Col. Ashok Tara in Australia*

L to R Anshuman Tandon, Col. Ashok Tara, Abha Tara, Saruchi and Arushi Tandon

CHAPTER 11

The Battle of Gangasagar and Veer Chakra

Sound trumpets! Let our bloody colours wave!
And either victory, or else a grave.

—William Shakespeare,
Henry VI Part 3

Gangasagar—A railway station becomes immortal

India Gate, New Delhi, 2019

On 25th February, 2019, Prime Minister Narendra Modi inaugurated the National War Memorial in New Delhi. Among the plaques of ten most notable battles was the plaque of the Battle of Gangasagar. The war memorial was termed as a National Pilgrimage Centre.

Jackpot of 1971

Autumn of 1971 saw tensions with Pakistan rise to an unprecedented high. The Battle of Dhalai, which ended on 3rd November, was a watershed, as it had put both sides on high alert. The month of November was a period of intense activity for the Indian Army and the Bangladesh Liberation Forces. Apart from regular skirmishes and raids all over the border, there were many notable battles. The Battle of Dhalai, however, was exceptional in terms of fierceness and causalities. Some of the other notable battles that took place are the Battle of Garibpur, and the Battle of Hilli or the Battle of Bogura. The Battle of Ajmiriganj (16th November) was an 18-hour encounter between the Mukti Bahini and the Pakistan Army, in which the famous freedom fighter Jagat Joity Das was martyred. He was awarded *Bir Bikrom*, Bangladesh's third highest gallantry award. Other notable happenings were the formation of Bangladesh Armed Forces on 21st November. On 9th November, six small patrol vessels made up the first fleet of Bangladesh Navy. On 3rd December, Bangladesh Air Force destroyed several Pakistani oil tank depots.

By the end of November, it was almost a state of war between the countries with action happening on an almost daily basis. Indian Armed forces and Mukti Bahini were nibbling away at Pakistan Army's controls all across the border. For the sake of military and guerrilla operations, entire Bangladesh was divided into eleven zones. The Eastern Corps, i.e., IV Corps was adjoining three of these zones. Gangasagar–Akhaura–Brahmanbaria axis area was in Zone 2. In October and November, guerrilla attacks in Bangladesh intensified and so did the retaliatory oppression by Pakistani forces and Razakar militia. Almost a quarter of the border outposts were lost by Pakistani forces. Some of these border outposts would later become launchpads to enter Pakistan. As many as 90 out of 370 BOPs had fallen before the war commenced. This aggression from multiple directions had the GOC of Pakistan, General Niazi, and his brass guessing where would the major thrusts come from in case of war.

THE STATESMAN

IT'S WAR

PAK PLANES BOMB MANY AIRPORTS

Heavy Shelling Of Border Posts

PRESIDENT DECLARES EMERGENCY

Country On War Footing, Says Mrs. Gandhi

AirCommander's Order Of The Day

MIDNIGHT PAK BOMBING

Agartala Airfield Raided Again

On 3rd December, Pakistan Air force launched Operation Chengiz Khan and targeted 11 of India's airfields and other positions with an objective to neutralise the Indian Air Force. The targets were the Indian airbases of Amritsar, Ambala, Agra, Awantipur, Bikaner, Halwara, Jodhpur, Jaisalmer, Pathankot, Bhuj, Srinagar and Uttarlai and air defence radars at Amritsar and Faridkot. The Indian Prime Minister Indira Gandhi addressed the nation on radio that same evening and held the air strikes to be a declaration of war against India. In response to the sadist murderous 'Chengiz', India launched Operation Jackpot.

November 7th–31st, 1971, Agartala

By 8th November, Dhalai was handed over to other units to secure its defences. 14 Guards moved back to Pratapgarh, near Agartala, for administration and training in case war took place. Dark war clouds were hovering over the Indian subcontinent, especially in the eastern sector. From our base in Pratapgarh, we would often visit BSF and state police posts at the border. These were both recce/acclimatisation and confidence-building measures. The BSF and state police had done an excellent job of cultivating local contacts and intelligence. These contacts were shared and passed onto the army.

14 Guards was stationed at Agartala, which was strategically an important town for India. Just 9 kms away from Agartala across the border was the Akhaura–Brahmanbaria area of East Pakistan. Brahmanbaria, a historical city, is one of the oldest municipalities in Bangladesh. Along with Comilla, Brahmanbaria also falls in Chittagong sector of eastern Bangladesh.

Agartala and Akhaura are on either side of the border, about 9 kms apart. Once you reach Akhaura in Bangladesh, the next important town, 22 kms away, is Brahmanbaria, and it further takes about 3-4 hours to cover 110 kms to Dhaka. The area was of mutual interest between us and the enemy.

On the Indian side, Agartala airfield was close to the border and was under fire from the enemy. India's IV Corps had considerable presence in Agartala. Pakistan Army could predict that India would launch its main attack in the east along the Gangasagar–Akhaura Upazila–Brahmanbaria axis, so Pakistanis moved their 27th brigade from Mymensingh to Akhaura, leaving only two battalions behind. Akhaura was an important rail junction and the Pakistanis had planned its defences immaculately. The fortifications were mainly along River Titas, which was on the west of the town. Some 4 kms south of Akhaura was Gangasagar station and village.

The army knew that an armed engagement was almost inevitable. East Bengal's Akhaura–Brahmanbaria sector right next to Agartala border was identified as one of the major thrust areas for IV Corps to press forward into Bangladesh. Further, security of Agartala as well as its airfield was vital to the strategic objectives of India. Agartala's airfield was in the range of Pakistan firing, but it was extremely important for supplies and logistics of Indian forces. On 1st December, 14 Guards was instructed to deploy itself and maintain a defensive line on the Agartala (Tripura) border facing East Pakistan, now known as Bangladesh. The troops were immediately moved to the border and the order regarding the defensive formation was complied with urgently. However, simultaneously, a top-secret plan was in motion: Orders were issued regarding infiltration of the enemy defences and taking control of the townships of Gangasagar and Akhaura. 57 Mountain Division, commanded by GOC Major General Ben Gonsalves, was tasked for the same. To accomplish this objective, a plan was devised wherein 73 Mountain Brigade, under Brigadier Tuli, was to capture Gangasagar while Brigadier Misra's 311 Mountain Brigade was to overrun enemy lines in Akhaura to the north.

IV Corps' plan was to be executed in four phases. Phase I was to capture Gangasagar, Phase II was to capture Akhaura, Phase III was to contain Brahmanbaria, Phase IV was to capture Daudakandi. Akhaura to Daudakandi was about 87 kms. From Daudakandi to Dhaka, the distance was about 60 kms. Phase I, capture of Gangasagar, was crucial to the entire plan. GOC from Pakistan was again Major General Abdul Majid Quazi, who Major General Ben Gonsalves had locked horns with in the Battle of Dhalai a month ago.

1st December 1971, Akhaura–Gangasagar Sector

Gangasagar was a small town strategically located at the crossroads between Brahmanbaria, Bhairab Bazaar, Kamalpur and the main

Akhaura Railway Station. A stronghold on this town, especially the railway station, would almost certainly ensure cutting off the enemy supply lines and delay re-enforcements from reaching their front lines. Gangasagar was just 6.5 kms west of Agartala, the capital of Tripura. The capture of Gangasagar, located 6 kms (3.7 miles) to the south of Akhaura upazila in the Brahmanbaria District, was crucial for the advancement of IV Corps. 14 Guards was tasked for this important job.

A contact told us about a deserted small hamlet of seven to eight pucca houses in Majigacha. This village was almost 3-4 kms inside the Bangladesh border.

On the evening of 1st December, 14 Guards was ready to cross into the border as soon as the sun bowed out. Indian Army logistics arrangement of trucks and jeeps were with us till the border. From the border through the BSF post, we were on our own, on foot, of course. It was too risky to travel further by regular tracks or roads, so we had to move off the track through trees and bushes. Enemy guns would have blown us away to bits. We intended to reach Majigacha by walking through the bushes. Winter had set in. The moon was in full bloom. As we started walking, we got the cover of clouds.

Our local guide was walking in front. We followed about 300 yards behind him. A lot of ammunition and other baggage was on mules and ponies, who are the most dependable companions of the army. From times immemorial, these unaptly called 'beasts of burden' have been the most reliable cohorts of many an army, in victory or defeat, in charge or in retreat. They have transported innumerable times both guns and gunners, rations and munitions, whenever needed.

However, a point came when the ponies refused to enter the pond of water, as it was about four feet deep. We had no option but to relieve them of their burden, as we waded into the water by ourselves. Nature was with us as mild fog began to set in. It was enough to obliterate our silhouettes.

As we walked in rank and file behind the spirited guide like a serpent, negotiating the turns, troughs and thorny bushes, the sheer grit of the man leading us for the unquestioned love of his motherland was not lost on us. As the guide moved forward and signalled us to follow, it was becoming clear that with every passing minute, deep into that foggy winter night, the enemy was drifting into careless slumber, oblivious of the hiss, venom and death creeping towards it.

It was a circuitous route to the desolate village. To my young readers, I reiterate that training never goes to waste. It prepares you for the surprises, and I had been through rigorous commando courses and also served the 9 Para Commando Unit. So were many of my illustrious colleagues, walking on unfamiliar terrain. The serpentine line kept moving. The eerie silence of that unusually quiet hamlet could be shattered by bullets and blood if the enemy came to know. Yes, training does help you a lot, but each actual situation in life or war is unique. No training can accurately predict as well as prepare you completely for the encounters that you face. It is your tenacity and resolve that makes you a winner, whether in life or in death, on battlefront or in civilian life. The war ultimately boils down to the manoeuvres of the men at the front lines.

After negotiating many twists and turns in and around the said area, we reached our destination—the deserted village of Majigacha—just before midnight. There was not a soul in the tiny hamlet; even stray animals had deserted it. The Pakistan Army's brutal repression had ensured that entire Bangladesh was littered with hundreds of ghost inhabitations where people had either fled in terror or were exterminated in cold blood. In Majigacha, we occupied the dilapidated rooms, and they became our makeshift headquarters for Operation Gangasagar. Our guide brought in another local man. He was to be our local guide from Majigacha to Gangasagar Railway Station.

In a lighter vein, young readers might argue that today we have Google maps to guide us, but in all times to come, such war games of nerve will not be controlled by meek geeky 'mouses' but by braveheart tigers who don't blink when faced with a challenge.

Decades later, when I visited Gangasagar in 2012 during my visit to Dhaka, to receive the award, 'Friends of Liberation War Honour,' by the Hon. Prime Minister, Sheikh Hasina, there was a buzz in town. An old man walked up to me, his eyes lighting up. He seemed to have been overcome with emotion. "Do you recognise me?" the frail man asked.

It was almost half a century ago in a dilapidated house of Majigacha when I flashed my torch on to the faces of my local guides. I marvelled at the bravery of the men who seemed to have lost the fear of death. They were risking their lives for their motherland and mother tongue. Without any material consideration, these were amongst thousands of nameless, faceless, impoverished semi-literate warriors who were challenging a powerful army that prided itself on technical, tactical, training, weapons… and last but not the least, racial superiority. For these semi-clad warriors, it was just their country and community. I never forgot the fire in the eyes of the guide who took us to Gangasagar station in the wee hours of the night. It may not be difficult for an ex-9 Para commando who has seen wars and death from close quarters to conceal his emotions. But that day I was overwhelmed as I hugged that man. His eyes had given him away. A young Major had flashed his torch on his face half a century ago.

We had to plan our next move quickly, there was hardly any time to sleep or eat. Time was running out. A select team was mobilised to form a reconnaissance party. The team comprised of Captain O P Kohli, Second Lieutenant Malhi, Hav. Girdhari, Lance Naik D N Das and Lance Naik Dara Singh (Radio Operator) and myself, as Major commanding the Alpha Company. Malhi was a strapping Jat Sikh who was with the intelligence office of the CO. His inputs were vital to formulation of any alternative plan. Captain Kohli like me hailed from West Punjab (Later Pakistan) and settled in Delhi. Hav. Girdhari was from Rajasthan, Lance Naik D N Das was from Orissa. The aim of the team was to assimilate ground intelligence and any visible signs of weakness in the enemy defences to consolidate the assault plan.

2nd December, 5:30 am—Majigacha to Gangasagar and back

The recce party set out a few moments before the first light on the morning of the 2nd. Winters had set in, and we were wearing woollen jerseys except for our guide, who was in a *lungi* and a thin white cotton cloth wrapped around his shoulders. He was a couple of yards ahead of us. He moved cautiously to spot any danger ahead and forewarn us if needed. There were areas where we had to wait for his signal to follow. We reached a place from where we could keep a close watch on the enemy line defences.

It soon became clear that the enemy was well-dug-in and had strengthened their defensive perimeter by extensively mining the area around the township, especially around the station. The railway station stood on a high ground along with some built-up area adjoining it. It was the centre of the enemy's defences. Adjacent to the station was a pond. The enemy was well-entrenched in concrete bunkers. The surrounding area, paddy fields, and marshes were heavily mined with anti-personnel and anti-tank mines. Other main defences were also extensively wired. It was apparent that the railway station area was very well-protected. But orders were firm and clear, we had to take Gangasagar, and the clock was ticking away furiously.

As I locked eyes with the binoculars and focussed on the enemy lines, none of us knew that this decrepit station of a sleepy village would be witness to one of the fiercest battles of the 1971 War. This battle would earn 14 Guards the highest war time gallantry award, the Param Vir Chakra, the third highest gallantry award, a Vir Chakra, and many other awards. This PVC would be the only one to be awarded in the Bangladesh campaign.

We were contemplating alternatives as we kept watch over the station from a distance. We came to know that the station had hardly any travellers or trains ever since the Pakistan Army had dug in. The enemy did not know at that point in time that both the angels of death and valour would visit Gangasagar station that very night and immortalise it.

As we focused our vision for one last time before returning, there was some noise on the tracks leading to the station. A bunch of Pakistani troops were pushing a rail-wagon over the tracks. To a civilian, it may be a routine move by the entrenched troops in the station. We watched them with bated breath. My stint with the 9 Para commando training came in handy. Something was amiss. It struck me that area between the tracks was not mined, and should be a strong contender for a possible breach-point and line of attack. We could reach the objective by walking along the railway tracks in a file without the fear of mines instead of charging head on. As we locked our eyes in the early morning pale light, there was no need to speak the evident. The alternative was before us. The morning activity in the enemy camp had started with full vigour. It was time to go back to the base.

Back at our makeshift headquarters at Majigacha, we assembled in the room of the commanding officer, Lieutenant Colonel V. N. Channa. A map of the area and the objective was hurriedly drawn on wax paper. We pondered over the idea of attacking the enemy in a single file. There was risk in approaching the enemy in a single file, walking along the track. In spite of the underlying risks, we were confident about feasibility of the plan and achieving success with minimal loss of life and equipment. Our CO pondered over the plan and almost dropped it for being highly unconventional. The plan was against known military norms and conventions, and absolutely contrary to the original plan. All of us at the operational level, especially Captain Kohli, myself, and strongly supported by Bn 2IC, Major P P Kshatriya persisted to go with the alternative plan. 14 Guards had been lucky with their adventures, as there were hardly any casualties until then. CO was finally convinced and came on board once he realised that the unconventional approach could minimise losses, but he was still hesitant and wanted to take the assent of higher command.

He reluctantly spoke to the higher level of command in chain. The plan was now relayed upwards at the brigade and division levels. This highly unconventional proposal was against all known military norms and conventions and was met with much apprehension at the higher levels, too. Finally, both Major General Ben Gonsalves and Brigadier Tuli were in the loop. At one point, we thought that the approvals would not come through.

The plan was risky and off beat. It was felt at the senior levels to have recce by another group. Another party was sent again in the evening to recheck the claims of the morning party. I ventured out again to have a look at the objective, accompanied by the new group. The evening recce allowed me to firm up the attack plan and direction of movement. We watched the enemy lines from a distance. I firmed up the plan for my company in my mind.

As we were walking back again behind the local guide, fog appeared in the sky. The sun's chariot had departed from the Bangladesh skies, leaving behind a maroon trail blazing in darkness.

In an almost unheard-of turn of events, the command obliged to the aggressive enthusiasm, determination and the confidence shown by the company commanders as well as pitch by the CO. They gave their consent for the battalion to go into full battle readiness and execute their plans to capture the objective—Gangasagar railway station and town. There was happiness in the ranks and we got busy in planning the attack. It was going to be a long day and a longer night. Alpha Coy, was to move along the tracks and on the right plank to attack the station. The Bravo Coy was to move on the left flank.

A premeditated assault was formulated:

- Alpha Company, under leadership of Major Ashok Tara, was to spearhead the attack over the railway tracks and take control of the railway station.
- Bravo Company, led by Captain O. P. Kohli and Lance Naik Albert Ekka, was to move west and clear the built-up area around the pond for dominance on the enemy bunkers.
- Delta Company, led by Major S. K. Kundu and company officer Lieutenant Bisla, was to move towards the Triangle—Mogra to secure a diversion move area around the station.
- Charlie Company, led by Major Balwant Rao with his company officer, Captain Ram Kumar, was in reserve with the commanding officer and was to move in for mop-up operations, if required.

Two companies were to launch an assault on Gangasagar Railway Station, while one company was to undertake the diversion move to secure and capture water pond complex. Though there was danger everywhere but the task for Alpha and Bravo companies was fraught with extreme risk and full of potentially fatal challenges. But that night the journey was magical. Everybody wanted to reach the station, knowing fully well that it may be the last time they would be visiting it. The planning had been meticulous; now it was over to execution.

On 3rd December, when most of the subcontinent was in deep slumber, some men in a remote East Bengal village were putting on war paint, checking their armour and pulling up their shoes. Friends, the devil of sleep is fiercest between two and four in the morning; your reason has to be extremely potent to keep you awake at that time. When 14 Guards operational group huddled together for the final briefing at 8 p.m. on 2nd December, there was a slight nip in the air. Around 3 a.m. on 3rd December, both the companies left Majigacha base camp for Gangasagar and followed the guide. He and I were venturing towards the Gangasagar railway-station for the third time in 24 hours.

We walked along the bundh in the paddy fields and marshy area, and reached the railway lines. From there, we started moving along the tracks in a single file, under the blanket of moderate fog. The plan was simple: pussyfooting to the prey's den while encountering minimal obstacles, and then springing a surprise. I could sense the enthusiasm of my men as I led them in the line. Right from my sporting as well as 9th para commando days, I loved leading from the front, leading by example, troubleshooting and playing a captain's knock when needed.

There was pitch darkness in the village. As we walked along the tracks, every step forward pumped up our adrenaline. Both companies were getting closer to their objective. Any wrong move or noise could have MMGs roaring at us. But step by step, we closed in on our quarry. Months of planning, mining, trenches, fencing and hard work put in by the Pakistani troops lay waste as we had reached the station walking along the tracks, with no stops in between. Our strategy had worked; we had reached our destination without any major obstacles except for some *punjis* and low-lying wire hurdles. There were two rooms in the railway station adjacent to each other, and concrete bunkers next to it. A building was behind them. We would soon face the blaze of the enemy's powerful MMGs.

Alpha Company steadily moved close to the first MMG bunker on the eastern side of the railway line. One of our men stepped on something, and it created a small sound. The silence was suddenly broken when an enemy soldier from within harked in a sleepy voice '*Koun hai utthe*?' (Who's there?) Subedar Hoshiyar Singh, the irrepressible Haryanvi Jat, was standing near to the door. He yelled back, '*Dekh Kaun Hai*.' (See yourself.) The enemy soldiers were quick to fathom that the Indian Army was breathing down their neck and almost instantaneously, all hell broke loose—the enemy opened fire. Hoshiyar Singh was critically wounded. We were all exposed and the enemy was entrenched in a bunker with a flashing MMG. As I saw Hoshiyar falling down, in a split second, I threw a Molotov cocktail followed by a hand-grenade into the bunker to subdue enemy offensive and prevent further casualties. Before the enemy soldiers could recover from the impact of the twin blasts, I grabbed the blistering barrel of the MMG and pulled it out from within the dugout. This move of mine had the enemy troops reeling in the bunker. I saw two panic-stricken soldiers who had survived the blasts running in sheer disarray. I and the jawans next to me aimed a rapid burst of our automatic weapons on the enemy soldiers. The Pakistani soldier closer to me took a volley of shots and slumped. As the corpse slumped and fell over, I got the second one, too, before he could either get me or escape. We had secured the position and silenced the gun and, sadly, the gunners forever. What started as a silent attack by us gave a not-so-silent heart attack to the enemy.

Parallelly, Bravo Company under Capt. O.P. Kohli had moved closer to the enemy lines next to the pond. The firing involving us at the first bunker had alerted the enemy. Bravo Company unfortunately lost the element of surprise. They came under heavy fire. The company pressed forward regardless of the odds. They upheld the assault and attacked with grit and determination under Capt. Kohli. In the ensuing epic battle, Lance Naik Albert Ekka was fatally wounded, yet he gathered all his courage to move close enough to destroy an MMG bunker on a two-storied fortified building that was causing heavy casualties on Indian troops and held up further advance. It was here that Albert Ekka silenced the MMG. He would create history after displaying remarkable heroics in a hand-to-hand contest. Unfortunately, he succumbed to the injuries with his boots on. He was conferred with Param Vir Chakra, posthumously.

BRAVEHEARTS OF 14 GUARDS

L/NK ALBERT EKKA, PVC(P)

Lt Col (Retd Brig)
VIJAY NARAYAN CHANNA,VSM
COMMANDING OFFICER

Maj (Retd Col)
PREM PRATAP SINGH
KSHATTRIYA
SECOND IN COMMAND

Maj (Retd Col) ASHOK KUMAR TARA,
VIR CHAKRA AND FRIENDS OF
LIBERATION WAR HONOUR -1971
BY BANGLADESH

Maj (Retd Col)
OM PRAKASH KOHLI,
SM

Maj (Retd Col)
BALWANT RAO

Maj (Retd Col)
SAJJAN KUMAR KUNDU

Maj (Retd Col)
SHANTI SWAROOP KHANNA

Capt (Retd Col)
NARENDRA BIR MANSINGH

Capt (Retd Col)
SURJIT SINGH

Capt (Retd Maj Gen)
HARA GOPAL MUKHOPADHYAY,SM

Capt (Retd Col)
KUTTAN MAHADEVAN,SM

2/Lt (Retd Col)
RAM KUMAR

2/Lt (Retd Col)
MAHINDER SINGH BISLA

2/Lt (Retd Col)
PARAMJIT SINGH MALLHI

2/Lt (Retd Col)
RATAN SINGH TANWAR

2/Lt (Retd Col)
NARENDRA SINGH

WILL ALWAYS LIVE WITH HONOUR

There was fierce resistance from the enemy. Alpha & Bravo company moved from one bunker to another, from one building to another. 14 Guards went about clearing the enemy lines—bunker to bunker. Hoshiyar Singh survived the battle and his wounds, to tell the tale to his grandchildren.

Gangasagar was a very difficult operation. There were blazing guns and fire everywhere. The core of this heavily fortified area would be around 2,000 sq. yards, while the entire area of operation was about a square mile. Complete control of the railway station, which stood at the heart of the core area, necessitated a bloody contest in close proximity with a determined enemy. Quite predictably, these close quarter duels, in many an instance, involved hand-to-hand engagement. 14 Guards kept on pressing forward despite deaths and injuries until they were victorious.

As Pakistani soldiers retreated, they resorted to Arty. SOS fire. SOS fire, in such instances, means 'save our souls' fire. This means that a retreating army continues the fire to stop the enemy from hot pursuit, even if it means hitting and sacrificing their own men. Both Indian and Pakistani soldiers died in this SOS fire. The ferocity of the Indian attack was so much that the enemy either abandoned

Ekka's statue at Param Yodha Sthal, National War Memorial, New Delhi.

its positions or was exterminated. The entire town was completely run over by Indian troops in the next couple of hours. The battalion captured a large quantity of arms, six prisoners, and also captured a flag of Pakistan's 14 Infantry Division. Our own casualties were 9 killed and 30 wounded, including one officer and three JCOs.

As the first light of the day illuminated Gangasagar, 14 Guards had extinguished all major enemy resistance, though some pockets of it were still there. A near impossible mission was accomplished and the bravery of 14 Guards of the Indian Army was at its finest display that turned the tide of the battle in their favour. During the reorganisation of defences at Gangasagar, then Lieutenant M S Bisla came with ten *jawans* to reinforce and deployed them at a small rail bridge to Akhaura. We had lost nine of our bravehearts including Albert Ekka. The wounded soldiers and the mortal remains of the martyrs were evacuated to our base camp in Agartala for prompt treatment and last rites.

The battle heroics of 14 Guards in this rare and unconventional piece of warfare was recognised by the Indian Army and the nation. Lance Naik Albert Ekka was decorated with the coveted Param Vir Chakra (PVC) posthumously. I was decorated with the Vir Chakra. Captain O. P. Kohli along with three others received the prestigious Sena Medal. After the war, 14 Guards was conferred with 'Battle Honour of Gangasagar'.

Victory in Gangasagar on the very first day of the commencement of the formal war was strategically of immense importance as it not only pre-empted any advance of Pakistani forces towards Agartala but also opened up the entire Eastern front of Bangladesh to Indian Army's IV Corps for its onwards march inside the enemy-held territory. The fall of Gangasagar threatened the rear of the Pakistani formation and later, Akhaura was vacated, too. Once Gangasagar was secured, we marched along with the railway tracks to Akhaura and then to Brahmanbaria. Our boots were destined to be unstoppable till Dhaka.

Memories of another era transported me back in time when I stood in front of the Gangasagar battle plaque in the National War Museum at India Gate. I wish to recall and share some of the valiant names of that glorious epic battle. As I stood in front of the bust of Albert Ekka at the War Memorial, I remember him as a man of few words, extremely energetic, and willing to take up even the most difficult of tasks and accomplish them with consummate ease. Albert Ekka was born on 27th December 1942, into an Oraon tribal family in Zari Village, modern-day Jharkhand. Growing up hunting with his bow and arrow, he developed a natural flair for sports. At the age of 20, he enlisted in the Bihar Regiment. In 1968, he was transferred to the 14 Guards. He gave his life for his country and brought glory to his Unit. Albert Ekka and all the other martyrs were given final farewell as per their traditional rites in Agartala. There is also a fitting memorial for Albert Ekka in Pratapgarh.

Official Citation for Albert Ekka's Param Vir Chakra

Lance Naik Albert Ekka was in the left forward company of a battalion of the Brigade of The Guards during their attack on the enemy defences at Gangasagar on the Eastern front. This was a well-fortified position held in strength by the enemy. The assaulting troops were subjected to intense shelling and heavy small arms fire, but they charged onto the objective and were locked in bitter hand-to-hand combat. Lance Naik Albert Ekka noticed an enemy light machine gun (LMG) inflicting heavy casualties on his company. With complete disregard for his personal safety, he charged the enemy bunker, bayoneted two enemy soldiers and silenced the LMG. Though seriously wounded in this encounter, he continued to fight alongside his comrades through the mile-deep objective, clearing bunker after bunker with undaunted courage. Towards the northern end of the objective, one enemy medium machine gun (MMG) opened up from the second storey of a well-fortified building inflicting heavy casualties and holding up the attack. Once again, this gallant soldier, without a thought for his personal safety, despite his serious injury and the heavy volume of enemy fire, crawled forward till he reached the building and lobbed a grenade into the bunker, killing one enemy soldier and injuring the other. The

MMG, however, continued to fire. With outstanding courage and determination Lance Naik Albert Ekka scaled a side wall and entering the bunker, bayoneted the enemy soldier who was still firing and thus silenced the machine gun, saving further casualties to his company and ensuring the success of the attack. In this process, however, he received serious injuries and succumbed to them after the capture of the objective. In this action, Lance Naik Albert Ekka displayed the most conspicuous valour and determination and made the supreme sacrifice in the best traditions of the army.

Citation for the Vir Chakra

The valour of Major Ashok Kumar Tara

Major Ashok Kumar Tara was commanding a Forward Company (Alpha) and was advancing along the railway line in the Eastern sector. The Coy was subjected to heavy automatic fire by the enemy who also used the artillery very effectively. With complete disregard for his safety, Major Ashok Kumar Tara, the right forward company commander took the lead in the Battle of Gangasagar. He crawled up to the leading medium machine gun (MMG) position of the enemy and in a flash threw the improvised Molotov cocktail and a grenade into the bunker and pulled out the MMG. The daring act of the officer so inspired the company that they assaulted the enemy with great determination. Major Ashok Kumar Tara, though wounded, continued to lead the assault till the position was captured.

In this action, Major Ashok Kumar Tara displayed courage, determination and leadership of a high order.

He was conferred with ‘Vir Chakra’ for this gallant act.

Awardees of the Battle of Gangasagar

- Lance Naik Albert Ekka, PVC (posthumously), Leading Section Commander, Bravo Company
- Major (Retd. Colonel) Ashok Kumar Tara, VrC, Company Commander, Alfa Company

- Captain (Retd. Colonel) O.P. Kohli, SM, Company Commander, Bravo Company
- Captain (Retd. Major General) M. G. Mukhopadhyay, SM (Regiment Medical Officer)
- Captain (Retd. Lt Colonel) K. Mahadevan, SM (Artillery Observation Firing Officer)
- Lance Naik (Retd. Havildar) Tilak Raj, SM (Detachment Commander of Recoilless Gun Section)

Other officers in the Battle of Gangasagar

- Lieutenant Colonel (Retd. Brigadier) V. N. Channa, Battalion Commander
- Major (Retd. Colonel) P. P. S. Kshatriya, Battalion 2nd in Command
- Major (Retd. Colonel) S. K. Kundu, Company Commander, Delta Company
- Major (Retd. Colonel) Balwant Rao, Company Commander, Charlie Company
- Major (Retd. Colonel) S. S. Khanna, Reinforcement in-charge
- Captain (Retd. Colonel) Ram Kumar, Company Officer, Charlie Company
- Captain (Retd. Colonel) Man Singh, Battalion Adjutant
- Captain (Retd. Major) Late R. S. Tanwar, Battalion Quarter Master
- Lieutenant (Retd. Colonel) M. S. Bisla, Company Officer, Delta Company
- 2/Lt (Retd. Colonel) Narinder Kumar, Company Officer Bravo Company
- 2/Lt (Posted to other Regiment) P. Malhi, Intelligence Officer

Martyrs of the Battle of Gangasagar

- Lance Naik Albert Ekka, PVC (posthumously)
- Guardsman (Gdsm) Gulab Singh.

- Gdsm Kashi Nath
- Gdsm Devid Tigga
- Gdsm Ram Deo Sahani
- Gdsm Udho Singh
- Gdsm Kesar Dev
- Gdsm Dal Singh
- Gdsm Malkiat Singh

❑

CHAPTER 12

The Triumphant March to Dacca

Do you hear the people sing?
Lost in the valley of the night
It is the music of a people
Who are climbing to the light

For the wretched of the earth
There is a flame that never dies
Even the darkest night will end
And the sun will rise.

—Finale of the musical
Les Misérables.

December 1st–17th

For the world, it was a war that lasted only 13 days, but for me it started a bit earlier and ended a couple of days later. For me, the Bangladesh action was for 17 days. A friend remarked after listening to my anecdotes, "It seems like you opened the locks and closed the doors." I told him I was only a minor component of a gigantic war machine with levers in various places, from Agartala to Calcutta to Delhi. My story of war starts from Agartala on 1st December and ends at Dhanmondi on 17th December.

1st December—Move to Majigacha from Agartala

The war started, for me, the moment we left Agartala for Majigacha in Bangladesh at the last light of 1st December 1971. It was a moon lit night. In poetic parlance, this perfect *Chaudvi ka Chand* played hide and seek to guide us and shelter us in the fog, depending on our requirements.

December 3rd–4th—Battle of Gangasagar and Forward March

In the wee hours of 3rd December, the attack along the railway lines was launched by us (14 Guards). The previous chapter talks about Battle of Gangasagar in detail.

Rail tracks crisscross the entire subcontinent, most of it through the countryside before passing through cities. Railway tracks seem to emerge from nowhere and are lost in the wilderness, seeming to be on an eternal journey, terminating at nowhere. But that winter night, the half-visible track was our marching track leading us to our goal, step by step, sleeper by sleeper, albeit sleep for the

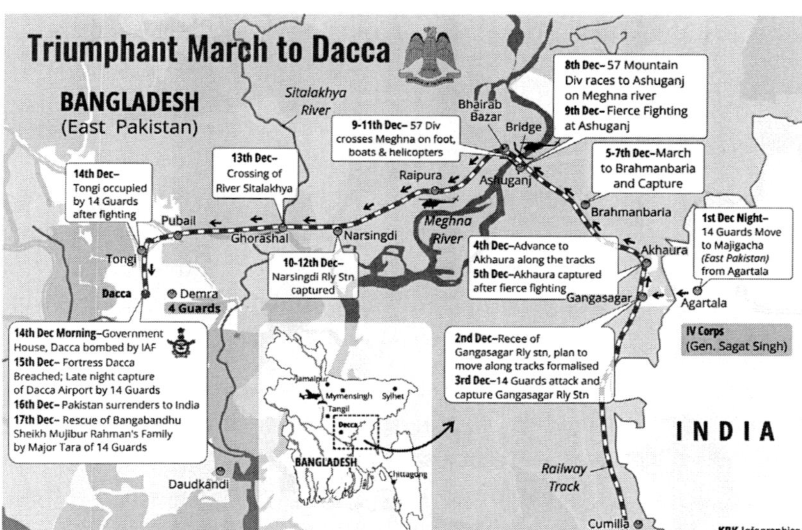

company would be a fortnight away. The innovative and unconventional Gangasagar attack along the railway tracks was the beginning of our glorious march to Dhaka. In a way, Gangasagar opened the gates to the grand arena. It was one of the toughest battles of the war and in a way set the mood, tone and tenor of the war right at the start.

On 4th December, mop-up operations were still going on in Gangasagar and other units had taken up defensive positions. However, we were ordered to march along the railway tracks to Akhaura. The mood in the company was upbeat. There were causalities, but much less than what was expected in a head-on combat. At that time, I had not reckoned that the Battle of Gangasagar would be considered as one of the fiercest battles of the war and a gamechanger. As I walked along the tracks, I remembered the fallen bravehearts. Given the level of enemy's defensive preparation and fortifications, a head-on assault as planned earlier would have ended in disaster. The offbeat plan proposed by me, along with other company commander, had worked spectacularly. Surprise in the battlefield is supreme. This surprise was primarily tactical in nature. A much bigger surprise was being readied at the IV Corps at operational level for General Niazi of Pakistan by General Sagat Singh. The railway track tactic had succeeded in Ganganagar. As we moved on the tracks to Akhaura, little did we know that the 'Track Trick' would ultimately lead us on to Dhaka.

December 4th and 5th—Battle for Akhaura

We, the 14 Guards, were approaching Akhaura from the south, as we moved on the tracks from Gangasagar Railway Station. Pakistanis had paid considerable attention to the defences of Akhaura, as it was an important railway junction. Akhaura–Brahmanbaria, a very well defended sector, was held by Pakistan's 12 FF/27 Brigade.

Akhaura proved to be a tougher nut to crack. 311 Mountain Brigade, under Brigadier Mishra, mounted and attacked as planned. The enemy defences were mainly based on River Titas, which ran west of the town. The battalions struggled against the enemy for three days, finally capturing it by the morning of 5th December.

The enemy had no chance in the end as more troops joined up with rest of the battalions from the rear of the town and 14 Guards had also moved from Gangasagar Railway Station to Akhaura along the rail tracks. Thus, Akhaura was caught in an Indian 'pincer'.

'Deception' in war is as important as 'surprise'. On the night of 4th December, as we closed in from the rear, we planned a deception move. The silencers of five-tonne trucks were removed, and they were manoeuvred in the north-east of the town. The resultant noise mimicked that of a huge number of tanks approaching the enemy position. A 'scarecrow' tactic. A roar sends all jungle animals, howsoever brave, scurrying for cover. This brilliant outmanoeuvring night-move, a faux roar, made Pakistani defenders believe that many tanks were coming to assault them. Akhaura fell on the 5th as the Pakistani garrison withdrew to Brahmanbaria.

4 Guards infiltrated the west of the Titas and found that the bridge over the river was intact. The enemy had forgotten to blow up the bridge while retreating. It is a standard practice for retreating armies to blow up bridges and other infrastructure so that the enemy in hot pursuit can be slowed down.

At this stage came the most important bit of news that was to impact the entire war.

It was reported by a patrol party that Pakistanis had removed one pair of lines of the double-track railway line leading to Brahmanbaria, and were using it as a motorable rail-cum-road track. The rail tracks and roads were not aligned. But by moving on the rail tracks, we could reach Ashuganj situated at River Meghna through Brahmanbaria swiftly. This innovative route change ultimately was to lead to a blitzkrieg-type rapid strike by IV Corps across the Meghna.

General Sagat Singh was on a helicopter spree, visiting all his battle zones. He was getting real-time inputs of the battlefront and was not afraid to take risks. The discovery of the intact bridge and the rail cum road tracks led to a change in the original plan. As per the original plan we, i.e., 57 Mountain Division under Lieutenant General Ben Gonsalves, were supposed to move towards Daudkandi, whereas 8 Mountain Division under Lieutenant General K. V. Krishna Rao was supposed to attack Brahmanbaria while coming down from

Sylhet. In a surprising move, General Sagat Singh along with his division commanders, had changed the attack line of 57 Mountain Division to north-west towards Brahmanbaria–Ashuganj axis instead of going south towards Myanamati–Daudkhandi. A ground level input had been exploited well. A battalion of EBR was left at Akhaura to contain the enemy and to look after the defences.

The next halt for us, as part of 57 Mountain Division, was Brahmanbaria, a town 14 kms north-west of Akhaura. Brahmanbaria had a strong natural defence as it lay in a loop of River Titas, and accordingly, the Pakistanis had developed it into a strongpoint.

December 5th–7th—March to Brahmanbaria and Capture

On 5th December, forward elements of 311 Mountain Brigade advanced towards Brahmanbaria followed by the 73rd Brigade, of which my unit, 14 Guards was a part. Major Marwah of 4 Guards with his company and Bn. HQ with the rest of the unit (4 Guards) under Major Chandrakant with a Squadron of armour moved ahead to Sultanpur (a suburb in Brahmanbaria). Later, upon the orders of GOC, General Ben Gonsalves, the unit moved to Brahmanbaria on the river of Pagla. Meanwhile, 73 Mountain Brigade was tasked to capture Brahmanbaria, while 311 Mountain Brigade secured the road leading to Brahmanbaria from the south. 73 Brigade pushed out two prongs: one to the town's south and another to its west.

Pakistanis were expecting the Indian move towards Ashuganj through Brahmanbaria, and it was no surprise. Pakistani troops entrenched in Brahmanbaria waited for a frontal assault by Indians from the south-east direction, however, 73 Mountain Brigade columns zeroed in from the west and south. Reacting to this manoeuvre, the Pakistanis evacuated the town, withdrawing towards Ashuganj. 73 Mountain Brigade had captured Brahmanbaria by the night of December 7th-8th, 1971.

The next objective for 57 Mountain Division was Ashuganj. It was an important town which was 13 kms to the north-west of Akhaura on the eastern bank of River Meghna. The Pakistanis were well-entrenched on both banks of the river. Ashuganj was on the eastern bank whereas Bhairab Bazaar was on the western bank. The banks were linked by a rail bridge. In case of any signs of dominance by the Indians near the eastern bank, the Pakistanis were sure to blow the bridge, thereby stalling any further advance of IV Corps. It was now a race against time. 7th and 8th December were very important days in terms of the next moves.

Lessons learned from the Sylhet heli-operation paved way for the next mega heli-operation 120 kms away in the Meghna–Ashuganj–Brahmanbaria sector two days later on 9th December. In the rapidly evolving battlefield, while the Liberation Forces were plotting, changing strategies, realigning, rescheduling based on events happening moment to moment, the Pakistani command was mostly unimaginative and was being manipulated to react to the moves of their adversary.

In his autobiography, Major General J. F. R. Jacob mentions interrogating the Pakistani GOC of the Sylhet–Brahmanbaria sector, GOC Abdul Mujeeb Quazi, regarding movement of the Maulvi Bazaar Brigade to Sylhet instead of moving to the Coronation Bridge over Meghna. Gen Quazi replied that they were determined not to surrender 'fortress Sylhet'. This unimaginative thinking coupled with Niazi's obsession with the fortress concept ensured that two Pakistani brigades were cut off from the centre of gravity, Dacca. This miscalculation was one of the factors which hastened the march of IV Corps across Meghna. In complete contrast to the Pakistan Army, the Indian side was quick to seize opportunities that came up and took calculated risks. The leadership styles were absolutely different for both the armies. (*For my young reader, there are some very important management lessons to be learnt here, especially regarding leadership styles.)*

8th December—Race to Ashuganj and Saving the Bridge on Meghna

Next stop was at Ashuganj, an important river port and industrial city on River Meghna. During the Liberation War, the Pakistan Army used to torture and kill suspected Bengali rebels at a place near Ashuganj Silo. Ashuganj is also called the daughter of River Meghna.

From Akhaura, the railway line went north-west towards Ashuganj and a railway bridge crossed Meghna. Once the mighty river was crossed, there would be no stopping. But there were three problems. One, to contain the enemy at Ashuganj, the other to cross Meghna, and third, to contain the enemy at Bhairab Bazaar once Meghna was crossed. The division had to reach the railway bridge before the enemy could blow it up. Major General Gonsalves ordered 311 Mountain Brigade to take up the pursuit of the enemy on the morning of 8th December. However, the build-up of the division at Brahmanbaria was not fast enough due to logistical problems. Bridges on route were either damaged by the enemy or not strong enough for rapid movement of vehicles and other equipment. A quick advance till Ashuganj by 311/73 Mountain Brigade, 57 Mountain Division could be possible only without any artillery support. The easy fall of Brahmanbaria showed demoralisation, confusion and disorganisation in the Pakistani rank and file. A calculated risk was taken to press forward to Ashuganj without artillery support. PT-76 tanks were dispatched for support. By 8th December, the Pakistani defences in the Eastern sector had almost collapsed. The brigade group at Laksham had disintegrated and almost 1,000 POWs were taken. Now, only the mighty River Meghna remained between Indian Army IV Corps and the road to Dacca.

The situation on the east bank of Meghna on 8th December was summed up by Major General D. K. Palit

"By the 8th, the fifth day of the war, Brahmanbaria had fallen, Comilla was encircled and the Laksham column was heading for Chandpur. The whole of sector opposite Tripura came under Indian control, while in the south—where the Feni salient had already been liberated before the commencement of the war—a column from the southern division raced for Chittagong."

Major General Sukhwant Singh writes,

"By 8th December, the Indians had reached all three river ports and key ports of communications along the Meghna at Chandpur, Daudkhandi and Ashuganj and had secured the vital Meghna bulge. All roads to Dacca from the east now lay open."

River Meghna as a Barrier to Dacca

Meghna is one of the largest rivers in Bangladesh, one of the three that form the Delta Ganga, and the only way to cross it was the Ashuganj railway bridge. This was the only bridge available across the huge river. It was heavily fortified, the Pakistan Army having dug in.

This was when Sagat Singh came up with the idea of airlifting the troops along with Major General B. F. Gonsalves. While General Sagat Singh was a paratrooper, Major General Gonsalves was himself a pilot. They, along with Group Captain Chandan Singh of IAF, explored the feasibility of airlifting troops across Meghna. 9th December was a day of major action. On one hand, plans were afoot to cross Meghna, and secondly there was fierce fighting in Ashuganj. Both instances are described as under.

9th December—Fierce Fighting at Ashuganj and race to Meghna Bridge

4 Guards kept on advancing under the worst conditions, i.e., marshy and broken areas. They captured the towns of Ashuganj and Talashar after little resistance from the enemy, about 20 km away, on the east bank of River Meghna.

After the fall of Brahmanbaria, the Indian troops, led by 311 Mountain Brigade of 57 Division, pursued the enemy who were now withdrawing to Ashuganj. As the enemy had evacuated its strongholds like Akhaura and Brahmanbaria in haste, no serious opposition was anticipated at Ashuganj, too. Further, sensing disorientation in the enemy ranks, heliborne operation to cross River Meghna was conceived to outmanoeuvre them. Accordingly, 4 Guards moved out from Ashuganj to Brahmanbaria for heliborne operation while 18 Rajput moved towards occupying Ashuganj with the assumption that Pakistan Army had left. This assumption was to prove costly.

The Pakistanis, however, had the time to reorganise themselves. They were well dug-in at Ashuganj by the time the leading elements of 311 Mountain Brigade with 18 Rajput got there on the night of December 8th–9th.

Pakistani 27th Brigade let the 18 Rajput reach within 50 yards of Ashuganj thermal power plant and launched a heavy attack on them. Taken by surprise, the 18 Rajput suffered heavy casualties and loss of equipment (120 men and 4 tanks). The CO blamed his seniors for leaving his unit alone to tackle the opposition from Pakistan Army, and that too without artillery support. Moreover, other Indian troops present just 2 km away also did not come to help extricate the Rajputs from the difficult situation they found themselves in. Later, 10 Bihar also arrived from the north but both the battalions had to fall back.

Pakistani HQ 14 Infantry Division, looking at the Indian build-up, started withdrawing to Bhairab Bazaar. In a premature action, the Pakistani divisional commander ordered troops from Bhairab Bazaar on the west bank of Meghna to blow up two spans of the Ashuganj railway bridge with a dynamite explosion. This resulted in Pakistan's 27th Brigade and its commander being stranded on the eastern side with Indians closing in fast. It was later learned that this incensed General Niazi so much that he sacked the Divisional Commander. However, Pakistani 27th Brigade successfully crossed over to Bhairab Bazaar side using country boats during the night of December 9th-10th. Pakistan's 27th Brigade had its moment of glory, but overall, with every passing moment, the situation was turning grim for their side.

Crossing the mighty River Meghna—a turning point

Jal—Thal—Aakash

Chol Chol Chol
Urddho gagane baaje madol
Nimney utola dharonee-tol
Aruno praater toruno dol
Chol re Chol re Chol
Chol Chol Chol.

—Kazi Nazrul Islam,
'*Notuner Gaan*'

March, March, March
By a drum beat to a heavenly height

The Triumphant March to Dacca

From earth beneath and soil's blight
Youth rise in the dawn's light,
Left, now, now, right!
March, March, March

—Translation by Kabir Chowdhry, 'Song of the Youth'

December 9th–11th—River Meghna bridges the gap

Crossing of the Meghna during the 1971 War is part of military folklore and is comparable to the lightning campaigns in the annals of world military history, especially the famed 'Deep operations' by Russians in World War II. It was one of the greatest logistical feats, and perhaps the first time in military history, that a brigade group crossed a major river through an air bridge—a remarkable combination of military ingenuity and daredevilry. Meghna was more than a mile wide at many places with rapid and massive flow. Any attempt to reach Dacca would require crossing this river. The mobility of IV Corps was greatly enhanced by the intelligent and effective use of helicopters in the riverine terrain. This was the first ever heliborne army air bridge operation known up till then. IV Corps had 11–13 helicopters mainly from units 105, 110 and 111 operating an ageing fleet of Mi-4s.

An amazing and daring feat

On 9th December, both 73 and 311 brigades under Major General Gonsalves were ordered to cross Meghna. 73 Mountain Brigade was to cross either through rivercraft or on foot on the remnants of the damaged rail bridge, while 311 was mostly heli-lifted. Thus, all three modes of transportation were used to cross Meghna—by helicopter, by rivercraft, and on foot. The speed, of course, varied in each case. Crossing the Meghna was not tasked to IV Corps as per the original plan. The move could have boomeranged, but war, nevertheless, is risky and is all about taking risks—calculated, measured, intelligent, and intelligence-based. It was the brainchild of Lieutenant General Sagat Singh and supported by Group Captain Chandan Singh (later Air Vice Marshal). They, along with Major General Gonsalves, get the credit for this unconventional move.

This operation was planned and executed against some reservations from Higher HQ. IV Corps was supposed to capture the area only up to Meghna and not cross it. The top brass at Fort William took notice of this deviation. General J. S. Aurora flew down to Agartala to be with General Sagat Singh. However, he relented when he saw the situation on ground. In a typical cricket parlance, the game had moved from the 'slog overs' and entered an adrenaline-pumping, high risk, high stakes, hard-hitting fast pace.

57 Division of IV Corps were now unstoppable. They were planning to spring a surprise not only for the enemy but had managed to surprise, to some extent, their own headquarters.

Lieutenant General Sagat Singh and Major General Gonsalves had out-witted and out-foxed Major General Quazi and Lieutenant General Niazi by crossing the Meghna.

Heli Bridge

This was a risky move as the airlifted troops had no artillery support. They could have been open to fire from the enemy upon landing in their territory. Brigadier Commander Mishra and Lieutenant Colonel Himmat Singh, Commanding Officers of 4 Guards, had reconnoitred earlier for possible crossing places at Meghna. A landing zone was chosen near Raipura, about 15 kms south-west of Bhairab Bazaar, where minimal opposition from the enemy was expected.

At about 9 a.m., 4 Guards of 311 Mountain Brigade was ordered to move to Brahmanbaria, and the unit reached by 1 p.m. Precisely at 4 p.m., four helicopters (MI-4) carrying a platoon of approximately 30 men plus some Mukti Bahini boys forming a sortie, took off simultaneously, after taxiing at short distances. Lieutenant Colonel Himmat Singh and Major Chandrakant were in the first helicopter. The pilot of the Squadron Commander of 110HU was under the command of Squadron Leader C S Sandhu.

Lieutenant Colonel Himmat Singh and Group Captain Chandan Singh had already carried out a recce of the landing zone. As soon as the helicopters were airborne, two Gnat Fighter Flying CAP (combat air patrol) joined them. It was evening and the sun was about to set. Within 15 minutes, they were hovering over Raipura after crossing Meghna, and landed at their designated LZ (landing zone).

Though the LZ was marked, the helicopters had to hover several feet above the ground because of uneven and marshy land, and troops had to jump out of the helicopters. For night-time landings, helipads were marked by torches with their reflectors removed.

Immediately, a recce party was sent under Major Chandrakant of 4 Guards to move to Methikhando Railway Station, which was reported to be defended by a platoon of paramilitary. There were no Pakistani troops. Instead, there were local Bengalis to receive them warmly. After hearing the noise of the helicopters and the crowd shouting *Jai Bangla* and *Jai Hind*, Pakistani troops in the vicinity withdrew to safety in haste.

Brahmanbaria was the base for heli-lifting that began during the afternoon of 9th December; it continued during the night till the moon set. The total number of Mi-4 helicopters in the fleet were 14, of which about 11–12 were used. In 36 hours, 110 sorties were flown, airlifting the entire 311 Mountain Brigade. MI-4 choppers could normally carry only 14 or 10 soldiers with equipment and weapons. That day, they carried as many as 23 per sortie. Around 600 troops were first airlifted on the night of December 9 to Raipura. Resistance from Pakistani forces was contained with support from IAF. Post-World War II, it was one of the largest airlifting of troops.

Steamers and country boats

73 Mountain Brigade moved across Meghna on boats and riverine crafts. 73 Mountain Brigade and 57 Mountain Division started crossing it in country boats south of Bhairab Bazaar and contained the Pakistani deployment there.

Hundreds of villagers were there to help with boats and rafts. Everybody pitched in —villagers, Jodhas, children, men and women. Rivercraft of all sizes available around the area were pressed into our service. Several steamers from the river port of Chandpur and River Titas were brought in. The simple boatsmen went about their task of transporting us with army-like discipline. Communication barriers had broken down. Rustic Bengali was conversing freely with colloquial Punjabi, Haryanvi, Rajasthani, Tamil, Odya, and vice versa. All part of the same subcontinent. On both the banks, every conceivable mode of transportation was deployed by the locals for our movement—cycles, bullock carts, rickshaws, boats and rivercraft of all kinds. I saw many a soldier passing by hitch-hiking a ride on the cycles. The locals were peddling furiously. A tsunami was building up across Bangladesh; they had had enough. Heavy guns were bundled over cycle rickshaws. Young children were helping soldiers carry heavy equipment as if they were light hay sacks. The rides were all gratis. There was light-hearted banter over the dues to be settled the next time, which, of course, is a common thing in these parts of the world. But in this case, the service was all gratis, 'charged' only with emotions and unmistakable nationalistic fervour of the locals. None of us present there on that night would ever forget those moments. It was as if God himself was guiding the colossal effort.

Tanks Swim Despite Odds

The airlifted troops did not have artillery or armoured support. Ferrying of artillery and tanks across the Meghna posed serious difficulties. Some of the recoilless guns were carried by the troops on their shoulders as they crossed the river on the surviving span of the bridge, while most heavy artillery and equipment had to be ferried across. The entire process was time-consuming. To provide support for the heliborne troops, PT-76 tanks were told to ford River Meghna, and a problem cropped up. The Russian PT-76 tanks were amphibian tanks, which could cross rivers also. However, they were designed for European rivers, which are much milder than the rivers of the Indian subcontinent, both in terms of span and flow. The tanks had trouble crossing a mega river like Meghna, which had massive flow and span. The tanks would overheat after half an hour of 'swimming'. This required out-of-the-box thinking and ingenious solutions by army engineers. In a lighter vein, no task is impossible for Indians, especially craftsmen who are now acclaimed worldwide with the invention of the word, philosophy, and science of *'jugaad'*. The tanks moved on their power for as long as possible, and later ferried by a bevy of country boats. The mighty tanks would have wanted to lower their barrels in respect.

The enemy stationed at Bhairab Bazaar observed the massive effort of the moving troops involving helicopters, steamers, boats and tanks fording Meghna.

Walking on the Damaged Railway Bridge

Morning of 10th December—Ashuganj Railway Bridge.

Although the bridge was damaged, we were able to figure out a way wherein the troops could still cross it slowly on foot in a column. Though a tad bit risky, I set out with my boys on foot to cross the bridge. Some heavy equipment was loaded on the boats. While 9 Punjab crossed the river using country boats, 14 Guards walked mostly on the bridge.

As I walked along the tracks of the damaged bridge with my company in the early morning chill, the hiss of the light breeze caressing the iron bridge, the river song of the mighty Meghna, the rising sun rays bouncing off the river waves, the mathematical notes of the oars of boats in the river, the half-measured thuds of soldiers' boots, the sound of breath while walking—all came together to conjure up a magical symphony that probably none of us would hear ever again in our lives. The clouds kept on playing hide and seek. Occasionally, the melancholic melody would be drowned in the distant noise of wind chopping, our heartbeats mimicking the sound of the choppers flown by Group Captain Chandan Singh's boys. It was a deluge of Indian soldiers whose movement was being facilitated by highly charged, enthusiastic nameless people of all ages—kids, adolescents, and men young and old.

I had enjoyed the hardy walk. The only serious competitor to British humour in the world is that of Punjabis. Both have their unique witticisms. As I walked along the railway tracks, I chuckled to myself in my mother tongue Punjabi, "*Yaar eh lineaa da changa panga le litta, kitte dilli tak hi na turaa maran, ehna de laage laage chalde.*" (Hope this self-created mess of discovering the railway tracks does not end up in walking all the way to Delhi alongside them.) Mercifully, the trek ended at Dacca and not Delhi, as everybody was now joking. Unfortunately for the Pakistan Army, the journey from Dacca to Dograi, Lahore was going to be very long and painful.

The strong Pakistani brigade at Bhairab Bazaar stationed just 2 kms away, was seeing what the Indian Army was up to, crossing the river on helicopters, country boats, walking in columns, but they made no effort to challenge them and preferred to stay in their bunkers. The demoralisation had fully made its way into the enemy ranks. Their chances of retreating to defend the fortress of Dacca were lost till the end of the war.

By 10th December, Ashuganj was occupied and Meghna crossed. Liberation Forces were now on both east and west banks of Meghna. The demoralised enemy stayed put in their bunkers, instead of challenging us once again. Probably General Quazi had had enough of Dhalai, Gangasagar, Akhaura, and Ashuganj. As long as they were not disrupting our march to Dhaka, they were safe from us. They retreated to their bunkers to safety from other deadly dangers such as the Mukti Bahini and Indian Air Force bombers. It was now almost sure that at least the Pakistani troops in the eastern sector would not be falling back to defend the 'Dacca Bowl' or to be a part of the fortress defenders.

The psychological tactics worked perfectly. The enemy thought that the Indian Army had put up a large force across Meghna and were attacking them. GOC Major General Abdul Majid, of Pakistan 14 Division, went in to a shell from which he emerged only on 17th December to surrender to General Ben Gonsalves.

The then Secretary of Defence Govt. of India K.B. Lal had an nteresting anecdote. "On 10th December 1971, at 1 p.m., there was a meeting being held in the South Block, *chaired by Sardar Swaran Singh,* Minister of External Affairs. Attending the meeting were the Defence, Home and Foreign Secretaries, Director of the IB, and the Principal Secretary to the Prime Minister. The meeting had just commenced when the message arrived that Sagat had crossed the Meghna. Defence Minister Babu Jagjiwan Ram rushed in soon afterwards while the Prime Minister's Principal Private Secretary ran to her office to inform her. According to Lal, very soon afterwards, Mrs. Indira Gandhi was seen running down the corridor, her hair and saree flying. They were all surprised to see her bubbling with joy, and for him, this was the most unforgettable moment of the 1971 War. This was also the one day that Sam Manekshaw could not take credit for having ordered the operation." *http://veekay-militaryhistory.blogspot.com/*

December 10th–12th—Narsingdi

On 9th December, after Raipura was secured, they moved further south, unopposed, and established a firm base near Narsingdi. From 10th December onwards, the troops were being flown directly to Narsingdi town, which is just 50 kms from Dhaka. It was found suitable to be developed as an advance base for the attack on Dacca.

The troops which had crossed the river either on foot or on boats, also started walking towards Narsingdi. These were mainly from the 73 Mountain Brigade, who were moving with recoilless guns and mortars on foot. Along 14 Guards, being Alpha Company commander, I was part of this movement which was entirely on foot. The Mukti Bahini guides were weighing a lot of permutations and combinations of safety, ease of movement, friendly territory, and avoidance of enemy strong points, as they guided us on a trek spanning railway tracks, paddy fields, marshes and through villages. I am sure sophisticated computer programs infused with principles of operation research cannot match the judgement of our guides from Mukti Bahini.

Sydney Schanberg of the *New York Times* who travelled with IV Corps Brigades described a scene where 20 local inhabitants were pushing and pulling a 5.5-inch medium gun across a boggy rice field and others ferried ammunition.

As Indian soldiers marched they were greeted by loud cheers by the locals - Jai Bangla, Jai Hind or Jai India.

The build-up of heliborne troops was too slow as only about ten helicopters were available. The troop movement with helicopters across Meghna was a major PSYOP (psychological operation) to unnerve the Pakistani commanders at Bhairab Bazaar. They were further kept in check by the deployment of two infantry battalions south of the town.

The build up at Narsingdi area was complete by 11th December with convergence of all elements of the two brigades. It was a sight to behold when Mukti Bahini brigades, too, joined us there.

With the capture of the railway station, Narsingdi was overrun completely on 12th December. Both rail and road bridges were captured intact. Narsingdi opened multiple routes to Dacca. All the routes to Dacca lay undefended for IV Corps to forge ahead.

Dhaka could be approached through multiple routes. It was decided that Alpha Coy under me and Bravo Coy under Major O. P. Kohli would lead the 73 Mountain Brigade to advance through the Tongi axis and 311 Mountain Brigade would advance on the Demra axis.

We raised our guns to the sky. "All roads now lead to Dhaka."

Eve of 11th December—The Tangail Airdrop by 2 Para

On 11th December, while 57 Mountain Division of the IV Corps was closing in Dhaka from the Narsingdi axis, 2 Para was being airdropped at Tangail some 113 kms north-east of Dhaka. It was led by Lieutenant Colonel K. S. Pannu. It is a matter of pride for me that I had served in 2 Para (now SF—Special Forces) between 1969-70 before being deputed to counter-insurgency in Mizoram with 32 Guards (now 14 Guards) where I served under Lieutenant Colonel K. S. Pannu (then Battalion Second in Command of 2 Para). Thus, the honour to reach Dacca on 16th December was shared by both my units. The main objective of the Tangail airdrop operation was to capture Poongli Bridge on River Jamuna in order to cut off the Pakistani 93 Brigade, which was retreating from Jamalpur and Mymensingh to defend Dacca and its approaches.

The battalion took off from Dum Dum and Kalaikunda airfields on 11th December at about 2:30 a.m. using two C-119 transport aircrafts. The drops were spread over a distance of 4 kms. The villagers initially thought that Pakistanis were being airdropped, and they ran in panic. However, when Indian soldiers shouted '*Jai Bangla*', there was jubilation among the villagers and suddenly, hundreds of helping hands were available to regroup, move packs and equipment, and of course act as guides.

The battalion assembled quickly and marched towards Poongli Bridge, which was captured after some resistance by 7 p.m. 2 Para dug in and waited for the Pakistani 93 Brigade retreating from

Jamalpur. At midnight, when the Pakistani brigade reached Poongli, it was surprised. The Pakistani brigade had suffered heavy causalities and disintegrated.

Captain Nirbhay Sharma (later Lieutenant General) who was part of 2 Para had a gut-wrenching story to tell. The advance elements of 2 Para were aghast to see mutilated bodies of women who were killed by Pakistani soldiers before fleeing Poongli. Commander Lieutenant Colonel Kulwant Singh Pannu was awarded the Maha Vir Chakra for his leadership in the battle. 2 Para received battle honours for capture of the strategic bridge and also theatre honours for Dacca. Lieutenant Colonel Pannu died a few years ago. Lieutenant General Sharma lives near my house and his anecdotes regarding the Tangail airdrop and the daring entry into Dhaka on 16th December is a part of military folklore.

December 13th and 14th—Crossing of River Sitalakhya and Battle of Tongi by 73 Mountain Brigade

"Bidrohi"
Bolo bir,
Chiro unnoto momo shir!
Ami jhonjha, Ami ghurni,
Ami poth-somukhe jaha pai jai churni.
Ami nrittyo-pagol chondho,
Ami apnar tale neche jai, ami mukto jibonanondho.

– Kazi Nazrul Islam, '*Bidrohi*'

Say, Valiant,
Ever high is my head!
I am the hurricane, I am the cyclone
I destroy all that I found in the path!
I am the dance-intoxicated rhythm,
I dance at my own pleasure,
I am the unfettered joy of life!

– Translation by Kabir Chowdhry

Crossing Sitalakhya

We were ordered to take the Ghorashal–Markuna–Tongi axis and reach the outskirts of Dacca as soon as possible. The distance between Ashuganj bridge and Tongi was about 70 kms. The terrain was typical of Bangladesh—a mesh of paddy fields and river bodies interspersed with small villages. The next big natural obstacle to cross after Meghna was River Sitalakhya. Though not comparable, it was nevertheless formidable too. On 13th December, some elements of 73 Mountain Brigade captured the rail bridge over River Sitalakhya which connected to Tongi. However, I, along with a sizeable number of troops, had to cross the river on local boats. The boats could carry only seven or eight troops at a time. As we were to climb onto a boat, the elderly boatman (known as '*mallah*' or '*manjhi'* in the Gangetic plains and delta) was overwhelmed at learning that I was the company commander of the troops. His boat was bobbing up and down on the river waves. He raised his hand in salute as he balanced himself on his oar with the other hand. Other boatsmen joined him as he cried emotionally, "Jai Bangla, Jai India." It was a Guard of Honour straight from the heart, and the best one I had ever witnessed. As boats bounced up and down the river, the *mallahs* broke into a traditional song. The background score was provided by splash of the nimble waves, the rhythmic swirl of the oars against a river that was happy to have us as her guests. A cheeky breeze after playing mischievously with our olives surrendered meekly to our helmets and barrels. I asked the boatman his name as I alighted. He picked up his oar and roared loudly as his gaze left me and took on the skies. "*Ami Bidrohi*" (I am a rebel). As his comrades and our Mukti Jodha friends joined him, the roar transcended each paddy field, each river, each rivulet, each mountain, each pond, each city, each town, each university, each school, each heart of Bangladesh East Pakistan and reverberated across the azure skies to be heard across the world.

However, a few people drunk on power wanted to shut their ears and stifle that roar, albeit unsuccessfully. Understanding Kazi Nazrul Islam's epic poem 'Bidrohi' written in 1922, would have been an uphill task for my Punjabi brethren from across the borders.

Battle of Tongi

We started moving towards Dacca on the Tongi axis. Tongi was on the outskirts of Dacca. A lot of development has happened since then. Tongi was only 6 kms from Dacca airport (now Hazrat Shah Jalal Airport). It was a small township at that point of time on the minor river of Turag. As I mentioned, Bangladesh is a riverine country and there are water bodies all around. Thanks to the local support, we could negotiate the challenges much faster, but nevertheless, being on foot, the overall march was only a few kms a day. Given the topography and war, our speed was considerable. We were greeted warmly by villagers at many places. Our rations were humble—rice and *dal*. Occasionally, villagers would get food for us. There was a stark contrast between the reception of soldiers of the two armies. While we were greeted warmly by the local populace and offered hospitality, Pakistan Army men were safe only in numbers; otherwise, they risked being lynched. The entire country was seething in rage. Our guide pointed towards an area where massacres had taken place. They had done everything possible to alienate the people of Bangladesh.

The entire Pakistani defence was built around the concept of 'Fortress Dacca.' 'The Dacca Bowl,' surrounded by a triad of rivers, made it almost invincible. The Indian Army deliberately avoided the monsoons when it would have been impossible to march in and attack the enemy due to rivers in spate and water everywhere. Even during non rainy season, the well dug-in Pakistani formations at the border and important towns across Bangladesh, beefed up by natural defences imparted by the water bodies, could supposedly halt any intruding army. If required, various Pakistani formations at the frontiers or other far-off towns could fall back and defend Dacca. The news that the Indian Army had crossed Meghna was a major psychological setback for the Pakistanis.

Sensing major trouble, Pakistan immediately withdrew its 120 Brigade for the defence of Dacca. 120 Brigade was facing India's 101 Communication Zone Area troops. But our pace was much too quicker than the Pakistani brigades that struggled to fall back.

As we neared the Tongi–Markun area, we got information about the movement of Pakistanis. An advance party was sent to the Markun area. It ran into Pakistani troops who were in a built-up area. The Pakistani troops were falling back to Dhaka via Tongi. The first burst by enemy took our troops by surprise, but they retaliated immediately. One officer, Captain Ram Kumar, and a *jawan* were wounded. However, the unit engaged the Pakistanis and kept them under pressure. It was then that Alpha Company, under me, was ordered to move to the enemy's flank to encircle them. We closed in and opened fire. The enemy was unnerved, realising they were being fired upon from multiple locations. Pakistani troops came out in the open and started running to save themselves from being captured. They intended to move to some other safe place. In this process, some of the Pakistani troops got into our firing range. Seeing their comrades falling to bullets, some six enemy troops came out with their hands raised and surrendered. The Indian Army prides itself on being one of the most professional armies in the world. All the prisoners of war were assured of being treated in line with the Geneva Convention. Unfortunately, we cannot say the same thing about Pakistani forces. The unfortunate case of Captain Saurav Kalia, martyr of Kargil War, is an example. He was captured alive, but his mutilated body was sent back with unspeakable barbarity.

While India's 73 Mountain Brigade of 57 Mountain Division occupied Tongi, Pakistan's 120 Brigade disintegrated before it could reach Dacca.

The roads to Dacca and the welcoming arms of its residents were wide open for us. It was time for food. As CQM (Coy Quarter Master) Havildar Kalicharan announced that he had brought dinner for the Alpha Coy boys, as did other CQMs for their respective companies, my gaze was focused towards the men who had kept the fire burning in their mobile makeshift hearths to keep us satiated. Thanks to the logistics and supply chain wings, we always had a fire in our bellies to achieve more. Before I move further, it is important to pay tribute to the people who ensured that logistics and provisions kept match with our pace.

An Army Moves on its Stomach—Logistics and Provisions

The science of logistics and supply chain management has military origins. Logistics has French–Greek origins and can be defined as the 'art of moving, quartering and supplying troops. The function can be traced back to the movement of Roman armies. Supplies, provisions and other logistics for an army on the move in a war can be a major challenge. A unit officer responsible for administering barracks, laying out the camp, and looking after supplies, is known as the Battalion Quarter Master. In our case, it was Captain R. S. Tanwar, who had done a wonderful job. Apart from ensuring the logistics, he also had a very important duty to perform. He was responsible for writing letters to our families regarding our well-being. He was doing this for the unit since our battle of Dhalai days. This was a major morale booster, both for us and our families. A family of the soldier is always on the edge. The casualties in my unit was relatively small. The number of wounded, was comparatively high due to fierce hand-to-hand and close combat battles; however there had been casualties in other units of IV Corps. Informing the family about the loss of their beloved son, husband, or father can be a heart-breaking job. Captain Tanwar was an energetic and jolly man. The person responsible for supplies and provisions at the company level is known as CQMH (Company Quarter Master Havildar). The Alpha Company's CQMH was Kalicharan. He was a wonderful organiser and ensured that none of us slept or went hungry. Legendary Napoleon Bonaparte is said to have remarked that 'an army marches on its stomach'. The food was mostly frugal *dal–chawal* (rice with lentils) but an occasional *macher jhol* (fish curry), too, was organised by Kalicharan, courtesy the friendly villagers and Mukti Jodhas.

The logistics had to match our steps, which Major Shanti Swarup Khanna and Major P. P. S. Kshattriya (Second in command) did remarkably well. Our forward march plans were changing every day because of the rapidly evolving war scenario. Meanwhile, though our appetites were satiated, the hunger of the top commanders to gain more control of Bangladesh grew by the hour, egged on by spectacular advances on ground.

14th December—The Longest Day of the War

The events of 14th December ensured that the war would end swiftly. We were now combing Tongi from where the Dacca skyline was visible. Advance elements of 65 Mountain Regiment under 311 Brigade, who had parted from us at Narsingdi and moved towards Dacca on the Demra axis, had also reached Dhaka outskirts. By the evening of December 14, Indian Army had started pounding targets in Dacca Cantonment. Both 73 and 311 Brigades were now firmly ensconced on the outskirts of the Dacca. Build-up, for the final assault on Dhaka had started. Other formations like 2 Para of the Tangail drop and 301 brigade were also inching towards Dacca. A full build-up of troops, artillery and tanks required at least two days, after which an assault could be launched.

The blitzkrieg of 57 Mountain Division was directly proportional to the rise of loss of willingness to fight by General Niazi till his complete moral collapse. His first big shock had come on 7th December with the news of the fall of strongholds of Brahmanbaria and Jessore. This was followed by the news of Indian Army crossing of River Meghna on 9th December. This proved to be a game changer and shook him completely. By 10th December, General Niazi had lost his will to fight and started to pitch in for a ceasefire. A factually incorrect report by BBC that the Indian Army had dropped 5,000 paratroopers over Tangail, whereas the actual figure was 540, led to complete politico-military demoralisation of the Pakistanis. On 12th December, Niazi sent an urgent message to Pakistani President Yahya Khan, urging him to save innocent lives. There was no reply. The events of the morning of 14th December delivered the final blow.

10:50 a.m. —Indian Air force Base, Guwahati

A cenar teco m'invitasti, E son venuto.

(You invited me to dine with you, and I came)

—Wolfgang Mozart's famous symphony,
Don Giovanni

Air Commodore (Retd.) Ishfaq Ilahi Choudhury, a prolific writer and a veteran who was commissioned into the Pakistan Air Force but retired from the Bangladesh Air Force, wrote about the 1971 War, "The IAF air operations went off like a symphony with the right notes striking at the right time."

I wish to slightly modify the sentence, "The entire war went off like a perfect symphony with Indian Army, IAF and others, the Mukti Bahini, Bangladesh Armed Forces all striking the right notes at the right time, and of course the icing on the cake was the wholehearted support of the people of Bangladesh to the Liberation Forces."

The most apt symphony that comes to my mind is one of the best operas in the world—Wolfgang Mozart's acclaimed score *Don Giovanni*. The villain of the opera, Don, is a libertine who lives an immoral life and is a murderer. He has lived a life full of sins. It is a gripping opera and story. In the final scene, the ghost of Commendatore, the noble man whom Don Giovanni had murdered, comes for supper to his house. He speaks the iconic lines, "Don Giovanni, *A cenar teco m'invitasti, E son venuto."* (Don Giovanni, you've invited me to dine with you, and here I am.) Commendatore's ghost asks Don to repent, but he is unrepentant. The opera closes with Don meeting a terrifying, fiery end.

On 14th December, the Indian intelligence intercepted a message regarding a high-level meeting to be presided by the governor of East Pakistan scheduled at the Government House in Dacca. This intercept resulted in a crucial turn in the war.

Very early in the war, Indian Air Force had attained complete dominance of the East Bengal skies by annihilating the Pakistan Air force. The runway at Tejgaon resembled a crater on the moon, and the entire Pakistani fleet of F-86 was grounded. While the helicopters enabled us to leapfrog insurmountable obstacles, the jets with their rockets and bombs supported the army by softening well-defended Pakistani fortifications in Comilla, Maulvi Bazaar, Narsingdi, Lalmai, Dhaka, Mainamati, etc. Although each sortie by the air force and each stride of army towards Dacca was sapping the Pakistani morale, the last straw on the camel's back was the bombing of Government House on 14th December.

10:55 a.m., 14th December, Wing Commander Bhupinder K Bishnoi 'Bhoop' had just come back from a mission when Group Captain Wollen, Station Commander, Guwahati, came rushing in with a crumpled tourist map of Dacca. Bhoop was to fly immediately for a critical mission and attack the Circuit House in Dacca, preferably at 11:20 a.m.—the reported time of the meeting. The flight time was 21 mins. The pilots rushed to their birds.

As Wing Commander Bishnoi all strapped up in the cockpit, revved up the engines, a flight commander came rushing with another paper. It read that the target had changed to Government House and not Circuit House. 4 MiG-21s were loaded with 32 high explosive rockets; each scrambled in no time. The team led by Wing Commander (later Air Vice Marshal) B. K. Bishnoi comprised of Flight Lieutenant Vinod Bhatia (Jimmy), Flight Lieutenant Malhi and Flight Lieutenant Raghavchari. The Indian Airforce was airborne within 15 mins of receiving the intelligence input.

Once in the Dacca skies, Commander Bhoop asked his colleagues to look for the target. Jimmy whooped as he spotted the proud dome of the beautiful old palatial building set in the middle of luxurious green grounds with rows of neatly parked cars. Bhoop took a *chakkar* to confirm the target.

11:20 a.m.—Government House, Dacca

Oblivious to the eagles in the sky, the puppet East Pakistan governor was walking slowly in the well-appointed impressive corridors of the Mughal-British building towards the conference hall. He was accompanied by his cabinet and a bevy of officers and one Mr. Kelly of the United Nations. The building had to be impressive. After all, it once served as a residence to the Viceroy of India. The legendary Lord Curzon had stayed in it. The 50 acres of gardens were aptly named '*Dilkusha*' (Pleasure to the heart.) Governor Malik and General Niazi were still hoping to hold out till Americans or the world powers would intervene.

United Nations, New York—Backroom Parleys

There were hectic backroom parleys in New York. Pakistan's team was led by the charismatic Zulfiqar Ali Bhutto. He had drummed up impressive support for Pakistan against India. The strategy of the Pakistan establishment in Rawalpindi and Dhaka was to prolong the war until intervention by the West led by USA or the United Nations or China enforced ceasefire. Though there was action in UN, and USA did move in its 7th fleet into the Indian Ocean, Soviet Russia checkmated all their moves. Apart from posturing, none of the powers wanted to be a part of the conflict. But one thing was sure—that Indians had to hurry up.

Mianwali Jail, West Punjab, Pakistan

Bangabandhu Sheikh Mujibur Rahman was transferred to Mianwali Jail from Faisalabad (Lyallpur) after the start of the war. Probably Faisalabad was deemed too close to the Indian border. He was in solitary confinement with his trademark pipe for company. His beloved country was burning, his people were being slaughtered.

US and Europe–Peshawar–New Delhi–Calcutta–Dacca Outskirts

It was 14th December. Away from the maddening heat and dust of the Indian subcontinent, the general public of the West would have been more interested in appreciating Mozart's Don Giovanni opera. Meanwhile, far away in Peshawar, preparations were on in full swing for the housewarming party of Yahya Khan. It was to be an exciting night of drinks and debauchery attended by Pakistan's who's who, including President Yahya's special friend—a lady known as 'Black Pearl' in power circles. While in South Block, the seat of power in New Delhi, the Indian political leadership led by Mrs. Indira Gandhi and diplomats were playing a game of nerves and deft diplomacy in the UN. Her hawkeyed cabinet colleagues and officials were monitoring the war by the minute, round the clock, and provided full support to the Indian armed forces. Indian Army Chief General Manekshaw was in the process of urging Pakistani commanders and troops scattered across Bangladesh to surrender through radio and pamphlets in Urdu, Pashto and Bengali. Lieutenant General J. S. Aurora GOC eastern front with his Deputy Major General J. F. R. Jacob at Fort William was finetuning and coordinating action across battlefields. There were almost 10,000 Indian troops within arm's distance of Dhaka. Right from India's topmost politico–military leadership till the last soldier, the mood was upbeat and focused. Add to this, the Bangladesh Armed Forces, Mukti Bahini and its Mukti Jodhas were all charged up. On the ground level, company commanders like me, expecting orders for the final assault, were huddled together brainstorming tactical strategies for the same.

The war's finale was building up akin to that of *Don Giovanni*, (Mozart air du Commandeur or Mozart's Grand Opera), and was reverberating across the world from New York to Paris to London to Moscow to New Delhi to Peking to Lahore to Dhaka. Like in the Opera Pakistan's sins were coming back to haunt them. In the Opera Commedatore's stone statue had come to life to torment the villian Don Juan for his sins and asked him to repent. When the unrepenting scoundrel Don Juan is told by the angry ghost that it is his last hour and his time is up, he cries dreadfully.

> *"Da qualtremoreinsolito, Sentoassalirglispiriti*
> *Dond'esconoqueivortici, Difocopiend'orror?"*

"What strange fear assails my soul, where do those flames of horror come from?"

Back to Dacca Skies

Bhoop in Tiger-1 (lead aircraft) jammed his target on a room below the dome and yelled fire. All hell broke loose in the highest seat of authority in Pakistan in East Bengal. There were flames, thunder and smoke everywhere as priceless chandeliers came crashing down. The elegant Durbar Hall lay in shambles. Two *chakkars* (passes) each by the sky Tigers and the entire payload of 128 57-mm rockets were emptied into the once-beautiful target. As the jets turned back towards India, the pilots looked back and smiled—wafts of smoke were billowing out of multiple points from the Government House.

In Paris, the audience was in a trance as the symphony notes were now louder than ever, the finale was near. Commendatore's eyes turn red with vengeance. Don Juan cries, "What a hell, what a terror," as he goes down in flames.

Chi l'anima mi lacera?
Chi m'agita le viscere?
Chestrazio, ohimé, chesmania
Che inferno, che terror!

The symphony becomes louder, and the crowd is rapturous.

The attack was so accurate that the rockets breezed into the ventilators of the hall where the meeting was to be held after a few minutes. The roof of the Darbar Hall had ripped apart, and it lay in shambles. The entire building was a smoking wreck. The governor of East Pakistan, Dr. A. H. Malik, went into a shock. Dr. Malik was yet to enter the conference hall. He was so shaken and rattled by the attack that he snatched a piece of paper from his aide and wrote his resignation with trembling hands. The resignation was handed over to Kelly, the UN representative, to relay it to the US Embassy in Islamabad (Rawalpindi) for onward transmission to the Pakistan Government.

The last semblance of Pakistan's authority in Bangladesh was gone. There was no official government in Bangladesh. Malik along with his cabinet and senior civil servants, many of them West Pakistanis, took refuge at the Intercontinental Hotel (now Sheraton) in Dacca, which was designated as a neutral zone under the UN Flag. He probably never came back to the Government House. General 'Tiger' Niazi retreated into a bunker. He sent another desperate plea to Rawalpindi. It was a night of horror for the West Pakistani establishment. West Pakistan officers with their families were huddled together in fear in safe areas. The Mukti Jodhas were all over Bangladesh by now and Dacca was the final frontier. They had seen their families and people in fear for far too long. The 'Royal Bengal Tigers' were now prowling in the hunter's backyard, but were still not close enough to stop Rao Farman Ali from scribbling, ticking and deleting a few names on the pages of a diary.

Shelling of Dacca Cantonment

It was evening and the Indian Army had started shelling positions in Dhaka. Indian Army further deepened its PSYOPs. General Manekshaw was on All India Radio, relaying his message. Major General Jacob from Fort William contacted General Niazi for the second time in 24 hours for a surrender.

Meanwhile, while General Niazi desperately waited for directions, the party at General Yahya's new house in Peshawar was at full swing as it entered the heady hour filled with fun and frolic, music, wine and women.

Night of 14th December—Massacre of Intellectuals

After the Government House attack, it was clear to the Pakistani establishment that they had lost the game. The Pakistani forces, along with their collaborators, mainly militia 'Al Badr', committed yet another horrendous crime against humanity. In a chilling Gestapo style operation, the Pakistan Army abducted 200 eminent Bengali intellectuals comprising of doctors, academicians, litterateurs, teachers, engineers, journalists, and other prominent thinkers. They were blindfolded, tortured, and killed mercilessly. The bodies were dumped in Rayerpur and Mirpur. One of the most bone-chilling murders was that of a young journalist, poetess, and a single mother Selina Parveen. She had pleaded with her captors to spare her for the sake of her seven-year-old son as there would be no one to look after him. Her body was found with two bullet injuries and had been bayoneted twice, once in the eye and the other in the stomach. It was a murder most foul. Her screams as the mother of a young child would have melted even the skies.

Equally foul was the murder of Prof. Munier Choudhury, Dean, Faculty of Arts, Dacca University, an alumnus of Harvard University and Aligarh Muslim University, a playwright, a literary critic, and an academician. The butchers had done meticulous homework to select their quarry—the curriculum vitae of each of the martyrs were second to none.

It is widely believed that the killings were planned and carried out at the behest of Major General Rao Farman Ali, a confidant of Yahya Khan, who was the military advisor on civil affairs to the Governor of East Pakistan, Dr. Malik. It was in the debris of his office in Governor House that two pages of his handwritten diary were discovered, which contained the names of leading intellectuals of Dhaka. The pages had survived, but not the intellectuals. General Niazi, in his testimony to Hamoodur Rahman Commission pointed towards Rao Farman Ali's direct complicity. Born in Rohtak in 1925, he kept a low profile for the last 26 years of his life till his death in 2004. He was buried with full military honours by Pakistan Army in Rawalpindi. He did not accept his role in the pogrom till the end, despite irrefutable evidence.

In New York, the Western world leadership led by President Nixon upped the pressure on India in the UN by introducing scornful resolutions.

Meanwhile, at Broadway, the elite horror-struck audience is stiff with scornful revulsion as the scoundrel Don Giovanni refuses to repent, even in his last moments.

[La statua] *Pentiti, cangiavita, nell'ultimomomento!*
[Don Giovanni] *No, no, ch'io non mi pento, vannelontan da me!*
[La statua] *Pentiti, scellerato!*
[Don Giovanni] *No, vecchioinfatuato!*

14th December is mourned every year in Bangladesh as the day of the martyred intellectuals, or *Shaheed Buddhijibi Dibosh* in Bengali.

Night of 14th December—Tongi

We had now occupied Tongi and cleared it of all resistance. After ages, we were not walking at night. Meanwhile, I sat in a rudimentary village hut, chatting with a well-informed Mukti Bahini friend about Dacca's cultural and literary life. He kept quiet when I asked about his family. The reflected fire in his eyes said everything as he slowly roasted a large fish on a skewer. I could hear the boom of the first shells being fired on Dacca cantonment. I checked with Kalicharan, our CQMH, if the troops could be given something better than the routine stuff. He went off to check with the villagers. That night, non of us —we, Mukti Jodhas, and the Pakistan Army—knew as to who would come out alive from the final assault. The war had entered a decisive phase. What if the Pakistanis decided to take a last stand? A war is never over till the last man surrenders and all guns cease to fire. It was an unusually dark night, but there were bright stars in the sky. As I lay on the ground on a humble bedding, I took out my purse, said good night to the photograph of my family, and dozed off, gazing at stars. It was almost midnight. I had to get up before the first light. There was an important pre-dawn meeting. At that moment, hundreds of Pakistani troops entered a particular Dacca University building to evade air strikes. As they were relocating, thousands of Indian troops were marching onto Dacca from all directions. Most Pakistani troops hailing from agrarian families, lay scattered, tired and despondent in their bunkers all over East Bengal, they were missing winters of North Indian sub-continent, longing to be in the midst of their fields, next to the ice-cold but motherly canals. It was time to sow mustard. The caravan of civil servants from West Pakistan posted in east poured into the red cross neutral zone—Dacca Intercontinental. Wives of Pakistani officers were trying to calm their kids in the relative safety and comfort of the hotel's compound as Pakistan's flags were being pulled down in major towns of East Pakistan.

The party in Yahya Khan's compound was now in full swing. Ladies' laughter mixed liberally with scotch as the world's finest bone china, silver cutlery, and exquisite crystal glasses rubbed noses with mesmerising music. Turbaned army of waiters served the most delicious kebabs and chutneys. As the elegance of the party unfolded into intoxicated, delightful debauchery, Saville Row bespoke suits and ties were competing with the strings of cheap Lahori baggy pants to outdo each other in loosening the heavy burden and pretence of propriety, not to mention the impending doom some 1,800 kms away. Gen. Niazi was waiting anxiously for directions from Islamabad.

US Embassy, Dacca, Evening of 14th December—The Ceasefire Proposal

With Malik's resignation, the reality finally dawned upon Pakistan's military *junta* and the following message was sent to General Niazi at about 1 p.m.

"You have now reached a stage where further resistance is no longer humanly possible nor will it serve any useful purpose. It will

only lead to further loss of life and destruction. You should now take all necessary measures to stop the fighting and preserve the lives of all armed forces personnel, all those from West Pakistan and all loyal elements."

Niazi and Farman Ali reached the US Embassy and handed a ceasefire proposal to American Counsel General Herbert Spivak. They had proposed ceasefire and cessation of all hostilities and handing over administration to the United Nations. There was no mention of India in the proposals and the word 'surrender' was deliberately avoided. It would take 19 hours for the proposal to reach the Indians.

Thus, 14th December may have been the longest day of the war with a lot of action spanning multiple cities across the globe. As Dacca went to an uneasy sleep, it was a cloudy winter morning in the UN headquarters in New York and the topic on everybody's mind was Bangladesh.

15th December—Fortress Dacca Breached

On December 15th, the chief of the army of Pakistan, General A. H. Khan, sent a message to Niazi: "I have seen your message sent to the president and I have also heard what you said to General Manekshaw [General Sam Manekshaw, India's army chief], which was broadcast on All India Radio. You are free to take a decision of your own but my advice would be to accept the terms and conditions given by the Indian force." A build-up of Indian troops was taking place. The buzz regarding surrender was there.

December 15th–16th night—Capture of Dacca Airport by 14 Guards

On 1st December, action shifted from the ground to the top commanders from both sides who had started to engage with each other regarding the ceasefire. Orders were received from the HQs to halt further advance. Accordingly, we stayed put in our position in Tongi. On the same day, tactical HQ 101 Communication Zone Area, 95 and 167 Mountain Brigade groups, and 2 Para were placed under the command of IV Corps. Thus, all the formations in the vicinity of Dhaka, including that of General G. S. Nagra, were under the command of Lieutenant General Sagat Singh, Commander of IV Corps. He ordered shelling of targets within Dacca to make it amply clear that Indians had closed in. IV Corps had closed in to Dacca from many directions. Had Pakistan not surrendered, a full attack on Dacca was almost a surety after 17th December.

It was late afternoon on 15th December that we (14 Guards/ 73 Brigade) were asked to explore the feasibility of closing in on Dacca airport. We pored over the map in our makeshift camp on the outskirts of Dacca. It was late evening when Major P. P. S. Kshattriya, accompanied by some jawans, was sent to recce the area and the airport and formalise the route to be taken by us. A city assault requires occupying and hoisting your own flags on important landmarks or buildings and letting the enemy know that the game is over. Airport is a very important landmark, which has a massive psychological impact on the morale of the enemy as the liberating army gets control over the airstrips. Our objective was just that.

Major Kshattriya spotted a few Pakistani soldiers guarding the airport entrance and there was no other major movement. He rushed back with the information. We were ready to march when he came back. It was late in the night when we (led by Alpha and Bravo Coys) started moving towards the airport, taking a circuitous route avoiding the main city, wherein we might have run into resistance. There were already small murmurs of Pakistanis giving up, but in war, conjecturing can be suicidal. We moved cautiously, guided by the Mukti Jodhas in pitch darkness. Nothing can be left to chance; absence of resistance can also be a trap. There had been major losses in Ashuganj power plant before it was run over. The full moon that had guided us in Machigacha on the night of 1st December had now waned. As we walked there was a nip in the air. A beautiful crescent moon appeared over the Dacca skies as if the heavens were smiling upon East Bengal. My Alpha Company being the leading Coy of 14 Guards, the first one to enter Bangladesh on 1st December, had been walking ever since, the only comfort being the wonderful boat rides. The rivers of Bangladesh had graciously borne us and the weight of our armour with a jolly welcoming bounce. We were moving mostly during the night time and resting sparingly at safe places near friendly villages. The Mukti Jodhas were guiding us well. The sky was our roof and the open grounds our beds. There was hardly a time to change uniforms or bathe or shave. However, the abundance of water ensured that we were able to splash our faces every morning or when fatigue set in. Being a commando, I was trained to survive against all odds. The comfort of well-furnished apartments with attached toilets and air-conditioned offices is unthinkable for a soldier on duty. The army recruits boys and makes men out of them—sturdy with nerves of steel and hardy; unflinching in hardships.

It was surreal. We were inside the 'Dacca Bowl', as the Pakistanis referred to it. Although not sure, we could sniff victory. The very fact that our objective was Dacca airport was a strong indication, enough that it was likely to be the last night of walking after 15 days. The mood was upbeat and cheerful as troops walked at a brisk pace towards the objective. If Dacca was the ultimate challenge and the crown prize, 73 Brigade was moving to occupy Dacca airport, the jewel in the crown.

As we reached the airport late night on 15th or in the wee hours of 16th December, we challenged the guards on duty who let loose a volley of fire on us. The befitting reply from our side was enough to make them scoot and vanish into the night. The roar of our guns ensured that all Pakistani troops vacated the airport before we started the room-to-room combing operations. The fleeing Pakistani troops had grabbed whatever they could lay hands on. A broken locker in the strongroom lay empty. Many almirahs were ransacked. A soldier must uphold the honour and dignity of his uniform. Unfortunately, the Pakistan Army, barring a few upright ones, had behaved like a medieval, marauding, barbaric army indulging in wanton killings, loot, rapine and plunder. It was hard to imagine that the top brass of all the three—India, Pakistan, and fledgling Bangladesh Army—were once batch mates in the same army. Pakistan Army came out of the war thoroughly discredited as a disciplined force.

We started the mop-up operation immediately upon entering the airport. By the first light of the day, we had secured the airport fully. 16th December 1971 was destined to be a day of festivities across Bangladesh, and year after year, subsequently.

Some of the almirahs escaped the wrath of the fleeing Pakistanis. Maybe our guns made them run hastily with whatever they had looted. We made an inventory of valuables and handed them over to a civil administrator. Among the valuables were gold coins, perhaps with Saudi inscriptions, and electronic items. Each and every valuable left behind was accounted for and handed over to the Bangladesh authorities.

The airport had a number of well-appointed rooms and barracks. I took up quarters in a comfortable room within the complex. We were at ease for the first time in many, many days. I took a warm bath and had a proper shave in ages. Most of us had not changed our uniforms since we set out. It was almost back to good old days as I donned my freshly-ironed, crisp uniform. My room had two glass tumblers with Pakistan International Airways (PIA) logo. Those two inexpensive PIA glasses still survive in my drawing room as souvenirs or trophies of the war, and were the only things I brought back from Bangladesh. Somebody jovially remarked that I should keep these glasses along with the ones with Air India Logo and Biman Bangladesh Airlines to complete the picture.

I will never forget the morning of 16th December 1971. The smiling crescent faded into the dark night pulling down East Pakistan, and a crimson red sun arose over the lush green landscape of Bangladesh. A very long and dark night was finally over for genteel folks who had struggled so hard, sacrificed so much for their motherland and mother tongue. That red sun flutters high, sitting proudly at the centre of their magnificent green flag.

It had been a long haul to Dacca as we had negotiated two large rivers and two small ones. The march to Dacca had been incredible. Ashuganj Bridge–Raipura–Narsingdi–Ghodashal– River Sitalakhya–Pubail–Markun–Tongi–Dacca Airport.

16th December—Endgame, Dacca Surrender

Later, other units started moving to Dacca. The surrender was to take place in the afternoon. Top military brass was expected to attend the surrender ceremony. Everybody seemed to be excited. The Mukti Jodhas were ecstatically moving around, as happy as busy bees attending a marriage.

Early on the morning of 16th December, General Niazi sought an extension of the truce by six hours up to 3 p.m. and suggested a preliminary staff meeting in Dacca and assured that they were going ahead with ceasefire formalities. Manekshaw agreed and told him that General Jacob would arrive by helicopter in the afternoon, with the condition that Pakistan must surrender by 4 p.m.

Gen. Manekshaw called up Lieutenant General Jacob. "Jake, go and take the surrender." General Jacob, who was already in touch with Niazi camp for the past two days, informed General Manekshaw that Niazi had invited him for lunch. There was a buzz in Fort William. Mrs. Bhanti Aurora informed General Jacob that she wanted to accompany her husband to Dacca. General Jacob switched his helicopter in Jessore to save fuelling time and reached Dhaka at 1.00 p.m. On landing, General Jacob was met by UN representatives Marc Henry and Kelly, who told him that they were accompanying him to take over the government and arrange the withdrawal of the Pakistan military. The wily general declined the offer politely. General Jacob had carried with him a draft instrument of surrender. General Niazi and his commanders, including Rao Farman Ali, were taken aback at the mention of surrender. General Jacob gave them the option of surrender with the guarantee of safety of the Pakistani personnel and families, or resumption of hostilities and bombing with no guarantee of safety. He gave Niazi 30 mins to decide, and went out of the room to puff on his pipes.

"You surrender, we take care of you, your families, and ethnic minorities. If you don't, what can I do? I wash my hands." General Jacob literally blackmailed him, "I'll give you 30 minutes, and if you don't agree, I'll give you 30 more minutes, and if you don't agree, I'll order the resumption of hostilities and the bombing of Dacca."

General Jacob mentions in his memoirs that the Pakistanis had laid out an elaborate lunch table with trophies, but he had no heart to eat.

Years later, when Hamoodur Rahman Commission asked General Niazi as to why he surrendered when he had 26,500 troops in Dacca and only 3,000 Indian troops were there, he replied, "Jacob tricked me into it."

At the end of 30 minutes, Jacob walked in and Niazi just kept quiet with teary eyes. General Jacob demanded a public surrender with a Guard of Honour. It was to be a public spectacle. The surrender was scheduled at the same Ramna Ground which was witness to so much, including the speech by Jinnah in which he had declined official status to Bengali.

There is much speculation about Niazi's surrender, but in my opinion, General Niazi did the right thing at the right moment. Any further fighting would have definitely led to loss of lives, and more so in the Pakistani camp. They were in a hopeless situation. Tiger Siddiqui, with his men, was already there with the Indian Army at the outskirts of Dhaka. Every heart, every mind, every hand wanted revenge.

4 p.m.—Ramna Ground

General Jacob and General Niazi rode out together to the Tezgaon airfield to receive the Indian entourage. Nine helicopters flying in a formation landed at 4:30 p.m. They were delayed because as a mark of respect and appreciation, General Jagjit Singh had gone to Agartala first to pick General Sagat Singh, the commander of IV Corps. Apart from the divisional commanders, Mrs. Jagjit Singh Aurora had accompanied her husband for the surrender. Thousands of Bengalis had poured into the grounds as the skies reverberated with the cries of 'Jai Bangla', 'Jai India'.

The Ramna race course ground (now Suhrawardy Udyan) had witnessed every moment of the Bengali struggle. It was a befitting grand finale. General Jacob had also demanded a Guard of Honour; he had witnessed the Japanese presenting on surrender during World War II.

At 4:55 p.m., both General Aurora and General Niazi sat down to sign the surrender. The iconic photograph has General Sagat Singh and General Jacob standing at the back and overlooking the papers. He was presented with a Guard of Honour by both Indian and Pakistani contingents. The Indian Guard of Honour was presented by Lieutenant Colonel K. S. Pannu of 2 Para. He was Battalion Second in Command during my tenure with 2 Para. Little did I know that a few weeks later, I too would present a Guard of Honour, to the acting President and Prime Minister of independent Bangladesh.

General Niazi then removed his epaulet and took out his revolver and handed it over to General Aurora. Tears rolled down his cheeks. General Jacob had kept the ceremony solemn. Surrender can be a soldier's most difficult moment. But General Niazi had saved the lives of his 93,000 troops, who were laying down arms with him. The entire city had erupted into joy, with people shooting bullets in the sky. General Aurora was hoisted on the shoulders of the crowd and cries of 'Jai Bangla' reverberated in the air.

Burly, turbaned sardar soldiers were carried on the shoulders of crowds. The Gurkhas marching with their trademark caps were showered with flowers. Jai Bangla was everywhere. The Indians had flowers in their barrels. General Niazi had to be whisked away under protection to save him. Anti-Pakistan slogans filled the air. It was the largest such event in history since General Paulus' surrender at Stalingrad in 1943.

The Indian Parliament was in session. General Manekshaw telephoned Indira Gandhi, and she informed the parliament, "Dacca is now the free capital of a free country. We hail the people of Bangladesh in their hour of triumph." There was a jubilant uproar in the parliament as members leaped out of their chairs and threw papers in the air.

Pakistan Army's superior martial race myth was given a ceremonial burial by a secular, diverse, multi-faith force comprising of Indian Army and the valiant Bengali Mukti Jodhas.

Night of 16th December—Tezgaon

The surrender ceremony was over. Thousands of Pakistani troops were surrendering. In a quick reversal of roles, we were to protect the Pakistani soldiers. They were eager to surrender to the Indians, knowing they would be safer in our custody. I had gotten used to sleeping lightly and in relative discomfort. My drift into sleep was disturbed by images of spattering blood, falling bodies, fields littered with uniformed corpses of friends and foes. Mass graves with bodies of children, women, and old people, piled up, wounded, dying, pleading for water flashed by. I got up in the middle of the night, thirsty and running a mild fever. I took a swig of water from my bottle as I rummaged my bag for an analgesic. I had not bothered about my wounds. I drifted into a semi-sleep again. The much-needed rest had been healing. I was feeling much better in the morning.

17th December—Rescue of Bangabandhu Sheikh Mujibur Rahman's Family

Even as General Niazi had surrendered, the message had not been conveyed to many Pakistani units who continued to fight or defend their positions. The news was slow to be conveyed as the Pakistani communication systems had collapsed.

I had not shaved properly for a while. Shaving with warm water in the morning was refreshing as I looked into the mirror and smiled at the handsome young man staring back. I was alive, and I hummed a favourite Bollywood melody. War can be psychologically and physically taxing; getting back to normal life is a perfect healer. I continued whistling as my orderly walked in with tea.

Barring small pockets of resistance, most of the Indian forces and leaders were relieved that the war was over. It was the end to a very stressful year and an excruciating fortnight. It was time to celebrate for some. It was time to rest for some. The Pakistanis were relieved, too. They knew most of them would be safe now, despite the terrible atrocities and crimes perpetrated by them against humanity. In many areas, they were more than willing to surrender to the Indian Army.

As I donned my uniform in my room in the building of Dacca airport, the most challenging moments of my life were going to unfold. By evening, my name was being announced on All India Radio and it was also shown on TV. My parents, especially my wife, Abha, saw me on TV. While a soldier in war has hardly any time for mushy feelings, it can be a harrowing time for his family. The reason for my name to be announced on the radio and splashed on TV is narrated in the next chapter in detail.

Night of 17th December

A lavish dinner and a warm, comfortable bed were still a few days away. Mop-up operations were to be finished. It would be at least a week later when we were able to uncork the bottles at a get-together. As I crashed into the makeshift bed that night, I yearned for my home, to be with my family. I longed to see my newly born daughter, Anshu. I smiled as I drifted into the realm of dreams. A young baby was chuckling. I had donned the costume of Santa Claus and flew the sleigh right over to my house in Delhi, near the cot of my first-born. I had loaded my cart with goodies and presents for the kids of the entire neighbourhood. The melody of 'Jingle Bells' started playing… and I slept soundly after ages.

That night, millions of East Bengalis would have slept with a smile. Their nightmare was finally over. Santa had come a week earlier in the eastern part of the subcontinent.

They will live again in freedom
In the garden of the Lord.
They will walk behind the ploughshare,
They will put away the sword.
The chain will be broken
And all men will have their reward.

—Finale of the musical *Les Misérables*

Hamoodur Rahman Commission, set up in Pakistan to investigate the debacle, severally criticised both General Yahya and General Niazi for their immoral acts. As per the report: "There is little doubt that General Niazi unfortunately came to acquire a bad reputation in sexual matters, and this reputation has been consistent during his postings in Sialkot, Lahore, and East Pakistan."

The ghosts of their sins against humanity will haunt the Pakistani generals and officers like Yahya, Niazi, Tikka Khan and Farman Ali even after they are gone.

❑

CHAPTER 13

The Bangabandhu Family Rescue

Fānūs banke jiskī hifāzat havā kare
Wo shama kyā bujhe jise raushan ḳhudā kare

(Sometimes even gusts of air protect a flickering flame by mimicking a glass shade

None can extinguish a lamp that has been illuminated by God's own hand?)

Rescue of Sheikh Mujib's Family at Dhanmondi

Prelude

If 14th December was the longest day of the war, an hour in the afternoon of 17th December was destined to be the longest hour of my life. In that one hour, everything that made 'Shokie' as Major Ashok Kumar Tara had suddenly converged. A 10 year-old had walked ten kms every day through the deep jungle to his school, having confronted wild animals. A nine-year-old mischievous boy would extinguish temple diyas *to pick up coins to show rebellion. An eleven-year-old had visited graves at midnight to prove he was fearless. Grandson of a fearless young widow of Rawalpindi, grandson of a shikari* nana *with a sense of fair play, son of an upright army officer. A student who shielded his professor from knife-wielding goons, son of a mother for whom duty was before self, husband of a strong lady who had left her family for love. A loyal friend who would stand with a friend, come what may. A sportsperson who was trained in swift planning and moved around the field in split seconds. A decorated army officer, ace commando, para trooper. A witty and happy-go-lucky man who could charm people at the drop of a hat or talk his way out of any situation. But still an extremely stubborn, unbending man when it was a matter of principles. His wit, his nerves, his personality, his family, his friends, his teachers, his city, his country, his ethnicity, his childhood, his student days, his army's philosophy, his commando training had all converged, maybe for that one hour, that moment. All his past had perhaps groomed him for this moment, to be a spoke in the giant wheel of time slowly churning into the future, to forever become a small footnote in the history of those tumultuous times.*

17th December, Early Morning—Dacca Airport

The orderly came in with my morning tea—a luxury I had after a long time. I had to get ready quickly as my CO had called for a meeting to assess the security. The battalion had implemented all the relevant protocols by now to secure the airport perimeter. Around 9 p.m. on the same day, while reassessing the arrangements along with Major Shanti Khanna and Captain O. P. Kohli, I was hastily summoned by my commanding officer Lieutenant Colonel V. N. Channa VSM (Brigadier Retd).

He introduced me to a visibly perturbed Mukti Jodha. I had picked up enough Bangla to understand him. He claimed that Begum Mujibur Rahman, along with other family members, was under house arrest in Dhanmondi, Dhaka, by Pakistani soldiers. Lieutenant Colonel Channa oblivious to the gravity of the situation, asked me to go and sort out the things. asked me to investigate the matter. I took a jeep and proceeded towards Dhanmondi. There were four of us in the jeep, I, two soldiers and the Mukti Bahini Jodha. I had a Sten gun, and both the soldiers had a rifle each. At that point of time, I was not aware that we were driving the jeep straight into the eye of the storm. Amongst the prisoners was Sheikh Mujib's daughter and current prime minister of Bangladesh, Sheikh Hasina with her three-month-old son Joy. Her younger sister Rehana and little brother Russel, too, were in the same house.

Through a newspaper article years later I came to know that the Mukti Bahini Jodha who had accompanied us was one of Sheikh Mujib's top aides, Hazi Golam Morshed. It was a pleasant surprise for me when he recalled the events of that day even after almost five decades and remembered my name in a recent interview. I gathered from his interview that he had first gone to the circuit house at Kakrail, where the senior officers of the Indian Army were camping. He recalled meeting Major General Gonsalves and another senior Sikh officer. General Gonsalves a tall handsome personality was my Divisional Commander. They came to the airport and spoke to Lieutenant Colonel Channa, who then called for me.

We set out immediately. One could hear firing sounds and occasional blasts around Dacca. In many cases, it was a celebratory fire by the Mukti Jodhas or minor skirmishes between them and some pro-Pakistan elements. The news of surrender had not reached many Pakistani units. There were isolated units of Pakistan Army who were yet to surrender and they continued to fight even on 17th December. Pakistan's 14th Div. surrendered on 17th December. The command and communication structure had completely broken down in the Pakistani ranks.

When we reached Dhanmondi, the Jodha pointed towards the house where the family was being held hostage. We had stopped about a hundred yards from the house. A crowd of locals had gathered there, emotionally charged and scared. A person with fear writ large on his face slowly lifted his hand and pointed towards a car near the gate and whispered in Bengali, " A driver and a media person has been killed by the Pakistanis." Some of them advised us against approaching the house from that direction lest we, too, met the same fate. They apprised me that there were about 14–15 trigger-happy enemy soldiers

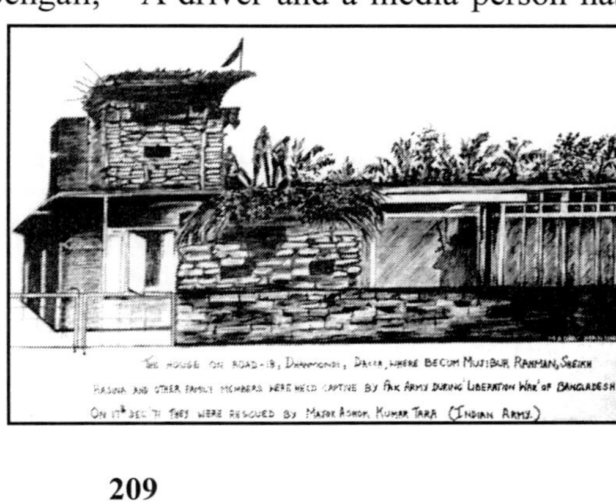

guarding the premises with automatic weapons. "They are firing at anybody venturing close to the house," somebody said in Bengali. The Mukti Jodha's intelligence input was right, and none of us at the 14 Guards and the higher commanders had bargained for this kind of a situation. It was indeed Bangabandhu's family being held hostage in the house.

I could not go back, it would have taken time to go back and brief my seniors and then come back with reinforcements. Time was of the utmost essence. Anything could have happened in the intervening period, especially since the crowd was building up. Further, a larger, well-armed contingent could have provoked the Pakistani troops, snowballing the situation into a no holds barred fight, endangering the hostages. My options were limited. The odds were stacked heavily against us. I had very limited resources at hand to take on a well-entrenched, heavily armed enemy ensconced behind sandbagged bunkers. Unlike the Battle of Gangasagar, my chances of charging and that too with just two men were not on the cards.

A poorly equipped, out-gunned, out-manned reconnaissance investigating jeepload was now at the forefront of one of the most important hostage rescue missions and operations in the history of the subcontinent.

Following my instincts, I decided to try and talk my way out. It was an audacious move, especially when my olive uniform proclaimed loudly that I was an Indian Army officer. I was presenting my head on a platter to the trigger-happy enemy. But taking calculated risks was part of my personality, whether on the playfield or otherwise. I handed over my weapon to one of my *jawans* and instructed them to take any advantageous positions they considered appropriate in case the situation got out of hand. Unarmed, I slowly walked towards the house. A hush descended upon the crowd. Almost everybody thought I would be killed.

It was an instinctive decision with perhaps least probability of being effective, but considering that time was of the essence, there were few options to juggle with apart from trying to tackle the situation psychologically.

As I slowly walked past the bullet-ridden car with corpses in a dried pool of blood, there seemed to be no doubt in my mind regarding the intent of the defenders of the house.

I hailed my Pakistani counterparts with full throttle of my lungs: "*Koi Hai*?" (Anybody there?)

I failed to get a response. The commando in me was careful to keep the car in between me and the direction of fire, lest I had to take cover. My soldiers were not in the enemy's view and could divert the enemy's attention, if needed.

I kept treading forward with cautious, slow steps and with my eyes firmly fixed on the house. My young readers can imagine themselves in my shoes and experience a moment when you are at the edge of your nerves and probably the only sound that you hear is your own heartbeat—a mildly paced, dull rhythm that can cease any moment in a situation like this. I hope that gives you a thrill more than the fast-paced 3D games you play on computers. If you want to experience it, join the Indian Army. If you don't think it matches, then, too, join the Indian Army. (Pun intended.) However, if you can't join one of the oldest, distinguished, noble and bravest armies ever in the history of mankind, do support it and appreciate its valour and values and stand by it, always. Please do read about its exploits right from World War I and World War II till today.

I walked slowly towards the house. There was a bullet-ridden car in between me and the house. I paused for a moment near the car. There were corpses lying in the car, shot dead by the West Pakistani soldiers positioned inside the house. I had been informed by someone in the crowd before moving ahead that some journalists who had ventured near the house had been shot dead by the Pakistani soldiers.

I later came to know through newspapers that the deceased lady was Dr. Ayesha Bedora Chowdhury, a gold medallist from the prestigious National Medical College, Calcutta. She had been actively but clandestinely involved in the treatment and shelter of liberation fighters. She was a close friend of the Sheikh Mujib family and rushed to the house to enquire about their well-being after the surrender. She was shot dead by the Pakistani soldiers guarding the house for daring to get too close to the house. Her chauffeur had also died in the firing. Unfortunately, she was killed after the surrender and ceasefire because many Pakistani soldiers were simply not aware of it.

I kept walking until I was about ten yards from the main entrance of the house. The cover of the car was gone. I had got no response from the Pakistani soldiers, either verbally or by trigger till then. Suddenly, a Pakistani soldier atop the roof of the house shouted in Punjabi.

"Otthe hi ruk jaa nahin te goli maar deyaanga." (Halt right there or I will shoot.)

It was a warning in our common mother tongue. Being a West Punjabi, I was well versed in their dialect and could completely appreciate nuances of tone and tenor in which he delivered the sentence. He was dead serious and meant business. I could fully comprehend the gravity of the threat. As a soldier and a commando, I had, by now, ample brushes with death. Fear is an emotion arising out of risk, which we are taught to overcome or sidestep. In day-to-day life of civilians, risk is mostly about money or material possessions. But for an army man, risk is mostly about loss of life or limb. It did not cross my mind that I was only 29 years old. Neither did it cross my mind that I was yet to see my first-born. My first-born, the apple of my eye, my beloved daughter Anshu was only three months old at that time.

There was a Pakistani sepoy sitting with his LMG on the roof of the house. I stood still as I looked towards him. The bodies outside were a testimony that the LMG and its bullets knew no compassion for men and women walking or driving towards the house. One of the Pakistan Army JCOs guarding the house later told me they had orders to eliminate the Bengali inhabitants of the house at the slightest provocation.

An eerie silence loomed there. It was a lone unarmed Indian soldier originally hailing from Rawalpindi, facing almost a dozen heavily armed Pakistani soldiers, all under Pak's Rawalpindi GHQ. One wrong move and the situation could be catastrophic. I kept on moving forward, slowly. Each moment seemed an hour, each step a mile.

Pakistani soldier: "*Rukk ja nahi te' goli maar deyaanga.*" (Stop immediately or I will riddle you with bullets.)

I took a small step forward and kept my eyes firmly on the house.

Pakistani soldier (angrily): *"Tu suneya nahi, oye maye..."* (Did you not hear me, ...Expletive)

Me: "*Mein nihattha aan, mere veer*." (I am unarmed, my brother.)

I stood still for the first time since I started walking towards the house. I was partially relieved that he had not shot me. On hindsight, I ponder why he didn't shoot me at sight. Perhaps my uniform prevented them from doing so, or maybe sheer luck or maybe he was surprised at my dare or maybe he thought I was a just the front of a bigger force. I can only recite an Urdu couplet here—"*Himmate' mardaa, madadde' Khuda*." (God helps those who dare.)

Pakistani soldier: "*Je tu hilya te goli maar deyanga*." (Freeze or I will shoot you.)

I knew it was time for me to engage the Pakistanis.

Me: "*Meri gall dhyaan naal sun, mere bhraa*." (Listen to me carefully, my brother.)

I had brought in a degree of compassion in my tone. I took a step further. It was now a battle of wits and guts.

The Pakistani sentry shouted in near panic, "*Jeh tu hun agge wadheya te jaano maar deyaanga.*" (This is the last warning. If you take one more step forward, I'll kill you.)

Me: "*Tuwannu pata te hovege hi ki Pakistani fauj ne surrender kar ditta haiga. Ceasefire da hukum ho chukeya haiga.*" (The Pakistan Army has surrendered and there are orders of ceasefire.)

Some other soldiers with weapons joined him and looked towards me. I could see them taking positions as their fingers clasped the triggers. The crowd was watching me from a distance. It was almost a scene out of a Clint Eastwood western, only difference being that this could be fatal. Everything was standstill, nothing moved, not even the mild breeze that had accompanied me since I had left the Dacca airport. The crowd could see me facing the soldiers alone. A hush had descended upon them. My soldiers later told me that some people in the crowd were praying to Allah for my safety and that of the hostages.

Pakistani post (All soldiers angrily, almost in unison): "*Jhoot, ae kade' nahin ho sakda.*" (You are lying. It is impossible.)

They probably thought that I was bluffing as there was disbelief on their faces.

Me: "*Tussi soccho mein Hindustani fauj da afsar twaade saamne khada haiga nihattha, Dacca de vichkaar, koi te gal hovegi.*" (Please think, there must be a reason why an officer of the Indian Army is standing unarmed in uniform in front of you, in middle of Dacca.)

I gestured with my empty palms stretched towards them. They could see that I did not even have my weapon.

Pakistani post (Shouting): "*Chup ho jaa oye, te apni bakwaas band kar*." (Shut up and stop this nonsense.)

It was followed by a barrage of expletives in Punjabi. Rustic Punjabi is a colourful language with an amazing range of expletives, which are almost alien to the cultured and urbane Bengali. The hostages were in the house, and were seeing the drama unfold. They had been living under the shadow of death.

Me: "*Mera yakeen karo, tussi mere Punjabi bhraa haige o. Mein tuwadde naal jhoot nahi bolanga.*" (Please believe me, you are my Punjabi brothers. I will never lie to you.)

For the first time, there was no retort. They kept mum and stared at me. I guess they did not have any words for the situation. I was spinning a web of words and they were speechless.

I could make friends in a jiffy. My peers would marvel at my ability to build reliable networks even in the most hostile environments. Throughout my school and college, I was always a loyal and popular friend. I could talk my way out of the most awkward of situations. I had honed my skills further as I joined the army. I had a very reliable network of local friends in the North-East, ably aided by the sportsman in me and my genuine sincerity and honesty in relationships. I continued the conversation.

Me: "*Sohn rab di, twaddi sab di jaan khatre wich haigi*." (I swear upon God, all your lives are in danger.)

They were listening now, fingers moved away from triggers. Some soldiers who had marked me had now raised their heads. Battle-hardened, trigger-happy, blood-thirsty soldiers were now metamorphosing back into hardy Punjabi farmers, simple village folk yearning to be amongst their kith and kin. But they still seemed unconvinced.

Me: "*Ghar baithe apne maa, pyo, bacche, tiviyaan de baare socho. Je tussi meri gall nahi suni te saare maare jaouge.*" (Think about your parents, children, spouses. If you do not pay heed to my counsel, all of you will be killed.)

I took a pause and let the logic sink in. I resumed after a poignant pause.

Me: "*Koi te gall hovegi je mein aethe apni jaan di parwah keete bagair twadde saamne khlota aan.*" (It is not without a reason that I am standing in front of you, while putting my life in danger.)

Just a day before, Indian generals had stood firmly up to the Pakistani generals, talking them into a surrender.

Pakistani post: "*Tu othe hi ruk jaa. Assi enna gallan da faisla nahi kar sakde. Sahnu koi vi gadbad hon te ahnaa qaidiyaan nu maaran da hukam hai.*" (You stay put. We cannot decide on these matters. We have orders to shoot the hostages at the slightest provocation.)

They did not seem to be convinced about the Pak Army surrender. Maybe their sense of pride did not allow them to. They told me that they would ask their Senior for further orders. The soldiers were soon joined by their senior, probably a JCO. There was disbelief on his face as he harked -

"*Bakwaaas bandh kar. Pakistan kadde' vi Jhuk nahi sakda. Tenu te ess saare siyaaape di jadd nu mukaa deyaangaa.*" ("Shut up, will you? Pakistan can never retreat. We will eliminate you and the root cause of this problem forever"- He pointed downwards towards Sheikh Mujib's family.)

It was clear that this unit had no knowledge about the surrender. This made my task even tougher.They were there to keep Bangabandhu's family under house arrest. They were trigger-happy and had orders to shoot the inmates or anybody coming near, if the situation warranted.

Me: "*Mein sachh bol rehyaan hainga.. General Niazi ne surrender kar ditta haiga. Mein fauji haan, te enna bewakoof nahin ki nihattha twaadi bandoookan de saamne khade ho jawanga. Agar mein ehte aa gayaan wa te ehdaa matlab hai ki ethe aale dwaale Pakistan fauj hai hi nahin.*" (I am speaking the truth, my brother, please believe me. General Niazi has surrendered yesterday. I am a soldier. Do you think I will be so naive as to come and stand in front of your guns? If I am here, it is a clear signal that the Pakistan Army is nowhere near.)

Me (In authoritative tone) :. *"Es vele Dacca wich charron paase keediyaan di terah Hindustan fauj te Mukti Bahini haigi.*" (At this moment Indian Army and Mukti Bahini are swarming around Dacca like bees.)

Both the soldiers and 1 were speaking in the same dialect. They were now listening to me intently. I had bluffed regarding the position of the Indian Army. Indian army personnel were yet to reach Dhanmondi, Dacca.

Pakistani post: "*Assi twada kinj yakeen kar laiyae? Pakistan fauj kadi vi jhuk nahi sakdi.*

oye, goli maar dushman nu, vekh ki rehyaan ae." (How can we believe you? Pakistan Army can never surrender. Sepoy, shoot the enemy.)

The soldier took his position and aimed his gun on me. It was an eyeball-to eyeball confrontation. I had not seen Anshu, my daughter, as of yet.

Me: "*Rab da vaasta e, apne bacchyeya da, bhaina bhravan da khyaal karo."* (For God's sake, think of your children, your family back home.)

I looked at the JCO.

Me: "*Ae galti na karo, twaaddi jaan kahtre wich haigi. Charron paasse vekho, aithe mere alaawa twadaa koi beli nahi.*" (Don't shoot, your lives are in danger. Look around, I am the only one who can save you.)

The Bengali crowd was staring at them from all over now. Bodies of long-dead people shot by the soldiers, perched in defiance giving them a scornful stare.

The seeds of hatred sowed by Pakistani Punjabi elite, emanating from a false sense of cultural and racial superiority, was coming back to haunt them. The hunter was now the hunted.

Pakistani post: "*Oye, dabb de ghodaa, uddda de ehnu."* (Sepoy, pull the trigger and shoot him dead.)

Me: "*Rab di sohn, mein sach aakh rayaa haan. Mein taa jaan hath te rakh ke aayaa wa. Zaraa socho, ehnaa sareyan Bangaliyaan ne twadde tote'tote'kar dene ne. Twannu sirf mein bacha sakda haa.*"

(Think for a moment. I have forsaken my life to come here. Imagine for a moment what this crowd will do to you if anything happens here. Only I can save you.)

JCO: (Angrily) "*Tenu Assi Maar Deyange*" *(We will kill you)*

ARSD College. I was playing as the captain of my college team in the football finals. I got a pass and sprinted towards the goal post. Somebody tripped me just as I had aligned the ball with the goal post, avoiding the goalie who was playing his first major tournament. He had naively come out to counter me. The final whistle was about to blow for a draw. As I was about to strike the ball, somebody pushed and tripped me. I got a kick in my groin as I rolled over. I got hurt badly. The referee saw it. We had earned a penalty stroke. The pain was excruciating, but it was now or never. I would not have been playing the university tournament next year. I had to win this match as I was graduating in a month. Moments later the primitive bell shaped speakers were blaring: 'Captain of the winning team, Ashok Tara, please come on the stage.' The spectators went berserk as I lifted the trophy. 'Shoki, Shoki, Tara, Tara'.

JCO screamed: "*Oye, maar goli.*" (Sepoy, shoot him.)

To my good fortune, at that very moment, an Indian Army helicopter flew overhead. The Pakistani soldiers and I looked up. The concentric circles of the tricolour were conspicuously shining bright in the backdrop of the midday sun. I grabbed the opportunity to re-convey the fact that the Indian Army was in control of the capital city, as was evident with the unimpeded flight of the chopper.

Me: (Pointing towards the IAF chopper) - "*Vekhya? O raehya Hindustani fauj da helicopter. Thode chir wich hi hazaaran di taddad wich faujaan aa rehiyaan ne. Tussi jinni cheti aithon nikal jaavo unna changa hai. Mera yakin karo, Veero*" (Do you see that? Indian Air Force helicopter hovering over us in the skies? It is only a matter of time before the Indian forces and Mukti Bahini overrun this place. You need to get out of here as soon as possible.)

This seemed to have struck a chord with the enemy, who asked for some time to speak to their command.

Pakistani post: "*Sahnu thoda waqt chaida hai apne commander nall gall karan vaste. Jo uhnaa da hukum hovega assi o hi karanage.*" (Give us some time to talk to our commanders. We will abide by their decision.)

To this, I re-asserted that all officers of the Pakistan Army were POWs and their communication grid had ceased to exist.

Me: *"Twadde saare afsar Hindustan di fauj di giraft wich haige ne. Na koi wireless hai na telephone.*" (Nothing is working, neither wireless nor telephones. All your officers have surrendered and are in the custody of the Indian Army. Who will respond to you?)

All this while, I steadily paced myself towards the enemy positioned at the front gate of the house.

Suddenly, a woman's shrill scream for help broke the silence. She waved frantically and shouted, "Do not believe them! If you do not save us, they will kill us." This reconfirmed my apprehension of the intention of the Pakistani soldiers in the building.

By this time, I was standing in front of the main entrance with a young Pakistani soldier nudging the cold steel of the bayonet of his rifle under my right ribcage. His trembling hand and his jittery finger on the trigger was an unmistakable reminder of the delicate position I was in. It was quite obvious that he had never been in such close vicinity of his adversary. Not wanting to give time to the enemy to consider alternatives, I continued to convince them to capitulate.

Me: "*Tussi meinu goli maar sakde ho, magar charo paase ghum ke vekho. Je ethe Mukti Jodhe aa gaye te twaddiyaan botiyaan vi nahin milni. Bhravo je Sheikh sahib de khandaan nu kujh ho gaya te tussan kise ne nahin bachna je. Twaadi zindgi te maut wich mein khada wa. Sirf mein hi twaanu bachaa sakdaa aan. Aur twade moye jisman da ki hal hovega tussi soch vi nehi sakde.*" (You can shoot me if you want. But have a look all around you. If Mukti Jodhas come here, they will hack you into pieces. Brothers, if anything happens to the family of Hon. Sheikh Mujib, then none of you will survive. And you cannot even imagine what will be done to your dead bodies.)

Gathering all my wits together, I continued to persuade the Pakistani soldiers to surrender while slowly pushing the barrel away from my body.

With the conviction that the enemy was almost swayed with my narrative, it was time for me to play the final card in the emotional salvo. I had engaged myself in inflicting constant reminders of their families back home and a safe passage back to their units, on one hand, as compared to certain death at the hands of the Mukti Bahini Jodhas as a consequence of non-compliance. This tactic finally brought about the realisation of the dire situation they were in, and eventually they yielded.

Me: "*Oye tussan Bangaal toh ki lena? Apne pindaan nu, apne gharran nu javo bharawo, apne khetaan wich, apne tabbaran kol. Jannatan vargi apni dharti wich apne bachaayaan te vohti kol. Oye sardiyaan aa gayiaan ne, maa de hattan da saron da saag te maaki di rotiyaan khaao jaake.*

"Tussi marran di zidd te kyun kar reye' ho jaddon aithon zinda bach ke nikal sakde ho, apne watan ja sakde ho?"

(What work do you have in Bengal? Go back to your villages, your homes, in the midst of your farmlands to be with your families. To your heaven, your motherland, to be with your parents, wives and children.

Why are you hell-bent on dying when you can go back to your native place?)

I was talking to the Punjabis in their own language, weaving an emotional narrative, playing on their fears interspersed with occasional funny nuances, which we Punjabis are quite capable of even in the most trying circumstances.

JCO: "*Lekin...*"

He was at a loss of words.

Me: "*Soch ki rahe ho, twaadde kol waqt bhaut ghat haiga.*" (What are you thinking, you don't have time.)

JCO (barely audible): " *Bandook thale kar.*" (Sepoy, lower your gun.)

The soldier at the gate was still pointing his rifle with the bayonet at me half-heartedly, and shivering even as I had gently moved the barrel away from my ribs. The JCO was crestfallen as he ordered his soldier to lower the gun.

I heaved a sigh of relief and smiled to myself. I had won one of the most thrilling battles without firing a bullet or getting one.

Cards and chess were important indoor games for our generation. There were many games that we played with those 52 cards. Kot pees, Bluff, Rummy, Flash. Mercifully, our generation did not have mobiles and iPads to play with. We were playing both physically and mentally challenging games. Physical games give you that killer instinct, physical fitness, split-second decisions, and planning new moves every moment. With cards, you are locking your brains with the adversary, trying to anticipate his next move. One of the most interesting games are Bluff and Flash. You need not have the best cards to win. It is all about how to outwit your rival.

The JCO was now gazing at me intently. The initial arrogance was all but gone. They all appeared anxious and worried now.

JCO: "*Tussi ki chahnde' ho?*"

I knew he had taken the bait. The arrogant defiance on his face had mellowed down, but an unmissable soldier's pride was writ on his face. The next thing was the hardest that a soldier has to say to another. I had to do it as delicately as possible, especially when the balance of power and guns were with them. I, of course, was empty handed.

Me: "*Tussi apne aap nu mere hawaale kar deyo. Aitho foran nikal ke mere naal chalo.*" (Give yourselves up to me and quickly get out of this place with me.) My voice was sincere and my expression sombre.

JCO: "*Assi twaadda kinj yakeen kar layiye. Jeh main te mere bande apne aap nu twaadde hawaale kar dinde aan te es gall da ki aitbaar hai ki assi bach jawaange?*"

(How can we believe you? If my men and I give ourselves up, what is the guarantee that we will be unharmed?)

Me: "*Mai, ek Hindustani fauj da afsar vayeda karda haa ki ager tussi surrender karoge te tusi sahi salaamat apne ghar vapas jaa sakoge. Saari Pakistaan fauj hathyaar paa chuki hai. Tussi jaande ho ki poora Bangaladesh intequam lenaa chahnda haiga. Twaddi hifazat sirf te sirf sadde naal haigi. O yaara, wapas apne pindaan nu jao, aithe Bangal wich ki rakheya twada*?"

(It is the word of an Indian Army officer that if you surrender, I will make sure you reunite with your families. Entire Pakistan Army has laid down their arms. You know that Bangladesh is seeking revenge. You are safe only if you surrender. Buddies, go back to your villages. There is nothing here left for you in Bengal.)

JCO (with a scared expression): *Tussi meinu kuch waqt deyoge?* (Will you give me some time?)

I declined with a warning that any delay will cost them their life.

The JCO confabulated with his soldiers. The bulk of the West Pakistan Army was in an alien land, and was hailing from Punjab. West Pakistan and East Pakistan were as different as chalk and cheese. There was nothing in common, from food to culture to dress to customs to ethnicity. The predominantly Punjabi West Pakistan Army was now homesick and stuck in a very hostile environment. There was zilch support for them in Bangladesh. They knew they were hated. The JCO agreed to surrender. I told them to leave their weapons there only.

The inmates of the house were observing the entire episode.

JCO: "*Mein te mere sipaahi twadde naal chalaan nu tyaar haige aa. Par tussi rab di sonh chukko ki sahnu kujh nahi hovega"* (My soldiers and I are ready to go with you, please swear upon God, that we will be safe.).

Me: (Nodding reassuringly) "*Aitho Pakistan fauj di vardi paa ke nikalna naa-mumkin haiga. Tussi kamizaan badlo*." (You cannot get out of this place in your Pakistan Army uniform. Please change your shirts.)

I heaved a sigh of relief. Mission was accomplished without any casualties.

Almost immediately, they came down after leaving their weapons at their location. I rushed in and pushed the doors open to secure the family and mitigate any chances of possible foul play. Mrs. Sheikh Mujibur Rahman embraced me and said, "God has sent you to save us... you are like my son."

After comforting the family and reassuring them, I went out and called for my soldiers to come forward to take over the surrendered Pakistani soldiers. When Pakistani soldiers came down, they were scared due to the uncertainty about their safety as their weapons were taken away. They were told to get in the vehicle and civilian clothes were given to hide their identity from the locals and Mukti Bahini. The grim situation was now clear to them, and they obliged willingly. The West Pakistan soldiers realised that I was right. We were now standing between them and the local Bengali mob. As they were in our custody, the mob could not take revenge. They looked sad, but relieved.

Mrs. Mujibur Rahman looked up at the rooftop where the Pakistani flag had been hoisted by the West Pakistan Army to humiliate Bangabandhu's family. I told her that Pakistan Army had surrendered to the Indian Army and Bangladesh was now a free country. She was overjoyed. Mrs. Mujibur Rahman gave me the flag of Bangladesh, and requested me to take down the enemy flag and hoist the Bangladesh flag over the roof of the said house. I was assisted by Mr. Mominul Haq Khokha, a close relative of hers. It is an honour that I will be proud of all my life. It was surreal as I climbed on to the roof and took down the Pakistani flag and hoisted the Bangladesh flag. It fluttered with pride in the joyful breeze of free Bangladesh as the Pakistani flag hit the ground. There were tears of joy in all eyes that were looking up. Sheikh Mujib was still in West Pakistan, under arrest. No words can describe the emotions in the heart of the first family of Bangladesh. No words can describe the valiant struggle of a nation and its brave people who were treated with unspeakable contempt and barbarity by their tormentors.

As the Pakistani flag bit the dust, it was trampled upon. Mrs. Mujibur Rahman, raised her fist, and roared with pride, '*JOY BANGLA*'. I could hear the joyous crescendo of '*JOY BANGLA*' from all over.

By that time a few media persons also came in. The JCO, the Pakistani soldier in-charge, had said a few words to the media before getting into the vehicle. They were sent to their headquarters. Later, when I enquired from the journalist, he told me that the JCO spoke in Urdu about me. *"Ya khuda yeh banda bekhauf hai."* (By God, he is a fearless man.)

Audentes fortuna adiuvat. (Fortune favours the brave.)

17th December— Rajouri Garden, New Delhi

Back home, Abha was in the house caring for my three-month-old daughter, Anshu, whom I was yet to see. My mother was in her school. Father was at home, tending to the children. My brothers and sister were busy with chores but glued to the battery-operated radios. My friends were planning to have a chilled beer with me and listening to wartime stories upon my return. I was in the thoughts of many, but none crossed me at that moment. Almost 6,000 soldiers from all three sides had died by now. I was lucky to have survived with a gallantry battle honour and a couple of brushes with death. Some of the most heroic in the battalion were dead. Albert Ekka and many other soldiers—Indian, Pakistani and Mukti Jodhas—were being laid to their eternal rest as per respective rites.

"Raah pe rehte hain, yaadon pe basar karte hain,
Khush raho ahl-e-watan, hum toh safar karte hain"

—Gulzar

(I travel forever on endless roads, living off memories
Wishing happiness to my countrymen, as I continue
my onward journey)

News of the rescue of Sheikh Mujibur Rahman's family had spread like wildfire in the continent, especially in India and Bangladesh, through local, national, international news agencies and electronic media.

My family came to know about it in a dramatic scenario, narrated to me later. On the eve of 17th December 1971, which was the last day of blackout, one of our neighbours came and told my parents to switch on the TV to hear the news about Ashok, but he did not disclose the news. Worried, they switched on TV . Abha, who was in the kitchen, came out, though tense, to watch the news. On seeing my picture with the news and that Mrs. Sheikh Mujibur Rahman had hugged me like her own son, my whole family was over joyed. My wife, who was standing quietly, was relieved and cheerful that I was safe and had done a glorious act. This was the first time that she had heard about me after many days. My father-in-law switch off the television & radio.

Later, I received many congratulatory messages from my family, relatives and friends. Even a cake was sent by some unknown person. I sent new year greetings to my parents and family members alongwith newspaper cuttings with my photo and the printed description.

After a few days, I was designated to accord reception to acting President, Mr. Nazrul Islam, and acting Prime Minister Mr. Tazzudin at Dacca airport, Bangladesh.

At the end of December 1971, my unit, 14 Guards, moved out of Bangladesh to Mizoram (India). But I was told to stay at Dacca because Sheikh Mujibur Rahman's family wanted me to meet him for saving them from the jaws of death. Bangabandhu was still in the custody of Pakistan. On 22nd December 1971, he was freed from solitary confinement and placed under house arrest at a guest house outside Rawalpindi. He was finally freed on 8th January 1972. The Father of the Nation arrived in London on the same day. Two days later, on 10th January, he flew home to a free, liberated Bangladesh.

My family had no information about my return to India. When I reached home and knocked on the door, everyone was pleasantly surprised. Abha, with her simple mesmerising smile and wet eyes, conveyed her feelings of deep love silently. That scene is etched in my mind.

On 24th November 1972, I was awarded the gallantry award Vir Chakra by the President of India, Shri V. V. Giri for the Battle of Gangasagar. After the completion of my leave, I left for Mizoram to join my unit, 14 Guards.

The lines of the Gracie Fields' song reverberated in my mind as I took my flight out of Dacca in January 1972.

"Wish me luck as you wave me goodbye.
Cheerio, here I go on my way
With a cheer, not a tear, in your eye
Give me a smile, I can keep for a while
In my heart while I'm away
'Till we meet once again, you and I
Wish me luck as you wave me goodbye."

❑

CHAPTER 14

Lifelong Memories of a Post-war Month

The fearless nationalist spirit among the Mukti Jodhas and locals, including women, before and during the Liberation War, had us all in awe. I cannot forget the burning desire in those anguished eyes to fight for their motherland, which was soon to be known to the world as Bangladesh. They volunteered to help the Indian Army and guided the movement of our troops through secure routes as well as identification of targets. During the entire war (December 3rd–16th, 1971) they helped and guided us, and often provided food, water, and shelter.

On 16th December 1971, the day Pakistan Army surrendered to the Indian and Bangladesh Armies, there were crowds everywhere shouting slogans of *Jai India, Jai Bangladesh and Jai Bangabandhu.* Even small children were bursting crackers and abusing the Pakistan Army with slogans like *Pakistan murdabad.* Enormous posters of Bangabandhu Sheikh Mujibur Rahman, India's then Prime Minister Indira Gandhi, Indian soldiers and Mukti Bahini Jodhas were displayed in many places. People turned out in their best dresses and carrying bouquets of flowers, presented them to the Indian soldiers wherever they went. They displayed great joy and were triumphant at overcoming an evil ruler. There were festivities everywhere. The dark days were finally over for them. Now the people of Bangladesh waited with bated breath for Bangabandhu, who had been incarcerated in Pakistan.

Since early morning on 17th December, there was a vast crowd rejoicing at Dacca airport to see their freedom fighters, the Indian Army. I, along with my men, was present to maintain the security of VIPs landing at the airport. I asked an ecstatic group of girls and boys what they were watching. Looking at the army personnel who liberated them, they said. At 11 a.m. the same day, when the family of Bangabandhu, Sheikh Mujibur Rahman, was rescued from the captivity of Pakistani troops, there was unbelievable elation among the locals, media and Mukti Jodhas. As soon as the news of the rescue spread in Dacca, it looked like everyone had come to see their Bangamata, Sheikh Faziilatunnesa Mujib, and family, including the present PM Sheikh Hasina. They were saved from the assassination attempt of the Pakistan Army. I had received many congratulatory messages from my family, relatives and friends. Even a cake was sent to me by some unknown person. I had responded to some of them, especially my wife and parents, by sending newspaper cuttings that had published my photos along with a description in their publications. I conveyed my thanks by writing 'Wishing Happy New Year' and signed as the new year, 1972, was approaching in a few days.

On 20th December, I was assigned to give Guard of Honour to acting President Mr. Nazrul Islam and acting Prime Minister Tajuddin at Dacca airport on their return to Bangladesh. It was an honour for me and an exciting experience to be leading the parade in front of senior army personnel, politicians and a big crowd of locals.

While most of my unit had left Bangladesh, I was directed to stay back. The Indian Army had acceded to the request of the Bangabandhu family who wanted me to meet Sheikh Mujibur Rahman. During this period, I was provided with accommodation in the MLA (Member of Legislative Assembly) residential area (mess) and a Toyota car with a driver. I was considered a guest by the Dacca Club. Locals used to look at me with respect and deep regard. Wherever I wanted to shop, they declined to take any money. In one case, I, along with Jamal, the younger son of Sheikh Mujibur Rahman, had lunch at a roadside restaurant. The owner did not take any money, rather insisted and gave me a ten rupee note and requested my signature on it as a souvenir. Such was the genuine and vivacious admiration I received for saving the first family of Bangladesh. During my stay up to 20th January 1972, before I left Dacca for India, many people kept on visiting me and conveyed their colossal warmth. I felt like a mini celebrity in Bangladesh during that month. I received so much love from the people of Bangladesh during that period. Wherever I went, people would mob me and cries of '*Jai Bangla*' and '*Jai Hind*' greeted me. As an army officer on duty, I was not supposed to react and just smiled and said 'thank you' for the adulation. Even after fifty years, that one month is etched in my memory as if it was yesterday.

An Illustrious Bengali Family's Humble Punjabi Son

The stick-together families are happier by far Than the brothers and the sisters who take separate highways are. The gladdest people living are the wholesome folks who make A circle at the fireside that no power but death can break. And the finest of conventions ever held beneath the sun Are the little family gatherings when the busy day is done.

It's the stick-together family that wins the joys of earth, That hears the sweetest music and that finds the finest mirth; It's the old home roof that shelters all the charm that life can give; There you find the gladdest play-ground, there the happiest spot to live. And, O weary, wandering brother, if contentment you would win, Come you back unto the fireside and be comrade with your kin.

—Edgar Guest, 'The Stick-Together Families'.

Rajouri Garden, Delhi—1960s and 70s

My generation grew up as parts of large families. The joint family system is unique to the Indian subcontinent. It is not uncommon for three to four generations to live under a single roof. Generally, relatives also lived nearby. Those days, it would not be uncommon during minor celebrations for an entire hall to fill up with hundreds of near and dear family members. Also, there would be close friends of the family too, at times, running in three generations. Unlike in the West, Indians have a unique name for each relation. The West has it much simpler—uncles and aunts. India has *Dada–Dadi, Nana–Nani, Bua–Phupha, Chacha–Chachi*, and so on. In any given year, there were several weddings, births and funerals in the extended families.

There were several rituals associated with them, and necessitated almost all the families to come together. Festivals like Holi, Diwali and Lohri brought the clans together to celebrate and enjoy good food and dance.

We were three brothers and one sister living in the same house with my parents and grandmother. My eldest brother had gotten married and my *bhabhi* had also joined our family. When I Iook back on those days, it seems like a different era, a different time. There used to be laughter and energy all around the house. Each one had his own stories of day-to-day struggles to share. My bhabhi was also working like my mother. My sister and brother-in-law would also visit us along with their children. While the ladies would cook up delicacies in the kitchen, my father would be sitting at the head of the dining table with his sons, engaged in animated discussions. The children would play and run around, shrieking away to glory. The walls of the house would shake with laughter and jokes. The warmth and glow of those days when large families consisting of four generations would be together is still fresh in my heart. We were like millions of middle-class families in the subcontinent, originating out of small towns and rural areas, now adjusting to the urban milieu. Thanks to the rapid proliferation of modern education, the story was the same in Delhi, Bombay, Karachi, Lahore, Calcutta, Madras and Dhaka. It was sheer magic when all brothers and sister with their spouses and children were together in the house, soaked in the glow of love and warmth of our parents. All this started to change when modern-day couples opted for smaller families. As the 60's generation bows out, those times are rapidly becoming a part of history and folklore.

The First Family

Keeping the safety of the first family after the 17th December episode in view, I was directed by the Indian Army to visit them on a daily basis for the next few days and to assess their safety and well-being. I cannot forget the time when I had rescued Mrs. Sheikh Mujibur Rahman (Bangamata) from the captivity of Pakistani troops and opened the door of the room where she, along with family members, was locked. She had put her hand on my head and said, "You are like my son and Allah has sent you to save us."

All the members of the family gave me lots of affection and respect. In fact, the younger sister Rehana of the present Prime Minister Sheikh Hasina, used to call me *Dada* (elder brother). I was told that I could visit them anytime, as I was a part of the family. She wrote me two letters, but I could not reply on grounds of security, as I was in active service in the army. Some other communications never reached me.

Meanwhile, Sheikh Mujib's two sons Kamal and Jamal, too, reached Dhaka and were reunited with their mother, sisters and younger brother Russel, who was about seven years old then. It was an emotional reunion. I was introduced to them and I became a part of their family. I hit off very well with the two elder sons. An instant brotherly bond was forged among us.

Both Kamal (born 1949) and Jamal (born 1954) were young men, full of life. They had escaped and crossed over to the liberated zones and joined the struggle to free their motherland. Kamal was an active organiser of the Mukti Bahini guerrilla struggle and had received a wartime commission in Bangladesh Army during the Liberation War. He received his training in Murtee Camp, in the Himalayan foothills in West Bengal. He was ADC to General Osmani, the commander-in-chief of the Mukti Bahini, during the Liberation War of Bangladesh.

Kamal was a versatile and handsome personality—tall like his father and amiable. He practiced playing the *sitar* at *Chhayanaut*, a music school. He was also involved in diverse cultural activities and was a keen sportsperson.

Jamal, the younger brother, was also detained with his mother and other family members at Dhanmondi. However, in a daring escape, he joined the Liberation Forces. He trained with the Special Forces in the Himalayan hills near Dehradun, Chakrata (in Uttar Pradesh, now Uttarakhand).

Kamal was an avid sportsperson with keen interest in cricket, volleyball and football. I told him about my achievements in cricket and football as a student of Delhi University. After the war, it was like a holiday for me. For the next one month, we would move around Dacca in an open army jeep or sometimes in a car. He would often take me to places of historical interest in and around Dhaka. Sometimes we played together. Like most Bengalis, he was also deeply in love with music and culture. Unfortunately, I had little to contribute on that front. There is a famous joke that the only culture Punjabis know is agriculture. Kamal had a magnetic aura around him. He was a tall, energetic, handsome young man with varied interests.

The Sheikh family treated me like their own and made me comfortable. It was normal for me to visit their house in Dhanmondi for casual conversations. I had been in war or in warlike conditions for almost a year and had not met my family. I felt as though I was with my own brothers, sisters and mother. Hasina and Rehana called me *Bhai*. Mrs. Mujib had kept her hand on my head and called me her son. The brave lady had kept the family and her nation together in such trying times. Her strength and courage are unparalleled, and part of folklore now. The family was erudite but grounded and tied to their culture. I was a soldier and sportsperson and not much into literature. But I could not help marvel at the diverse collection of books by renowned authors in their house. I was told that Bangabandhu was very fond of reading. Almost all books read by him were diligently preserved by Bangamata. She was extremely meticulous and disciplined. The entire family, and of course Bangladesh, was waiting with bated breath for Bangladesh's most illustrious son. I had heard so much about Bangabandhu that I looked forward to meeting him, the 'Tiger of Bengal.'

I was invited regularly for meals to their house and treated to excellent Bengali dishes, all supervised by Bangamata. She came to know that I was very fond of seafood, especially prawns. Bangamata told me that Sheikh Mujib, too, liked prawns. She would make sure that I was comfortable and treated me at par with her sons, sitting next to me at the dining table. She was very dignified and in control of the house, with a strong sense of duty. I could not help comparing her to my own mother. Then finally, the news came that the family and the people of Bangladesh had been waiting for anxiously—Bangabandhu was coming back. I later came to know that meeting me was on the priority itinerary of the great leader.

10th January 1972 was the day Bangabandhu returned from incarceration in Pakistan. His flight itinerary was from Pakistan to

London to Dacca, with a brief stopover in Delhi. Dacca was the city of the moment in the world, and Bangabandhu was the man of the moment. There were people everywhere. Huge crowds moved towards Dacca airport with large posters and Bangladesh as well as Indian national flags, singing patriotic songs and shouting slogans of '*Jai Bangabandhu*', '*Jai Bangladesh*' and so on.

At the first sight of the beloved leader, the waiting crowd burst into jubilation. It was a historic occasion. The people had united with their leader after 292 days. They had suffered so much, and now it was time to celebrate. From the Tejgaon airport, Bangabandhu was taken in a procession to the Race Course ground (now Suhrawardy Udyan). It took two and a half hours to pass this four-mile-long route. Chants of '*Jai Bangla*' reverberated across the skies. The crowd was ecstatic on seeing their beloved leader. Some wept, tears of joy overflowing from their eyes. I was witnessing history in the making. That day would become a golden leaf in the history of the proud and valiant people of Bangladesh. He was finally united with his family at his Dhanmondi house.

On 12th January 1972, I was called by Bangabandhu to his residence. I was probably amongst the first outsiders, apart from other senior Indian officers, to be called to meet him. I was told that he wanted to meet the saviour of his family. I was nervous about meeting the great man. I saluted him as I saw him. He instantly said, 'You are like my son,' and embraced me. He conveyed his gratitude for saving his family. He said that I could visit and meet him any time without any reservation or appointment.

16th January 1972, Dhanmondi, Dhaka—A Breakfast to Remember

It was early morning on 16th January 1972. I got a message that Bangabandhu wanted to have breakfast with me. That meal with his family, just before I left Bangladesh, is still fresh in my memory, like it was yesterday. They were a remarkable and noble family. Bangabandhu and Bangamata, their three sons and two daughters, were a perfect picture of bliss like any other family on the subcontinent, and yet extraordinary in some unspoken way. The house seemed less like that of a political leader and more of a professor. There was joy in the family as their patriarch had come out from the jaws of death. It was a portrait of bliss—a happy and contented family.

They were very polite and grounded. The Sheikh family seemed like my own. I had not met my family for almost a year and they made me feel at home. While in the battlefield, there were times when I would hurriedly consume my modest army rations, I could feel that my mother was standing there next to me, keeping an eye on the white aluminium plate and exhorting me to eat more, not knowing when I would get food next or whether there would be another meal at all. I am sure that most other army men had the same feeling.

Mrs. Mujibur Rahman exhorted me to eat. During breakfast, Bangabandhu had repeatedly conveyed his thanks and gratitude for saving the family and we had a very cordial talk.

I was just an army man from a modest middle-class background; they were big people for me. They were amongst the most influential, respected and noble families of the subcontinent. I was initially hesitant to go to their house, but they made me feel like one of their own. The cultural, class and linguistic barriers melted with their affection.

A General's Visit and a Nervous Major

When Bangamata Mrs. Mujibur Rahman addressed me as 'son' and exhorted me to have the delicious breakfast, I could not help comparing her to my own mother—very dignified, very articulate, with a strong sense of duty. While the entire family was joking and treating me like their own, the head of the Indian forces in Dhaka, General Jagjit Singh Aurora, came to the ground floor reception. I became nervous, as a young major. I thought he may come upstairs and see me enjoying having a hearty breakfast. I could feel beads of perspiration trickling down my forehead. This was a situation more difficult than any of the assaults or charges. Most of the time, on the battlefront I was in charge. Here, I was a young novice officer in front of my general, snacking away to glory. I quickly rehearsed the sequence in case I came face to face with my top commander. I would get up in a flash, click my boots and give the best military school salute —*Jai Hind,* sir. In a split second, I rehearsed my lines in all the three probable languages—Hindi, English and Punjabi and the likely questions that General Aurora may ask. Punjabi could have been the medium, as nobody else present there could have understood it. With a half-eaten sandwich in my hand, ready to take another bite, I froze as I rehearsed a hypothetical encounter in my mind the moment I heard General Aurora was there. It was a terrifyingly comical situation for me. Mrs. Mujib, with her motherly instinct, could sense my discomfiture. She said, "Don't worry, Bangabandhu will take care of everything." Bangabandhu left for the ground floor reception to meet General Jagjit Singh.

My mind was racing for a hypothetical encounter with the legendary general. I imagined him entering and myself after getting rid of the sandwich; standing instantly to attention, drawing myself to my full height and presenting the smartest salute ever.

General: "…and you are?"

Me: "Sir, Captain Ashok Tara, sir, 9 Para, IV corps, sir!"

General: "Why are you here?"

Me: "Sir, I was ordered to be here." (with a click of heels)

General: "Meet me once you are through with this."

I rehearsed the imaginary lines in Punjabi too.

General: *"Tu kaun hai?"*

Me: "Sir, Captain Ashok Tara, sir, 9 Para, IV corps, sir"

General: *"Tu aithe ki kar raeiya haiga?"*

Me: *"Mainu hukum hoya, sir"* (my boots clicking in rapt attention)

General: *"Shaami report karo"*

Me: *"Ji,* sir" (with salute and boots clicking)

I was thinking furiously about getting out of the tricky situation.

Bangabandhu came back after some time and told me that the general had left. I heaved a sigh of relief. Bangamata smiled and said, "I told you not worry, Bangabandhu will take care. Have something more to eat." I could not believe that the first family of Bangladesh and the man of the moment who had just led his people to independence after an unbelievable struggle, was making me such an important visitor to his house. Mrs. Mujib had briefed him about the rescue. He asked me about my family and thanked me for saving his. Two of my photographs with the family have been displayed in the National Museum in Dhaka. The family bid me an emotional goodbye. I was hugged by Bangabandhu as he said thanks once again.

23rd January 1972, I was to leave Dacca for Delhi. Bangamata and family wanted me to join them for lunch before I left. On my visit to the house on 19th December, she presented a Tissot wrist watch to me as a gesture of affection.

Sheikh Hasina gave her photo with her three-month-old son as a souvenir to my wife Abha, duly signed at its back—*'Dear Bhabhi'*. Abha cherishes it, and she has still kept in safe custody. It was an emotional goodbye. I did not know when I would come back again.

Next day, on 20th January, I took a flight out of Dacca for India. One of their relatives and close associates of Sheikh Mujibur Rahman, Mr. Khokha, came to Dacca airport with a bouquet of flowers to see me off.

15th August, 1975, 5 a.m.—Humanity is Shamed

I was posted in Bagalkot, Karnataka. I got up early, did my stretching and got ready for the Independence Day functions to be held that day.

A fellow officer broke the news to me. The architect of Bangladesh and the Father of the Nation, Bangabandhu Sheikh Mujibur Rahman, along with his family members was assassinated by a few treacherous military officers in cold blood. I was in disbelief. The next few hours were the toughest moments of my life. They were my family and a family to millions in the subcontinent. Crestfallen, I sat glued to the radio set in the faint hope that the news was false, but BBC had confirmed our worst fears. There were not many channels of information those days. I frantically tried to get to my contacts in Delhi to know about the survivors in the family. I came to know that only Hasina and Rehana had survived the tragedy.

In total, 16 people were martyred on that day. Bangabandhu Sheikh Mujibur Rahman and Bangamata Begum Fazilatunnesa, their eldest son and freedom fighter Sheikh Kamal, second son Lieutenant Sheikh Jamal, two daughters-in-law Sultana Kamal and Rosy Jamal, Bangabandhu's brother Sheikh Nasser, brother-in-law and Minister of Agriculture Abdur Rab Serniabat and his daughter baby Serniabat, Arif Serniabat, grandson Sukanto Abdullah and nephew Shahid Serniabat, Bangabandhu's nephew and youth leader and journalist Sheikh Fazlul Huq Mani and his pregnant wife Arzoo Mani, Bangabandhu's security officer Brigadier Jamil and a fourteen-year-old boy, Rintoo, were killed.

The killers did not spare even the youngest son, ten-year-old Sheikh Russel. Heavens would have cried that day. My friends, my brothers Kamal and Jamal were gone. Abha and I were not able to eat or sleep that day. I mourned the deaths of my family. We were worried about the well-being of my sisters from across the border. I heard that both were out of the country and had survived the dastardly act.

I was shaken to the core and could not sleep and eat properly for days. I had lost my family members in Bangladesh.

Immortality

Do not stand at my grave and weep,
I am not there, I do not sleep.
I am a thousand winds that blow;
I am the diamond glints on snow.
I am the sunlight on ripened grain;
I am the gentle autumn rain.
When you awaken in the morning's hush,
I am the swift uplifting rush
Of quiet birds in circled flight.
I am the soft stars that shine at night.
Do not stand at my grave and cry.
I am not there; I did not die.

— Clare Harner,
Immortality

❑

CHAPTER 15

A Forgotten Soldier, Long Lost Sisters and Recognition

Time has unique qualities. It seems to move fast in the long run, and appears to move very slowly in the short term. The journey of life mimics a river that gushes energetically down the mountains in rapids, in the falls with a youthful force, and maturing slowly to settle down in a benign flow that sustains and nurtures other lives before emptying itself into the ocean of eternity. In 1951, I was a little prankster kid walking miles through a jungle to reach school. In 1961, I was in college, an ace sportsman and NCC cadet, leading both football and cricket teams. In 1971, I was a young 29-year-old, a veteran of two wars—a battle-scarred decorated major. In 1981, I was 39 years old and posted in a peaceful posting and father of two young children. At 42 as a Lieutenant Colonel, I was promoted to be Second in Command of 14 Guards and after three months promoted to full colonel to take over the command of 14 Guards. Commanded 14 Guards from 1984 -1987, at Nasirabad(Raj) and Punch (J&k). In 1990, I was posted at Quarter Master General Branch, Army Head Quarters (AHQ), New Delhi. My children were growing up fast and the elder one was in college., On 31st January 1994' at the age of 52 years, I retired from Army and joined the civilian sector

By 2001, at the dawn of the new millennium, I was 60 years old and retired, leading an active social life, contributing to the society while living in a retired army personnel suburb of Delhi. By 2011, at 70 years, Abha and I were shuttling between India and Australia where my children had settled. The lives of my children had started in another land in full swing. My generation had taken their premium seats in the audience to watch the next generation play in the arena of life. Colonel Ashok Tara (Retd.), like all soldiers, was fading away slowly and suddenly there was a buzz, a knock at my door. People wanted to know about me, my times and my story. I was remembered, recognized and my past recalled. The print and digital media covered my story extensively on both sides of the border. Time and life are both linear and multi-dimensional.

My rescue of the Bangabandhu family earned me a lot of fame in 1971 and as it is, with most things in history's course, it faded from everyone's memory but for the ones involved. Over the course of time, the Bangabandhu family faced immense tragedies. His surviving daughters were exiled and the famous Dhanmondi house was locked up by successive regimes. It would be an eternal wait for the books of the house's well-stocked library for both their keeper and reader—Bangamata and Bangabandhu.

1972—An Award Gets Lost in Rules

I was back in India and joined my unit in January 1972 after meeting my family. Within the army, there were talks about appreciating my heroics in saving the Bangabandhu family. There was a section in the army who thought that I deserved an exemplary award for the 17th December episode. I was later told that since the war had ended on 16th December, a wartime gallantry award was not possible. Later, I was told that after two months, gallantry awards are not considered per se. One of my seniors said that my Vir Chakra in the war for the Battle of Gangasagar should serve as a consolation. I heard that my case got buried in the dusty labyrinth of files, rules, regulations and bureaucratic indifference. At the end of the day, I was doing my duty, which, in any case, is not performed by keeping awards in mind. I feel that awards and recognitions mean more to the family and friends than to the individual concerned. I retired from the army as a very proud and satisfied soldier. I am thankful to my destiny that took me to serve in one of the most glorious armies of the world, during a very eventful era. I gave my best to live up to its reputation.

A Brave Daughter's Lonely Battle

Sheikh Hasina's brave struggle in the aftermath of the bone-chilling tragedy that had befallen her and her family is stuff that folklore and legends are made of. Despite all odds, she came back to reclaim her father's legacy and led his party. Abha, my wife, is an avid reader and would point out all the news pertaining to her in magazines and newspapers. Life had come to a full circle when she became the prime minister of Bangladesh in 1996. During my service, my replies to the letters received from the family were not sent by the authorities to them. I guess there could be political or security reasons behind this.

Prime Minister Sheikh Hasina Wajed visited India in 1998. She had enquired about me from the authorities, who could not locate me. Unfortunately, Abha and I were out of the country and we could not meet her.

From 2001–2008, she was in the opposition. She became the prime minister for the second time in 2009. Under her leadership, Bangladesh, today, is one of the fastest growing economies of the world. It is a garment powerhouse and has made phenomenal strides on all fronts. In many social indicators, it has overtaken its cousins, India and Pakistan. Ladies form a sizeable chunk of Bangladesh's workforce. On the sports front, Bangladesh is emerging as a cricket powerhouse.

Prime Minister Sheikh Hasina Wajed has been voted as one of the most powerful women in the world by the Forbes Magazine. She has also been in the list of '100 Global Thinkers' of the decade. Bangladesh continues to rise as an economic powerhouse under her stellar leadership. She has redeemed her pledge to her nation, and to the memory of her noble parents.

Friend of Bangladesh Liberation War Honour

On 1st October 2012, one of my friends rang up and asked me to turn on the radio news—I was invited by the Bangladesh Government to receive the prestigious 'Friend of Bangladesh Liberation War Honour'. It was a pleasant surprise for me. Memories from another era came by as if it was yesterday. Later, it was confirmed by Bangladesh High Commissioner's Office,

New Delhi, and also through a message from the Bangladesh Government. A representative of the High Commission Office made all the arrangements in respect of my visa, return tickets and transport from my residence to Indira Gandhi Airport. Mr. Sayed Muntasir Mamum from Bangladesh's Delhi High Commission was at the airport to escort and see us off.

As the plane touched the Hazrat Shah Jalal International Airport at Dhaka (formerly Dacca), I was eagerly looking out of the plane window to catch a glimpse of Dhaka after 40 years. Abha and I were accorded a warm welcome by the government officials, coordinators, and media personnel. I was interviewed by the media in the VIP lounge. There was an excellent arrangement of high tea and snacks. A few more guests were invited from India and other countries, from different fields, who had supported, directly or indirectly, the people of Bangladesh during the Liberation War. I was accompanied by Albert Ekka's widow, Balamdini, and his son. Late Lance Naik Albert Ekka, PVC, was my comrade-in-arms in the epic Battle of Gangasagar, in which I was awarded the Vir Chakra.

We were put up in the prestigious Hotel Intercontinental. A liaison official was there to guide us to the areas and to take care of other needs. The transformation of this city and country, which was ravaged by war and brutality, was remarkable. It had metamorphosed into a thriving economic power, bubbling with boundless energy and enthusiasm for overall development. Dhaka is a city on the move. The future belongs to the young nation and its youth.

On 19th October 2012, we visited the War Memorial and Bangabandhu Museum. Warm thoughts filled my heart as I visited the revered Dhanmondi bungalow after 40 years. It was almost in the same condition as I had last visited it on 19th January 1972. I stood mesmerised in front of Bangabandhu's library, all the books neatly laid out by Bangamata herself. The breakfast table was laid out as it was decades ago. For a moment I could hear peals of laughter from the happy family enjoying itself. I could sense the family's benign presence at every step. At the photograph gallery of the museum, I stood still, gazing at a photograph of the family with a young Indian army major with a Tissot watch presented to him by Bangamata. 'He' was I in another era. I stood by Kamal's *sitar* in his bedroom. It seemed as if the strings were waiting for their master. It was the bedroom of Kamal and his young wife Sultana Kukhi, an ace sportswoman of the Dacca University with a national record in her name. Time had stood still till it was shattered as I spotted the blood-spattered walls with bullet marks. Abha and I could not speak during our journey back to the hotel. I recalled my journeys around the city with Kamal and Jamal. My eyes were moist with emotion and my heart full of grief. Memories haunted me.

On 20th October, it was a glittering awards ceremony at Bangabandhu International Conference Hall, I was awarded 'Friends of Bangladesh Liberation War Honour' by Hon'ble Prime Minister Sheikh Hasina, in the presence of the President of Bangladesh. The Hon'ble Prime Minister narrated the rescue episode to him. The audience sat mesmerised, and a huge applause greeted the friends of Bangladesh.

Whenever Abha and I went to Bangladesh, we found lots of warmth in people, especially in youth born after the Liberation War. The young boys and girls gave us bouquets and welcomed us with respect. They were, for the first time, seeing soldiers and others who had helped their nation in the Liberation War, at a time when their parents and grandparents went through unspeakable atrocities.

On 21st October, we were honoured by the Natundhara Foundation. It is a renowned publication house based at Dhaka. They invited me along with my wife to Dhaka University. They distributed leaflets, printed my photo between flags of Bangladesh, with a description about me and the role I played in the Liberation War. A sizeable crowd of students, professors and some other important personalities of Dhaka University welcomed us. Dhaka University had seen a despicable massacre of young students in 1971. An awe-inspiring statue of the Mukti Jodhas stands at an important intersection of the campus. I had the opportunity to deliver a talk on the Liberation War and role of the Indian Army, Mukti Jodhas and the locals. They presented me with a souvenir.

In the evening of 21st October, Prime Minister Sheikh Hasina invited my wife and I to her residence. There, we also met her younger sister Rehana, and her son and daughter-in-law. It was an emotional get-together as we reminisced about the old days. We were touched by the respect and personal warmth accorded to us by the first family of Bangladesh. We exchanged gifts between us, especially, a painting of PM Sheikh Hasina with her three-month-old son and Rehana (1971). Later in the evening, there was a dinner in a hotel where the PM came to meet all the invitees. I had requested the Bangladesh authorities for a visit to Gangasagar. It was promptly agreed to.

22nd October 2012—Gangasagar, A Battleground Revisited.

While the other invitees took their flights out of Dhaka, we proceeded to Gangasagar. The authorities were gracious to let me visit the place where the December action had started on 2nd December 1971. I had taken Albert Ekka's wife and son along with me. They had to visit the place where he was martyred and was accorded the Param Vir Chakra. It was an epic battle fought at the Gangasagar Railway Station, where I was awarded Vir Chakra. En route, people stopped us to offer their gratitude and respect. Lt. Col. Sajjad Ali of Bangladesh Army accompanied us to Gangasagar railway station.

A large crowd was there to receive us at Gangasagar Railway Station. A frail old man came forward and saluted me. His eyes gave him away. Even after 40 years, none of the fire and zeal he had for his motherland had diminished. He was the guide on that night of 2nd December, who had fearlessly guided us into the town towards the railway station. Neither he nor the soldiers he was leading knew that the serpentine line would finally stop at Dacca 15 days later, and unfurl the flag of the new nation. We hugged each other like long-lost brothers. He told me that the other guide, unfortunately, was no more. I went around the station and explained the events of that fateful night.

The local MLA and other senior dignitaries were present. We went to the graves of the freedom fighters and paid homage to the martyrs, accompanied by a local *maulvi*. A *fateha* was read, and I bowed my head to the sacred memory of all the fallen soldiers–from Bangladesh, India and Pakistan. A gala lunch was organised in our honour. We got a warm send-off.

In Dhaka Mr. Khoka and his wife had arranged a dinner at the century old prestigious Dhaka Club for us. I recalled being an honorary guest to the club on 22nd,January 1972.

(It was a sad day for me and my family when my dear friend Mr. Mominul Haq 'Khoka', veteran freedom fighter of Bangladesh, passed away in Singapore on 23rd May 2014)

On 23rd October we had a morning flight back to home, Delhi. Liaison Officer Lieutenant Colonel Sajjad, was there at the hotel to take us to the Dhaka airport. A few other officials and representatives of Indian High Commission in Dhaka came to see us off. I once again peered out of the window to say goodbye to a city that marked an important chapter in my life. We arrived at Delhi by 12 p.m. Mr. Sayed Muntasir Mamun, representative from the High Commission, Delhi, was there to receive us. In the evening back at home, there was a crowd of friends, neighbours and children waiting to meet us. They arranged a get-together and everyone wanted to listen about the visit and the ceremony. The media also came to know, and I had a few interviews about the award ceremony. Since then, I have been interviewed several times by the print and digital media. The young reader just has to google my name and many of these articles will pop up. The love and affection that I have received from both sides of the border is the biggest recognition that I could ever hope for.

8th April 2017—A Tale of Two Prime Ministers

Hon. Prime Minister Sheikh Hasina was on an official visit to Delhi. Amongst her itinerary was a visit to the army's Manekshaw Centre in the Delhi Cantonment on 8th April 2017. A 'Sommanona Ceremony' was to be held to honour the families of the martyrs of the Liberation War 1971.

In the first week of April 2017, an army officer called and requested my presence at the Manekshaw Centre. I asked if my wife could accompany me. The authorities allowed the request. The events of the day turned out to be one of the most memorable events of my life. The army functions follow strict protocols. Both the prime ministers were to grace the occasion–Prime Minister Narendra Modi and Prime Minister Sheikh Hasina. Amongst the esteemed guests were the senior ministers, the three defence chiefs of army, navy and air force, senior officers, both serving and retired, and war veteran's families. We accidentally landed at the VIP gate from where the prime ministers were supposed to come. I was politely guided towards the entry for other guests. Abha and I took our seats in the designated row in the Zorawar Hall auditorium behind the senior officers. The auditorium was jampacked. The armed forces are a punctual lot. We heard that the prime ministers had arrived and were viewing the photo exhibition about the 1971 War. Just before the start of the event, I saw a Senior officer enquiring about someone from the guests. One of the retired officers pointed at me. The officer came to me and said, "Colonel Tara?" I nodded; a bit surprised that I would be picked out in an auditorium full of luminaries. He requested Abha and me to follow him. We were escorted to the gallery of the photograph exhibition.

Both the prime ministers were there. Prime Minister Sheikh Hasina acknowledged us warmly. Apparently, we were called there at her request. We greeted Prime Minister Sheikh Hasina, who then introduced us to Prime Minister Modi. As we followed them through the exhibition, Sheikh Hasina stopped at a 1971 photograph which featured me and her family. She then made an unparalleled gesture when she narrated to Hon. Prime Minister of India how I, then, Major Ashok Tara, had rescued her family. Prime Minister Modi, too, in a wonderful gesture, asked me and Abha to stand next to the photograph in the gallery and asked the official cameraman to take a picture.

We then entered the auditorium and the prime ministers took their seats on the dais. We went and sat in our designated place. The auditorium was full of senior dignitaries from both the countries, Bangladesh war veterans and their families, ministers from either side, serving chiefs of army, navy and air force, and other senior officers.

Both the prime ministers gave excellent speeches on Indo-Bangladesh ties and recalled the sacrifice of the armed forces in the historic struggle. PM Sheikh Hasina mentioned that the history of Bangladesh is written in blood, and the blood of countless Indians had mingled with that of the people of Bangladesh and flowed down Padma, Jamuna and Teesta. PM Modi, in his speech, paid tributes to Bangabandhu. He praised the rapid progress made by Bangladesh on all fronts. He recalled the valour and sacrifice of the Indian forces. Just in the middle of the address, PM Modi paused and took my name in front of the august gathering and said, "Today we have in our midst, Brother Ashok Tara who saved the life of the Bangabandhu family." He asked me to stand for recognition of the audience. I stood up, followed my protocol and saluted the prime ministers, and bowed to the audience. I was overwhelmed at the recognition and ovation. The clip is available on YouTube for the readers to see.

I was also invited to India Gate for Army Day celebration on 15th January, 2019.

16th December 2020—Swarnim Vijay Mashaal

National War Memorial, India Gate, New Delhi—Tributes on the 50th Anniversary of 1971 War.

It was an early winter morning on 16th December, 2020 when Hon. Prime Minister Modi along with the Defence Minister Raj Nath Singh reached the National War Memorial to pay tributes to the heroes of the 1971 War to mark the 50th anniversary of India's win over Pakistan. PM Modi lit the '*Swarnim Vijay Mashaal*' (Flame of Glory) at the eternal flame of the National War Memorial.

Four war veterans were present with torches in hand. PM Modi lit those torches. My name was the first one to be read out. I stepped out, and the PM lit the flame of the torch in my hand.

The veterans handed over the torches to the youngsters who, in turn, started a relay race in the four directions of the country. The torches were to be carried to all the four directions and every nook and corner of the country, and return to Delhi.

17th December, 2020- Virtual Talk between Prime Minister Modi and PM Sheikh Hasina.

On 17th December 2020, Virtual Bilateral Summit between Hon'able PM Modi and Hon'ble PM Sheikh Hasina was held to honour the "Martyrs of Liberation War, Bangladash". During summit Hon'able PM Sheikh Hasina, Bangladesh, stated, in Bangali, that "17th Decenber was a special day for her and her family as it was on that day in 1971 when Major Ashok Tara of Indian Army freed her, her mother, sister and brother from Pakistani forces. Bangladesh was freed on December 16th but we were freed on 17th December, 1971.

I have been a part of many celebrations by Civilian and Army authorities and felicitated. There has hardly been a month in the last decade when my life and story has not been covered by the print and digital media on either side of the border. I am thankful to the almighty that I have been able to pass on the tales to future generations.

I sum up this chapter with a beautiful verse on the relation between 'Duty and Reward' from a verse from the Bhagavad Gita:

Karmanye vadhikaraste ma phaleshu kadachana,
Ma karmaphalaheturbhurma te sangostvakarmani!!

(You must perform your duty without any expectations.)

❑

CHAPTER 16

The Tara Family & Friends

Late Shri Chattarpati Tara (Father)

Shri Chattarpati Tara was born on 1st August 1908 in Sagari, a village near Rawalpindi. He did graduation from Govt. College Lahore (now in Pakistan). In 1942, he joined the Indian Army. During his tenure in the army, he fought on behalf of the British Crown at Burma border. Once the World War II was over, he decided to retire from army life in 1945 and took up a role in SPCA (Society for Prevention of Cruelty to Animals) at Delhi. He used to be fondly called *'Papaji'* by everyone. *Papaji* believed in service to humanity and treated everyone fairly. He was very fond of animals and hence his role in the SPCA was perfect for him. After retiring in 1968, *Papaji* kept himself busy with his family and emotionally supporting his cousin's family who lived next door. *Papaji* passed way in 1980 after an ailment but lived a content man who saw his children well established in their lives, married and enjoyed spending time with his grandchildren.

Late Mrs. Damyanti Tara (Mother)

Shrimati Damyanti Tara was born on 20th January 1917, at Rawalpindi (in Pakistan). Her father was a Tehsildar in Maharaja Hari Singh's kingdom of J&K. Damyantiji married Shri Chattarpati Tara in 1936 in Rawalpindi and he lovingly called her Daman. In 1942, Ashok's parents Damyanti & Chattarpati Tara moved to Maharashtra, where Ashok was born. While living in Maharashtra, everyone started addressing Damyantiji as Baiji. She was a dedicated teacher. Damyanti Tara was a teacher by profession and taught for over 25 years at Lahore Montessori School, initially based at East Patel Nagar and then moving to the Rajouri Garden Branch. In her spare time, Baiji tutored students weak in studies so they could achieve their potential. Once there her second child, Kirti was electrocuted by a live wire while flying the kite. Baiji ran from her school and took him to Wellington Hospital (now Jai Prakash Narayan Hospital), however after ensuring the doctors were managing Kirti's care, she went back to her school. When the Principal advised her to go back to the hospital, *Baiji* commented that the students were her children too and how could she leave them without support during their final exams. *Baiji* too like *Papaji*, always believed that duty came before faith and self-concerns. For those times, *Baiji & Papaji* were progressive in their thoughts and fully supported their daughter, Upma's (the youngest of their children) desire to pursue her Master's in Physics from BITS Pilani. After the loss of her older son, Ashwin, and sale of her ancestral home, Baiji was lost her spirit to live. Baiji passed away on 20th January 1999 while living with Col. Tara had his family at Noida. She was still wearing her revered parandi in her hair when she died.

Abha Tara (Wife)

Born on 12th November 1948, New Delhi. She did her schooling from prestigious Auckland School, Shimla (HP) up to 8th class and later 11th (ISC) from Presentation Convent School, Delhi. A good student from the beginning, she did her B.Sc. from Miranda House College, Delhi University and her B.Ed from Jama Millia Islamia College, Delhi. She has been a dedicated teacher and taught for about 28 years in various schools due to her husband's postings. She retired on 31st March 2009 from Vishwa Bharati School, Noida (UP). After retirement, she has been keeping herself in touch with School activities. She voluntarily guided and taught the students weak in studies.

She is a true symbol of old saying "Silence is stronger than Noise." She is quiet by nature but very strong from inside. During the India – Pakistan (liberation of Bangladesh) War in December 1971, when her husband was in the thick of war, she knew that anything odd could happen to her and her 3 month old daughter Anshu. She neither panicked nor was petrified. When people quizzed her about Ashok Tara's safety, she would stoically reply that her husband is a soldier and would discharge his duties sincerely and come back home safely. There was no communication from him for a long time. She got news about him for the first time during the war on 17th December 1971, when it was shown on TV that Major Ashok Tara had rescued the family of Sheikh Mujibur Rahman from the captivity of Pakistan Army.

She has been a close companion to Col. Tara in his Social and Welfare activities and has always stood like a rock with him during his army life and till date. Despite being from non-army background, she adjusted herself to the Army life which required her to move from one station to another with her children. She groomed her children, daughter Anshu, and son Ashish with sterling human values.

Anshu Tara (Daughter)

She was born when Col. Tara was posted in Mizo hills, North East. He saw her for the first time in January1972 when he returned from Bangladesh War. He had to report to his unit in Mizo hills immediately. The family was reunited in the summer of the same year at Kanpur Railway station when his unit moved there. She studied in about 12 schools and passed her 12th standard from Army Public School, Delhi. She did her B.A. in Russian language from JNU. She did her post graduation Diploma in Travel and Tourism from IITM, Delhi. She has a tall and pleasing personality with a friendly nature like her father. After her PG she joined Scandinavian airline service (SAS) in Delhi. Being in Airlines, she ensured that her parents visited many countries across the world. After a few years, she went for further studies to Australia, where she eventually settled. She has worked with HR department, Melbourne University and is now with Eastern Health, Melbourne. She is well travelled and a very adventurous person. She likes adventure sports such as sky diving, bungee jumping etc. Taking after her father, she likes to go on expeditions. She is extremely fond of cooking. She has recently travelled to South America and Antarctica to be with pristine nature and in the company of icebergs, penguins, whales and seals in a 'once in lifetime' trip.

Ashish Tara (Son) & Dr. Sanyogita (Daughter-in-Law)

Ashish was born on 12th December, 1973 at Kanpur. He went to many schools depending upon his father's postings. He passed out from Army Public School, Dhaula Kuan, New Delhi. He did B.Tech in Computer Engineering from Bharti Vidyapeeth, Poona. After working for a few years in Delhi, he joined his sister and wife in Australia where he is settled now. He was an avid swimmer during his school days. His mother recalls him as a child full of life, naughty and an intelligent one. His daring adventures was to amaze and startle his Mother many a times. He grew up to be a strapping 6 ft 2 inches tall handsome young man. Unlike his sister, he is reserved in nature like his mother and takes his own time to open up. He is a very hardworking and a sincere person. He is now working with Telstra in networking department, Melborne. He married Dr. Sanyogita, daughter of Dr. Ashok & Dr. Deepa Singh in the year 2000, whom he met while studying in Bharti Vidyapeeth in Poona. Sanyogita hails from a family of Doctors. Her parents have a nursing home and a hospital in Krishna Nagar, Delhi. Her Sister Sangamitra & her husband Dr. Rakesh Bilwani are settled in Australia. Her brother Dr. Gautam Singh and his wife Dr. Roya Singh run their nursing home in Delhi. Sanyogita has very amiable down to earth, helpful caring nature. After completing her MD in India, she moved to Australia where Anshu joined her after one year. Later Ashish also joined them. She is a popular Doctor and has her own practice in Melbourne. She is also attached with other hospitals in the Eastern Health. She gets along very well with one and all. It is a close knit family and stays together with Anshu also staying with them. Abha & Col. Tara stay with them for about 6 months in a year.

Rhea Tara (Granddaughter)

Born on 12th August, she is apple of the eye of Tara family. A soft spoken, well behaved and an adorable child, she is an avid reader. A quiet, intelligent child she has recently finished her 12th Standard and is amongst top 2% students in Australia. Like her father and grandfather and mother, she is also a sportsperson. She is good swimmer. She is very attached to both her paternal and maternal Grandparents. She is always keen to learn new things. She recently learnt crochet and knitting from her Dadi. She is also daring like her father and Grandfather. Col. Ashok Tara calls her an angel. She is learning Japanese language and has visited Japan on a study tour.

Ekta Gupta

She is an invaluable family friend of Tara family. She belongs to Moradabad (UP), was born on 05.08.1974 to Mr. N.C. Gupta and Mrs. Sudha Gupta. They run a chemist shop. She has one elder brother Dr. Nischal Gupta. She did her schooling and passed 12th from Prabha Devi Girls College and her, BSc, from D.A.K.Degree College at Moradabad. She did a Diploma course in Computers and later taught this subject. During her spare time, she helped her parents in running the chemist shop. She got married to Captain Vikas Gupta in 1998, who later left army after serving for a few years. She has stayed at Delhi Cantt and Sagar (MP) military cantonments. A graceful lady with a charming smile and an extremely helpful attitude towards one and all, makes her popular among relatives and friends. She is very close to Abha Tara, both being inseparable souls. She looks after Abha and Colonel Ashok Tara like her parents irrespective of the time of the day. She has very good relations with their children too. They are grateful to God to have Ekta as their Family friend and neighbour.

Ashwani & Kirti (Brothers)

Col. Tara had two elder brothers, Ashwani & Kirti Tara. Unfortunately, both are no more. Ashwani was 5 years elder and was married to Madhu, both were working in India Airlines where they met and got married in 1965. They had two sons Anurag & Anuj both of whom are no more. Kirti was two years elder to Ashok Tara. Both shared extraordinary camaraderie and were inseparable during childhood. He initially joined Navy which he left to try his luck in films. He was extremely handsome and did odd roles in Hindi films.

Upma Chopra (Sister)

She is the youngest Tara sibling. She did her MSc in physics and retired as Principal of 'Golden Jubilee Air Force School' Delhi Cantt. She got married to an Air Force Officer, Group Capt. Shiv Lal Chopra. Both of them were in Khalsa College, Delhi. They are blessed with two daughters – Deepti & Pragati. Deepti is a senior Teacher in Air Force Bal Bharti School and is married to Air Vice Marshal (Retd.) Harry Kamal. They stay in Vasant Kunj. They have a daughter Rubeena who is working in London. Upma's younger daughter Pragati is a Dentist. Her husband Manmeet Aneja works with Nestle. He is now posted in Kuala Lumpur. Their daughter Riddhima has recently finished her Masters from London School of Economics.

Late Shanta Pal and Prof. BN Pal

Abha's mother Shrimati Shanta Pal, was the eldest daughter of the five children, and was born in Multan (now in Pakistan) on 16 July 1925. Early on in life Shantaji took on the responsibility of the household and took exceptional care of her younger siblings. Despite growing up in the pre-independence ere of India, Shantaji's parents encouraged her to pursue a Bachelor's of Art. Abha's father, Mr. BN Pal, was born in August of 1919 in Punjab. He pursued his academic career at various institutes from Nowshera, to college in Lahore, MA from Punjab University at Lahore.

At the age of 21, Shantaji married Bhupinder Nath Pal in a simple ceremony at Lahore. Before partition, they relocated to the then summer capital of India, Shimla when Mr. BN Pal secured a role as a Professor of Economics at BM College. They had three children, Bipan, Abha and Nipun, who lovingly called her Ammiji, reminiscent of the pre-independence era. Thereafter, Shantaji was known as

Ammiji by one and all and across generations. Despite living a simple life, Ammiji & Palji (as her husband was fondly known as) ensured their children were educated in the best Institutes both while at school and in college. The family moved to Delhi in 1962, and between Shimla and Delhi, the children grew up during their formative years to become independent thinkers. Ammiji supported her children through the education and career decisions they made.

Despite the strong opposition of her husband, Ammiji played a very crucial role in getting Abha & Ashok married. Ammiji passed away peacefully on 8th June 2011, a contented family lady who saw the birth of her great grandchildren and continued to enjoy her Gol-gappas till the end. After Ashok and Abha's wedding Prof Pal did not communicate with either Abha, Ashok or their children until the day he died on 4th June 2003.

Bipan & Nipun Pal (Abha's brothers)

Bipan, born on 5th October 1947 at Shimla (HP) is the eldest of Pal siblings. Father Bhupinder & Mother Shanta Pal had shifted from Lahore to Shimla in 1946. The family shifted to Delhi after his father Prof. Bhupinder Pal got a job as Reader in NCERT, Delhi. The family had a tough time to adjust from quiet and hilly Shimla to the hectic life of Delhi. He often reminisces about the old, well spread green Delhi. He did his graduation from Khalsa College, Delhi University. He was close to his sister, Abha and brother Nipun. The family lived near Long Wood, Shimla. He stays in Hauz Khas. He got married on 1st October 1976, to Dr. Kiran Pal who is a PhD in Political Science and teaches university students. He worked initially with the prestigious Institute of Mass Communication, New Delhi. He superannuated as General Manager from PEC (Projects & Equipment Corporation Of India) Ltd. in October 2007. They are blessed with two children Hansika and Himanshu who are both well settled in their lives. Puneet Sharma, her husband is a banker and they live in Zurich. They are blessed with two school going daughters Nayonika & Siddhika. Himanshu is an environment engineer working with an NGO.

Nipun was born on 29th November 1950 and did his initial schooling from St. Edward's School, Shimla and from St. Xavier's

Delhi. He did his graduation from Ramjas college and post graduation from Kurukshetra University. He also did a course in forensic science from Delhi University. He is married to Sarita who was initially a teacher and now has joined his business. He has pharmaceutical company. Nipun and Sarita have two daughters Ruchika & Kanika both of who are excelling professionally and making their parents proud. She is married to Prashant Verma. They are blessed with a son Neel. Kanika works for Unilever and has recently got an award in Davos. She is married to Shriskhandh who is an environment engineer and they have a 3year old son Avyut.

Lt. Col. S.S. Khanna

Lt. Colonel Shanti Sarup Khanna is a dear army friend of mine. He is a 'friend of friends'. He was born in Peshawar (now in Pakistan) in 1938 and later his parents moved to Delhi in 1944. He completed his education in Delhi. He was an excellent player of cricket. He captained his school and college teams. He represented St. Stephens College and the Delhi University Cricket Team.

Shanti was commissioned in to Territorial Army (TA) in 1962 which was converted to regular army in 1965. In 1970, he was posted to 32 Guards (14 Guards) - A Counter Insurgency Unit in Mizoram. During December 1970, I was also posted to 32 Guards from 9 Para Commando.

During the Liberation War of Bangladesh, 1971, both of us took active part in 'The Battle Of Gangasagar' (Bangladesh). I was the Commander of the assaulting 'Alfa' Company and he was the Commander of the Support Company and in addition, also carried the duty of Quartermaster. He did an excellent job by ensuring the availability of ammunition and supplies at the right time at right place. He was also sent on a special patrol duty which he carried out very successfully. It further brought both of us close to each other.

Later we served together in Pune and Kanpur etc. Both families become very close to each other. His dedication to army motivated both his sons to join army. One of his sons, Colonel Savit Khanna even commanded 14 Guards.

He retired from the army on 31st July 1989 and settled in Pune (Maharashtra). Families of both of us are in touch with each other.

Col. Prem Kshattriya

Col. Tara first met him during 1963 and he became an invaluable part of his life. They were together in the battle of Gangasagar (1971). He was born to a renowned freedom fighter cum politician parents of Bundelkhand on 10th October 1941 at village Mangarauth, Distt Hamirpur, (U.P.) An NCC 'C' certificate holder, he was selected to undergo commissioning training at IMA Dehradun. He was commissioned on 11th December 1962 in the Brigade of the Guards. He got married to Mrs. Amita Kshattriya, a graduate from famous Banasthali Institute, Rajasthan on 24th November 1968. He, with only 9 years of service, was the Second-in-Command of the 14th Battalion Brigade of the Guards which captured the 'Gangasagar' objective during the Bangladesh liberation war, 1971 with a record number of lesser mortal casualties than expected. He retired on 31st October 1993 and settled in his ancestral village.

My college and school friends have been covered in chapter 4.

Col. Shashi Vaid

Col. Shashi Vaid belongs to Distt Kangra in Himachal Pradesh. After his birth in the year 1944, he did his education from GAV High School Kangra and Govt. College Dharmshala. He joined the Army and was commissioned in to Corps of Engineers in 1968.

He has had a very eventful and memorable journey in the Army, where he mostly served in the Combat units and also in Border Roads and Military Engineering service and Army Welfare Housing Organisation. During the service, he was honoured with the Chief of Army & Chief of Air Staff and AOC in Cs Commendation cards. After retirement, he served in the Real Estate industry for 12 years.

On the family front, his family consists of his wife, Indira, two daughters and a son. All children are happily married and doing extremely well in their professions.

Presently, he is devoting his time to the social service. After having done as Chairman of Arun Vihar RWA and Senior Vice President of Federation of Noida RWAs, he is now giving his services as President of Arun Vihar Sanatan Dharam Mandir Noida.

I am blessed to have a wonderful association with him & his family since 1992. Me and my wife Abha have a very close family bond with Vaid Parivaar. I regard him as my true friend, philosopher & Guide. More so, we both have been contributing our humble bit in various social activities of Noida.

❑

Revisiting Alma Maters

I & Abha and our parents were lucky to go to some of the best educational institutions in the subcontinent, which moulded and prepared us for our future lives. I fondly recall the days I spent at SD college, Delhi university (Now ARSD). I scouted for the right advice for the younger generation . What better than listing the mottos of the institutions that have been mentioned in this book:

Atma Ram Sanatan Dharam (ARSD) College (estd. 1959): *Tejasvi-naav-adhitam-astu* (May our learning be endowed with radiance)

Auckland House School (estd. 1836): *Altiora Peto* (I seek the higher things)

DAV Schools and Colleges (estd. 1886, Lahore): *Tamso ma jyotirgamaya (*Lead us from darkness to light)

Delhi University (estd. 1922**):** *Nishtha Dhriti Satyam* (Dedication, Steadfastness and Truth)

Dhaka University (estd. 1921): *Shikshai Aalo* (Education is light) শকি্ষাই আলে ।

Dyal Singh College (estd. 1910): Gather Ye The Wisdom of East And West.

Dyal Singh College now a 100-year-old institution owes its origin to the extreme generosity and foresight of Sardar Dyal Singh Majithia, founder of The Tribune and Punjab National Bank, who willed his vast wealth in 1895 for the setting up of an education trust for a truly secular college. Consequently, Dyal Singh College was established at Lahore in 1910. After partition of India, Dyal Singh College was established in Karnal and in Delhi. Today Dyal College exist both in Karnal and Delhi.

Forman Christian College, Lahore (estd. 1864): By love, serve one another

Government College, Lahore (estd. 1864): Educating people for tomorrow

Indian Military Academy (IMA) (estd. 1932): *Veerta aur Vivek* (Valour and Wisdom)

Jamia Millia Islamia (estd. 1920**):** *Allam al insaan amaa lam yalam* (Taught man that which he knew not)

Miranda House (estd. 1948): *Swadhyaya pramaditavyam* (Learning through self-education)

OTA (Officers Training Academy), Madras (estd. 1942/1963): Serve with Honour

Punjab/Panjab University (estd. 1882, Lahore): *Iman, Ittehad, Tanzeem (*Faith, Unity, Discipline)

Punjab University, Chandigarh*:* *Tamso ma jyotirgamaya* (Lead us from darkness to light)

Presentation Convent, Delhi (estd. 1924**):** VIRTUE and LABOUR

Rashtriya Indian Military College (estd. 1922): *Bal Vivek* (Strength and Conscience)

The reader may have noticed that the above institutions have been run by various different religions and sects, all imparting education to children of the subcontinent to make them worthy human beings serving society and humanity irrespective of gender, faith, caste and creed. I bow to the visionaries of our shared heritage of undivided India who contributed so much towards shaping up the future generations.

Dear readers some of the mottos may have changed during the course of time. In case you come across the original mottos, you can email them to us.

I sum up this book with a verse from two-thousand-year-old 'Taittiriya Upanishad'

Vedamanucyacharyo ante vasinamanusasti: Satyam vada; dharmam chara; Swadhyaya pravachanabhyam na pramaditavyam.

A teacher after imparting knowledge gives final advice to his students -

Be truthful, stay on the path of righteousness

Never neglect (self) study and teaching.

(A part of this verse was adopted as the motto by Miranda House in 1990, during the time of Principal Dr T. S. Rukmini—a Sanskrit scholar and Miranda House alumnus)

❑

Notes

Chapter 1

Correspondent, H. T. (2022). HT This Day: May 22, 1973 -- Army moves into Lucknow varsity. *Https://Www.hindustantimes.com/India-News/Ht-This-Day-May-22-1973-Army-Moves-into-Lucknow-Varsity-101652795738299.Html*. Retrieved 2023.

David, S. (2003). *The Indian Mutiny: 1857*. Penguin.

Reuters. (1973). Death Toll Is 40 in Indian State As Revolt by Police Continues. *New York Times*. Retrieved 2023, from https://www.nytimes.com/1973/05/24/archives/death-toll-is-40-in-indian-state-as-revolt-by-police-continues.html.

Spilsbury, J. (2008). *The Indian Mutiny*. Orion Publishing Group

Chapter 2

Rakesh Anand Bakshi (2021). *Nagme, Kisse, Baatein, Yaadein: The Life & Lyrics of Anand Bakshi*. Penguin Ebury Press

Pike, J. (n.d.). *Military*. Rawalpindi Cantonment. Retrieved April 29, 2023, from http://www.globalsecurity.org/military/world/pakistan/cantt-rawalpindi.htm

Chapter 3

Dalrymple, W. (2011). *City of djinns*. HarperCollins Publishers.

Hasina thanks New Delhi for naming road after Bangabandhu. (2022). *The Statesman*. Retrieved 2023, from https://www.

thestatesman.com/india/hasina-thanks-new-delhi-for-naming-road-after-bangabandhu-1491671555.html.

Chapter 4

Atma Ram Sanatan Dharma College – University of Delhi. (n.d.). Retrieved April 29, 2023, from https://www.arsdcollege.ac.in/

Chapter 5

Army, I. (n.d.). *History of The Brigade of the Guards*. Indian Army. Retrieved 2023, from https://indianarmy.nic.in/Site/FormTemplete/frmTempSimple.

x?MnId=xLdSmbl/8UnUnTMGyWSanA==&ParentID=h5t-9cUv6BW26ROVvYBmWcA==#:~:text=Brigade%20of%20The%20Guards%20which,in%20the%20last%20four%20decades.

Army, I. (n.d.). *OTA Chennai*. Indian Army. Retrieved 2023, from https://indianarmy.nic.in/Site/FormTemplete/frmTemp-Simple.spx?MnId=K7BbVGAhL8Y9P77+kuU8gQ==&ParentID=qcvs8e5GdFsvbvb3o6Pn/Q==

YouTube. (2019). *OTA: The Saga Of Excellence | Patriot With Major Gaurav Arya*. Retrieved 2023, from https://www.youtube.com/watch?v=hicnjBjWp5Q.

Chapter 6

Army, I. (n.d.). *Indo Pak War 1965*. Indian Army. Retrieved 2023, from https://indianarmy.nic.in/Site/FormTemplete/frmTempSimple.aspx?MnId=zWoYgLaJ4Hep3xXfTXfpoQ==&ParentID=UPO9d-Q6OEhnUFTioK7z0qg=.

Bharat Rakshak. (n.d.). Retrieved April 29, 2023, from http://www.bharat-rakshak.com/

Black, J. (2016). *War in the early modern world*. Routledge.

Carpenter, W. M., Wiencek, D. G., & Lilley, J. R. (2016). *Asian Security Handbook: Terrorism and the New Security Environment*. Routledge.

Chavan, Y. B., & D., P. R. (2007). *1965 War: The inside story: Defence minister Y.B. Chavan's Diary of India-pakistan war*. Atlantic.

Gallantry awards: Ministry of Defence, Government of India. Gallantry Awards | Ministry of Defence, Government of India. (n.d.). Retrieved April 29, 2023, from https://www.gallantryawards.gov.in/

Gokhale, N. A. (2015). *1965 turning the tide: How India won the War*. Bloomsbury.

Jamal, A. (2009). *Shadow war: The untold story of jihad in Kashmir*. Melville House.

Of 1965 Indo-Pakistan War- indiancc.mygov.in. (n.d.). https://indiancc.mygov.in/wp-content/uploads/2021/07/mygov-9999999991444044806.pdf

Palit, D. K. (1998). *The lightning campaign: The indo-pakistan war, 1971*. Lancer.

Praagh, D. V. (2014). *Greater Game: India's race with destiny and China*. McGill-Queen's University Press.

Pradhan, R. D. (2007). *1965 war, the inside story: Defence minister Y.B. Chavan's Diary of India-pakistan war*. Atlantic.

Prasad, S. N., & Thapliyal, U. P. (2011). *The India-pakistan war of 1965: A history*. Published by Natraj Publishers on behalf of Ministry of Defence, Govt. of India.

Sarkar, B. (2000). *Outstanding victories of the Indian Army, 1947-1971*. Lancer Publishers.

Sethi, C. K. (2018). Lt. Gen Zorawar Chand Bakshi, the greatest wartime hero who 'just faded away.' *The Print*. Retrieved from https://theprint.in/theprint-profile/lt-gen-zorawar-chand-bakshi-the-greatest-wartime-hero-who-just-faded-away/63532/.

Subramaniam, A. (2017). *India's wars: A military history, 1947-1971*. Naval Institute Press.

Verma, S. K. (2021). *1965: A Western Sunrise*. Rupa & Co.

Chapter 7

About Jamia. Welcome to Jamia Millia Islamia - A Central University. (n.d.). Retrieved April 29, 2023, from https://www.jmi.ac.in/

House, M. (n.d.). *Miranda House*. Miranda House - University College for Women. Retrieved April 29, 2023, from http://www.mirandahouse.ac.in/

Netflix. (2023). *The Romantics. The Romantics by Yashraj Productions*. Retrieved 2023.

Chapter 8

A collection of eye witness statements from Liberation War of Bangladesh. Witness statements of Bangladesh Genocide. (n.d.). Retrieved April 29, 2023, from http://www.1971archive.org/

Abdul Gaffar Chowdhury. (n.d.). Retrieved 2023, from https://dbpedia.org/page/Abdul_Gaffar_Chowdhury.

Ahmed, I., & Liton, S. (2015). Pakistanis tried to keep foreign journos away. *The Daily Star*. Retrieved from https://www.thedailystar.net/frontpage/pakistanis-tried-keep-foreign-journos-away-184396.

Ahsan, S. B. (2020, March 4). When Mr. Jinnah came to Dhaka. *Dhaka Tribune*.

Bass, G. J. (2013). *The blood telegram: India's Secret War in East Pakistan*. Random House India.

British journalist Simon Dring, a true friend of Bangladesh, passes away. (2021, July 20). *BSS*. Retrieved from https://www.bssnews.net/news-flash/6449#:~:text=British%20journalist%20Simon%20Dring%2C%20a%20true%20friend%20of%20Bangladesh%2C%20passes%20away,-BSS&text=DHAKA%2C%20July%2020%2C%202021%20(,at%20the%20age%20of%2076.

Concert for Bangladesh. George Harrison. (2020, February 25). Retrieved April 29, 2023, from https://www.georgeharrison.com/films/the-concert-for-bangladesh/

Dummett, M. (2011, December 16). Bangladesh War : The article that changed history. *BBC*. Retrieved from https://www.bbc.com/news/world-asia-16207201.

Ferdous, H. (2016, October 8). *Remembering Sydney Schanberg*. The Daily Star. Retrieved April 29, 2023, from https://www.thedailystar.net/op-ed/remembering-sydney-schanberg-1260304

Genocide - cbgr1971.org. (n.d.). Retrieved April 29, 2023, from http://www.cbgr1971.org/files/SundayTime/GenocideAnthonyMascarenhasDocx.pdf

I&B Ministry Government of India. (1972). *'Dateline Bangladesh' – Documentary. Films Division.*

In Dacca, troops use artillery to halt revolt - The daily star. (n.d.). Retrieved April 29, 2023, from https://www.thedailystar.net/sites/default/files/genocide-in-newspapers-pages.pdf

Kennedy, S. E. (1971) *Crisis in South Asia – A report to the Subcommittee investigating the Problem of Refugees and Their Settlement, Submitted to U.S. Senate Judiciary Committee*. U.S. Govt. Press.

Mazumdar, S. (2015, February 21). This day, that year: When they gave away their lives for mother tongue. *The Indian Express*.

Notebook. (2021, January 3). *1971.03.28: In Dacca, troops use artillery to halt revolt civilians fired on sections of Dacca are set ablaze: New York Times*. সংগ্রামের নোটবুক. Retrieved April 29, 2023, from https://songramernotebook.com/archives/309143

Published: March 30, 1971 The New York Times. (n.d.). Retrieved April 29, 2023, from http://docstrangelove.com/uploads/1971/foreign/19710330_nyt_heavy_killing_reported.pdf

Raghavan, S. (2015). *1971: A global history of the creation of Bangladesh*. Permanent Black.

Rahman, T. (2006). Language policy, multilingualism and language vitality in Pakistan. In A. Saxena & L. Borin (Ed.), *Lesser-Known Languages of South Asia: Status and Policies,*

Case Studies and Applications of Information Technology (pp. 73-106). Berlin, New York: De Gruyter Mouton. https://doi.org/10.1515/9783110197785.1.73

Salik, S. (1998). *Witness to surrender*. Oxford University Press.

Schanberg, S. H. (1971, March 29). *Sticks and Spears against tanks*. The New York Times. Retrieved April 29, 2023, from https://www.nytimes.com/1971/03/29/archives/sticks-and-spears-against-tanks-in-east-pakistan-sticks-against.html

Sengupta, N. K. (2011). *Land of two rivers: A history of bengal from the Mahabharata to mujib*. Penguin Books India.

Shariff, M. (2010). *Admiral's Diary: Battling through Stormy Sea Life for decades*.

Sisson, R., & Rose, L. E. (1992). *War and secession: Pakistan, India, and the creation of Bangladesh*. Oxford University Press.

United Nations. (n.d.). *International mother language day*. United Nations. Retrieved April 29, 2023, from http://www.un.org/en/observances/mother-language-day

Chapter 9

Correspondent, S. (2012, March 20). *Liberation War in sculpture*. The Daily Star. Retrieved April 29, 2023, from https://www.thedailystar.net/news-detail-227070

Chapter 10

1971: Making Bangladesh A reality - II. Indian Defence Review. (2012, December 14). Retrieved April 29, 2023, from http://www.indiandefencereview.com/spotlights/1971-making-bangladesh-a-reality-ii/2/

Chapter 11

Battle of Gangasagar. National War Memorial. (n.d.). Retrieved April 29, 2023, from https://nationalwarmemorial.gov.in/murals/details/10

Chapter 12

14, M. E. on N., 30, F. on J., 17, S. W. on D., 16, Kishore Thakrar on D., 16, A. on D., & 15, S. on D. (2022, December 16). *14-16th Dec 1971 - inside enemy camp*. Indian Defence Review. Retrieved April 29, 2023, from http://www.indiandefencereview.com/news/14-16th-dec-1971-inside-enemy-camp/

Air Aspect of the liberation war 1971 Air Cdre Ishfaq Ilahi Choudhury (retd). (n.d.). Retrieved April 29, 2023, from https://mm-gold.azureedge.net/Articles/ishfaq/air_aspect71.html

Hamoodur Rahman Commission Report - dunya news. (n.d.). Retrieved April 29, 2023, from http://img.dunyanews.tv/images/docss/hamoodur_rahman_commission_report.pdf

India in Un 1971| Liberation War Of Bangladesh, talk by Asoke Mukerji . (2022). *ndia in UN 1971| Liberation War Of Bangladesh, talk by Asoke Mukerji* . Retrieved from https://www.youtube.com/watch?v=bi_85_hNCn0.

Jagan Mohan, P. V. S., & Chopra, S. (n.d.). *Eagles over Bangladesh*. News article in depth. Retrieved April 29, 2023, from http://www.bharat-rakshak.com/archives/1971/Dec14/Art04.htm

Maj Chandrakant Singh, V. C. (2021, June 4). *The Schanberg story and Dacca's liberation*. Salute. Retrieved April 29, 2023, from https://salute.co.in/the-schanberg-story-and-daccas-liberation/

News article in depth. (n.d.). Retrieved April 29, 2023, from http://www.bharat-rakshak.com/archives/1971/Dec14/Art04.htm

Official 1971 war history. (n.d.). Retrieved April 29, 2023, from https://www.bharat-rakshak.com/archives/OfficialHistory/1971War/

Prasad, S. N., & Thapliyal, U. P. (2014). *The India-pakistan war of 1971: A history*. Natraj Publishers, Publication Division on behalf of Ministry of Defence, Government of India.

R., J. J. F. (2015). *An odyssey in war and peace: An autobiography*. The Lotus Collection.

R., J. J. F. (2011). *Surrender at dacca: Birth of a nation*. Manohar.

Raj, R. (2018). *Indo-Pak War Of 1971*. Prabhat Prakashan.

(Retd), L. G. N. S. (2019, December 12). *As a young captain in 1971 Bangladesh War, I gave Pakistan's Lt-Gen the letter to surrender*. ThePrint. Retrieved April 29, 2023, from https://theprint.in/opinion/in-1971-bangladesh-war-i-gave-pakistan-lt-gen-letter-to-surrender/333068/

Singh, R. (2013). *Talent for war - the military biography of lt gen Sagat Singh*. Vij Books (India) Pvt. Ltd.

Subramaniam, A. (2017). *India's wars: A military history, 1947-1971*. Naval Institute Press.

The centre of South Asian studies. " Collections " K.B. Lall. (n.d.). Retrieved April 29, 2023, from http://www.s-asian.cam.ac.uk/archive/audio/collection/k-b-lall/

The Parachute Regiment. Page is unavailable. (n.d.). Retrieved April 29, 2023, from https://indianarmy.nic.in/Site/FormTemplete/frmTempSimple.aspx?MnId=NdBdDo%2Bw%2FUDX-uIi4ElKqqQ&ParentID=CCAio%2FJMRcL5mIp1c4fyrQ

Tiwary, A. V. M. A. K. (2013). *Indian Air Force in Wars*. Lancers Publishers.

Veekay. (n.d.). *Veekay's history book*. Veekay's history book. Retrieved April 29, 2023, from https://veekay-militaryhistory.blogspot.com/

Chapter 14

Father of the nation Bangabandhu sheikh Mujibur Rahman Memorial museum. (n.d.). Retrieved April 29, 2023, from https://bangabandhumuseum.org.bd/en/

Rahman, M. (2012). *Sheikh Mujibur Rahman the unfinished memoirs*. Oxford University Press.

Schanberg, S. H. (1972, January 11). *Mujib, stopping in New Delhi, vows eternal amity with India*. The New York Times. Retrieved April 29, 2023, from https://www.nytimes.com/1972/01/11/archives/mujib-stopping-in-new-delhi-vows-eternal-amity-with-india.html

Chapter 15

YouTube. (2017). *YouTube*. Retrieved April 29, 2023, from https://www.youtube.com/watch?v=5MJQaa4xJrw.

YouTube. (2020). *YouTube*. Retrieved April 29, 2023, from https://www.youtube.com/watch?v=dujY9ua02PA.

❑